RIDING
THE
UNICORN

Perfect fuel for a hungry, hungry founder.

—**Nina Juhl, UNSW Founders**

Like its title, *Riding the Unicorn* is a rare breed. It's a time-travelling journey through startup history, from solving problems no-one asked to be solved, to why we should be obsessing over customers who know more than we do. This book is a masterclass in getting out of your own way, especially if you are chasing the unicorn, and it leaves you wondering, are the real unicorns the companies and their celebrated success or the quirky geniuses behind them?

—**Jodie Siggers, Transformer Program Manager, Bond University**

Fun, insightful and beautifully written, *Riding the Unicorn* is brimming with optimism about Australia's dynamic startup landscape. Packed with stories and lessons from Australia's most well-known startups (and many others), this book is a must-read for Aussie founders, business leaders and capital allocators.

—**Tom O'Neill, Co-founder of Vale**

From children's books to 80s music to biblical character analogies, this book was informative and relatable. If you want to know more about the world of entrepreneurship while reminiscing past trends, this book is for you.

—**Kai Man Yuen, Organisational & Program Lead, INCUBATE**

RIDING THE UNICORN

THE STARTUP GUIDE
YOU'LL WANT TO READ

WENEE YAP • THOMAS DERRICOTT

WILEY

First published 2026 by John Wiley & Sons Australia, Ltd

ISBN: 978-1-394-36768-9

A catalogue record for this book is available from the National Library of Australia

Registered Office
John Wiley & Sons Australia, Ltd. Level 4, 600 Bourke Street, Melbourne, VIC 3000, Australia

For details of our global editorial offices, customer services, and more information about Wiley products visit us at www.wiley.com.

Wiley also publishes its books in a variety of electronic formats and by print-on-demand. Some content that appears in standard print versions of this book may not be available in other formats.

Cover design by Wiley
Cover Images: Neon: © Danial Chaudhry/Shutterstock; Wall: © Amax Photo/Getty Images
Author photo: © Felipe Jara Saba

Set in 12/16 pt and Warnock Pro by Straive, Chennai, India.

CONTENTS

ABOUT THE AUTHORS

Wenee Yap and Thomas Derricott are entrepreneurs and authors from Sydney, Australia. Together, Wenee and Thomas co-founded Catmosphere — Sydney's first dedicated cat cafe — in 2015. The cat cafe's launch followed a successful crowdfunding campaign and a partnership with cat rescue charities.

Wenee's first venture took flight during law school when she founded Survive Law — an online community for law students. Within four years of its launch, Survive Law became Australia's highest traffic law student website. In 2015, Wenee sold Survive Law to the College of Law Australia.

Wenee has also worked as a law academic and a legal technology expert. Her previous book — *Social Media Law and Marketing: Fans, Followers and Online Infamy* — was published in 2014. Wenee is a budding sailor, and won Line Honours in the 2023 Sydney to Hobart yacht race. (Just don't quiz her on any nautical terminology.)

Thomas began his editorial career in Chile, where he wrote for the English language newspaper *The Santiago Times*. After returning to Australia, he became an award-winning journalist for a range of industry publications. In recent years, he has forged a career in the startup ecosystem, having joined multiple leading startups as an early employee.

Outside of work, Thomas is an avid martial artist. He holds a purple belt in Brazilian Jiu Jitsu, and is a former national and Oceanic sumo wrestling champion. Thomas speaks minimal Japanese and fluent Spanish (although his Latin American friends would doubtless disagree).

Wenee and Thomas met while studying undergraduate degrees in writing at the University of Technology, Sydney. However, their romance didn't blossom until some years after they had graduated. They have been married since 2020, and live in Sydney's CBD with their West Highland White Terrier, Schnoozy MacDuff.

INTRODUCTION

The legends are true — the unicorn is out there.

If you're looking for a business mentor, you can't do much better than *The Very Hungry Caterpillar*.

Yes, this book is off to a strange start, but bear with us for a minute. He's a caterpillar. He's small. He makes some smart decisions, and he grows larger. He does some things he shouldn't do, but he learns from his mistakes. His journey isn't one without issue, but by the final page, he has morphed into something beyond his wildest dreams. Should you have been lucky enough to read his story as a child, you likely didn't realise its entrepreneurial merit. Even so, we're confident in saying *The Very Hungry Caterpillar* — and many works like it — stoked that urge you're feeling right now.

Within this book, you'll find exclusive access to some of Australia's most successful founders, leaders and **venture capitalists (VC)**. You'll hear from those who have reached the finish line, and those who are still running the race. Teachings, research and business best practices will abound from across the globe. But more than anything, this book is a Rosetta Stone. It seeks to unearth and translate the lessons you've learned from your hungry caterpillars, your favourite bands, your after-school specials and Saturday morning cartoons. And, so you know we're not talking out of our hats, we'll cross-section each insight against various leading CEOs' lived experiences.

Perhaps you're keen to launch your own business, but you're not sure where to begin. Maybe you're curious about these mystery ventures that always seem to report multimillion-dollar raises. Perhaps you already have your own business, and you'd like to learn what you can apply to your own hustle. Whatever the case, without knowing it, you've been preparing for this next step your entire life. Every song, story and fable you've ingested has readied you for this moment. We're just here to give you a well-researched nudge.

This isn't the first book about startups and business, and it sure won't be the last. But hopefully, it will be the one you actually want to read.

What does a unicorn have to do with business, and why should I care?

White horse. Pointy horn protruding from its head. Features in countless myths, *Blade Runner* and the Harry Potter series. Same page, yes? Good. Now, how did the concept become a byword for a successful startup?

'Unicorn' first appeared in this context in a 2013 TechCrunch article by Aileen Lee, founder of seed-stage fund Cowboy Ventures. In the article, Lee used the word to describe **scalable** businesses — or startups — that reach a **valuation** of $1 billion.

By her calculations, only 0.07 of venture-funded software startups from the 2000s reached such a valuation. Between

2003 and 2013, that equated to an average of four per year. As such, Lee reckoned that these startups were as rare and precious as the mythical creatures that bore their name. In the same article, startups like Facebook — which exceeded a value of $100 billion — enjoyed the mantle of 'super unicorn'.

We don't know what went through Lee's head when she first used 'unicorn' in this context. Perhaps she was a *Mean Girls* fan, and she wanted to make her own version of 'fetch' happen. Maybe she just loved unicorns, and wanted to see the horned myth receive its due. Whatever the reason, startup life would never be the same.

Why is Oceania the right climate for unicorns?

Looking at Lee's reasoning (and the startup scene in general), you might feel that the unicorn concept is very...*American*.

And if you do, your gut has aligned with the market. In 2022, of the world's top-10 privately owned unicorns, five were US-owned and operated. By contrast, Australia and New Zealand looked lonely, with only one Aussie startup — Canva — making the list. At a glance, then, you'd be forgiven for thinking unicorns hadn't taken to the trans-Tasman landscape.

However, while Silicon Valley often hogs the spotlight, there's a lot to like in our corner of the world. In fact, venture capitalist Kylie Frazer regards Australia as one of the most capital efficient places in the world to find a unicorn. What she means is that it's an easy place to start a business — indeed, by global rankings, we're one of the easiest places in the world.

Having said that, we're arguably one of the hardest places to *grow* a business, because we aren't a cash-rich innovation hub like Silicon Valley, Shenzhen or Singapore. These locations nurture new ideas by allowing venture capital, government investment and a business-friendly regulatory environment to converge — with staggering success. By contrast, our capital and regulatory frameworks are still playing catch-up.

So what can we take from this? That whatever survives in some of the world's southernmost nations might be a little remarkable.

Sure enough, ANZ has a storied history of innovation — one that spans beyond Vegemite and the Bungy Jump. The bionic ear, the egg beater, polymer bank notes, the jet boat, wifi technology, tank-bred tuna, kite surfing and the black box flight recorder — all of these inventions call New Zealand and Australia home. In fact, the depth of our countries' ingenuity is only outstripped by their breadth.

In 2003, a Sydney-based company called Where 2 Technologies began to explore the idea of digital mapping; by the end of 2004, the founders had sold the startup to Google, and Google Maps was born. Two years later, a world-first cervical cancer vaccine created by two researchers in Brisbane was approved for widespread use; since then, it has protected millions of women from the second-highest cause of female cancer mortality. Around the same time, organic gardeners the world over were living by the tenets of permaculture — a nature-led, chemical-free approach to farming, community and resource management. It was two Aussies who nurtured the idea to life in 1970s Tasmania.

Cross the ditch to Aotearoa and you'll find similar stories. In 1994, a pair of Kiwis forever changed the relationship between humans and hills when they invented the ZORB. A plastic, transparent orb designed to cushion its users within, the ZORB lets its users tumble down hilltops in comfort. 'Zorb' has since become a verb, and footage of people beach-balling down inclines has become a common sight online.

Let's just hope zorb-ers don't crash into any electric fences; they were invented in New Zealand nearly 60 years earlier, to the relief of livestock farmers the world over. Speaking of farmers, Kiwi inventors also gifted them with a non-lethal means of sedating rowdy animals. Not content with inventing the disposable hypodermic syringe, New Zealand vet and pharmacist Colin Murdoch also created the tranquiliser gun. As a byproduct, he irrevocably changed the action movie genre. Don't want your hero to die in a firefight? Simply hit them with a tranquiliser gun and they'll live to fight another day.

As you see, our nations' new ideas don't only present as lines of code or iPhone updates. They exist everywhere, from garage work benches, to chemist shelves. If you look at our countries' great inventors, you'll see doctors, hippies, tradies, scientists and sailors. Whatever colour your unicorn may be, it can thrive across our borders.

In fact, New Zealand founder Nick Whitehouse thinks our constraints are our advantages. He should know: his legal AI startup, McCarthyFinch, **exited** in a record three-and-a-half years through an acquisition. In the parlance of finance, this meant his deal size went from around $3000 per deal before acquisition to $400 000 on his first deal post-acquisition. How? McCarthyFinch was acquired by US legaltech Onit, giving its market-leading AI massive credibility in the vast North American market.

'Constraint is the mother of all invention,' Whitehouse said to us. 'Constraint creates creativity. In Australia and New Zealand, people don't think casually about startups because they need a job to pay the bills; there's not enough funding here to fail at something in three months, then fail into something else. The risk for us is much higher. So, the people you attract to startups are way more engaged on the mission — they're more loyal and passionate — because they're putting far more at risk.'

Unlike the multimillion-dollar cheques their American peers might receive, McCarthyFinch kickstarted with $2.5 million in **pre-seed funding** from law firm MinterEllison and New Zealand VC Goat Ventures. Comparatively speaking, it's not a lot of money to fail, or succeed, but it's a huge amount in the New Zealand start-up scene, especially pre-seed.

'The cash situation here is actually an advantage and disadvantage,' said Whitehouse. 'It's an advantage because you have to be way, way more tactical with what you do. In New Zealand and Australia, if you blow through a million dollars, that's it. You're dead and you're not getting another cheque from anybody ever again. We want to fail fast, but we have to be very judicious too.'

To some, Nick's take might sound like a crisis dressed up as an opportunity. In his eyes, though, it's simply another reason to approach a startup with both eyes open.

'It's like going to a casino,' he said. 'Everything you do is a bet. In our part of the world, you can't be a high roller like in America. You have to be way more tactical about what you're doing and who you have at the table with you, and how much you put down on each bet.'

Echoing Kylie Frazer's insight, Whitehouse thinks it's our threadbare funding that make us efficient at finding, and nurturing, unicorns.

'Any idea that makes it past the first six-month window in New Zealand and Australia ends up being a great idea that can *really succeed*,' he said. 'In America, I think that process is a lot more inefficient. They create great companies — massive companies. But the hit rate is so low.'

What's more, our nations possess the right kind of people power.

In 2020 (a famously challenging year for new immigration), Australia was home to 7.7 million people who had been born overseas — over 30 per cent of our population. New Zealand's 2023 census paints a similar picture, with 1.4 million people (nearly 30 per cent of the population) hailing from a different birthplace. That equates to over 150 languages, and over 200 countries and regions of origin. Globally, Australia ranks ninth for the total number of migrants, and New Zealand hovers between the late 20s and early 30s. As a percentage of their overall populations, though, ANZ both beat the leaderboard's victor — the United States — by nearly 15 per cent. This doesn't just mean that our nations' identities are as varied as our census. It also propels our cultures of innovation to places they otherwise wouldn't reach.

With diverse populations, we see fresh perspectives, an array of knowledge backgrounds and novel answers to current problems. A multicultural region gives us more thinkers, makers and doers — all of whom think, make and do in different ways.

Of course, this doesn't even account for Australian and Aotearoan First Nations cultures, whose 60 000-year track record of land management is already helping to mitigate climate crises (arguably the greatest scalable problem of our age).

Again, we don't raise these facts to push a civil rights agenda, but to stress our region's competitiveness. If ever there were a people, culture and economy fit to welcome unicorns, it's Australia and New Zealand.

Okay, ready? Let's begin. And, at the risk of fanning our readers' *schadenfreude*, we'll begin by detailing what *not* to do.

PS: Throughout this book, you'll occasionally see words marked in **bold**. For a deeper insight into what they *really* mean, head to the glossary at the back of the book!

CHAPTER 1

HOW TO MAKE MISTAKES (BECAUSE YOU WILL)

Everyone loves watching businesses self-destruct, right? It's okay, you don't need to feel guilty — there's an entire subgenre dedicated to it. From *The Dropout* to HBO's *Silicon Valley*, people love watching over-achievers screw up.

At the risk of seeming callous, we're going to jump on this bandwagon. And while this book is filled with first-hand success stories, we're going to begin with some home-grown stumbles.

To be clear, with one exception, we don't reflect on these case studies with any judgement. The startup landscape is a minefield of unknown unknowns, and nearly anyone could have stepped on the landmines these founders triggered. What's more, by making these mistakes, they've ensured you won't need to.

Once we've shared their stories, we'll also extract a few key lessons from each startup. That way, you'll be able to apply these learnings to your own journey. And we'll begin with a startup that dripped with the social promise of the early twenty tens: the aptly named Roamz.

Roamz

Launched: 2011

Closed: 2013

Location: Sydney, Australia

For any social media watchers, 2011 must have felt like a milestone year. Facebook, having exceeded 800 million users, had just launched Timeline. With this feature, the platform shifted their focus from static info to dynamic updates, creating a crack house of user stickiness. Their progress sounded the death knell for MySpace, who had been the reigning social media champs only four years earlier. Too young to remember MySpace? All you need to know is that a group of devs crammed the mid-noughties into a social media platform.

Back in 2005, News Corporation had bought MySpace for US$580 million. At the time, Rupert Murdoch probably thought he was getting hip with the kids. Fast-forward to 2011, and MySpace had just been co-bought by singer/actor Justin Timberlake for around US$35 million. Murdoch, it seemed, had been outfoxed by the guy who'd played a startup shyster in *The Social Network.*

During the same year, a scrappy young upstart named Instagram was making waves (and sharing photos of them). They'd only launched the year prior, and had raised US$7 million in **Series A funding**. Knowing what we know now, we can picture the execs at Facebook licking their lips in yearning. *Soon, my pretty. Soon, you will be mine.*

In short, the air was rife with the promise of change. And change is like catnip to would-be founders, because it creates opportunity. Enter Roamz.

If Daredevil were a foodie

Roamz began its life in February 2011 in Surry Hills, Sydney. Not quite a social media app, Roamz instead built a user experience from the data of other platforms. First, they would access Instagram, Twitter, Facebook and (blast from the past) Foursquare. From there, Roamz would compile photos, updates and other user-generated content. Then, via geolocation witchcraft, an in-app news stream would showcase events and attractions in a user's nearby area. All of the info Roamz sourced was publicly available, so users would receive insights from friends and strangers alike.

Think of the app as a sonar sense for venues and businesses in a neighbourhood. With Roamz, you could live like Marvel's Daredevil — if Daredevil was more focused on finding local cafés than hunting criminals.

Against 2011's backdrop of social media growth, Roamz saw an encouraging start to life. Their founder, Jonathan Barouch, bore many of the hallmarks of a winning entrepreneur. He'd launched his first business (an online and retail florist) as a teenager, and sold it in 2010. He'd earned two Masters, and served as Director of the Australia–Israel Chamber of Commerce. He was old enough to be a veteran, and young enough to be a prodigy.

Clearly, the market backed both the founder and the vision. VC firms invested $3.5 million into the business, confident that they would ride the headwinds of New Social Media. The app then garnered attention when its team presented at the Web 2.0 Summit in San Francisco (the Woodstock of 2011 tech startups). They showed potential on the consumer front as well, and attracted a quarter of a million app users.

From these early accounts, many could fairly assume that Roamz bore the makings of a success story. But by July 2013, the app had closed its doors to iOS and Android users alike. So, what went wrong?

Hype doesn't pay the bills

Perhaps no-one has offered a better answer to this question than the founder himself. While founders from Elizabeth Holmes to Adam Neumann field accusations of delusion, Jonathan Barouch should suffer no such slight. In fact, in reflecting on his failures, he was refreshingly self-aware.

In an interview with the *Australian Financial Review*, Barouch likened it having an ugly baby.

> *You don't want to see it, but after hundreds of comments you realise you can't lie to yourself anymore... What we were offering just wasn't resonating. No-one needed it. We just kept getting the same feedback: they wanted to use the data we were collecting in a different way.*

Thanks to a growing base and ample media buzz, Roamz saw no shortage of would-be client meetings. Brands from the Commonwealth Bank to Qantas agreed to sit-downs, doubtless eager to capitalise on the next social media trend. Through these meetings, Roamz hoped that brands would pay for promotional space on Roamz.

However, by Barouch's own admission, few were eager to pay for promotion on the platform. Despite their laurels, Roamz couldn't squeeze a cent from advertisers. That's why, after around two years of fruitless sales meetings, Roamz conceded defeat.

No doubt Barouch has wondered countless times what could have steered those meetings towards a happier mooring. Perhaps they may have secured paying clients if the app had been a bit slicker or busier. Maybe these would-be clients simply weren't ready for another social media–adjacent platform; remember, eight years prior to Roamz' launch, MySpace didn't even exist yet, and Zuckerberg was still in high school. It's even possible that the market was waiting to see whether Roamz would thrive or crash. After all, MySpace's costly decline still felt fresh, and Instagram was still proving its commercial mettle.

In the end, though, these potential reasons played a supporting role to the star. It was a truth that, to his credit, Barouch came to recognise: Roamz offered a solution to a problem no-one needed to solve.

Key takeaways

- *Measure the right metrics.* A robust user base is great—but only if you can monetise it. Ensure that the numbers you're tracking equate to increased value for your business.

- *Focus on solving a problem.* As obvious as this might sound, many would-be startups fail in this regard. Instead, they focus on a solution they *like* — even if it doesn't solve a problem people are facing.

- *Listen to your clients and customers.* Obsess over learning from them. Find the common ground in what they're all saying. Apply those insights to your business.

Guvera

Launched: 2010 (having incorporated in 2008)

Closed: 2017

Location: Gold Coast, Australia

Remember how we said we didn't judge these case studies — with one exception? Welcome to the 'one exception'. Now, we're not trying to be armchair critics when we say this. On the surface, the idea could have been a sound one. After all, the concept of a new online streaming platform made sense when Guvera incorporated in 2008. Spotify had only launched that same year, and was millions of users away from the market-leading status it enjoys today.

At first glance, the founders also looked like the right pair for the job. Claes Loberg, a Swedish–Australian entrepreneur, shared the same birth nation as the Stockholm-based Spotify. Having launched a feted ASX-listed IT company in the 1990s, Loberg boasted a proven business track record. He also sported long hair, sleeve tattoos, a devil beard and all the trappings of a latter-day Metallica member.

For VCs who drew comfort from a more vanilla co-founder, Guvera had Darren Herft to proffer. Ever clean-shaven, with a Wharton MBA-approved haircut, Herft's idea of casual dress involved a suit with no tie. The intended optics were clear: Loberg was the mad genius; Herft was the numbers guy. Herft would work like crazy, while Loberg's vision was just crazy enough to work. Or, in the nomenclature of this book, Herft would train a workhorse; Lobang would ensure a magic horn sprouted from its head.

Of course, that didn't happen. If it had, they wouldn't feature under the 'learn from mistakes' section of this book. Indeed, by May 2017, Guvera had ceased all operations. What killed their vibe?

A most expensive jukebox

Without knowing any more about the startup, one might be tempted to blame Spotify, Soundcloud or even Pandora. 'The market was too crowded,' they might say. 'Another music streamer couldn't hope to compete.'

Other industry pros may point to the unique hardships of music streaming. Music licensing always poses a challenge, and it's one that usually requires large piles of money. The tech demands are also legion: if your platform fails to stream dependably, users will simply download another app.

These issues may have hobbled Guvera if they had struggled to attract funding. But before they shuttered their offices, Guvera had wooed over 10 million users and secured around 30 million songs. They had also shunned a subscription model in favour of advertising-funded free access. In doing so, they set themselves apart from Spotify at the time.

But perhaps most remarkably, Guvera had banked over $180 million from 3000 investors. To put that figure into context, Atlassian — *the largest tech company in Australia* — raised US$210 million (almost AU$314 million) before going public on the NASDAQ in late 2015. Over the same time frame, Guvera convinced its backers that they were worth nearly two-thirds of a pre-**IPO** Atlassian.

At this point, the question of whether there was room for another music streamer becomes less relevant. The more pressing concern becomes, 'How could Guvera get it so wrong after raising so much?'

And *this* is the reason why Guvera isn't on our 'nice' list.

Songs to make commission to

For starters, Loberg and Herft had clearly never read Simon Sinek's 2014 hallmark management book, *Leaders Eat Last*. Despite raising their $180 million-plus war chest, Guvera burned through $81 million in the 2015 financial year. In the same window, they only scraped in a revenue of $1.2 million. Against this grim backdrop, Herft and Loberg it seems saw no problem in making salaries of $264 000 and $300 000, respectively.

'Okay,' you might say, 'that seems like pretty poor form. But that doesn't account for the $80 million deficit.'

Fair point — but it gets worse. See, Darren Herft's fundraising efforts didn't stop at a clean shave and a corporate wardrobe. From day one, he was the linchpin of Guvera's search for investors. In fact, he was so crucial to their capital campaign that he pulled double duty: Guvera CEO and sole director of AMMA Private Equity. AMMA, as you may have surmised, played a key role in raising the $180 million from an array of investors. The twist? For their labours, AMMA claimed over $22 million in commission from Guvera.

If we were to look up 'conflict of interest' on dictionary.com, we wouldn't be surprised if we saw a picture of Herft.

So, we can see that the founders enriched themselves while their startup floundered. But that isn't where the issues end. Problems also emerge when we assess the *types* of investors they courted.

The bank-of-mum-and-dad investors

When you wade into the startup ecosystem, you're likely to hear the term 'sophisticated investor'. At first listen, it may sound like a smug title that VCs cooked up to bignote themselves. In reality, it's an important distinction that exists to protect everyday mum-and-dad investors. And it's one that many, including the plaintiffs of a class action lawsuit, believed was intentionally ignored for Guvera's gain.

Instead of focusing on VCs and **angel investors** (which this book will cover later), Guvera cast a wider net. Namely, they partnered with a series of accounting firms across Australia.

Some of these firms would then earn shares in Guvera whenever they compelled their clients to invest.

Details differ over the tactics these firms employed to sell the Guvera investment. In a since-defunct class action lawsuit, burned investors claimed their accountants pitched the startup as a sure thing. They also maintained that these firms failed to stress the risk involved when investing in a startup. The firms, meanwhile, insisted they had simply passed on details about Guvera. They also maintained that they had never given their clients what would legally constitute financial advice; that part was handled by — you guessed it — AMMA Private Equity.

Whether these accountants acted in bad faith is a matter for the legal system, not this book. Even so, it seems clear that Guvera (through its fundraiser, AMMA) targetted regular investors. This matters, because when you pocket VC money in good faith, you're not hurting anyone. According to the *Harvard Business Review*, VC funds only require 10–20 per cent of their backed companies to succeed. They expect to lose money on most of their ventures — and more importantly, they can afford to.

When you court fund from private citizens, though, you deal in much more personal stakes. If your startup fails, you're not simply adding a forecasted loss into an investing firm's books. You're depriving a person, couple or family of their savings. That's money they could have channelled into a mortgage, school fees or a retirement fund. It's a buffer they can no longer access if they lose their job, or face a health scare. And there's nothing sophisticated about that.

Burn, baby, burn (discography inferno)

These slippery funding strategies didn't just carry moral weight. They also ruined the startup's hopes of launching an IPO — or, indeed, of staving off failure. By 2016, with an eight-figure **burn rate**, Herft and Loberg it seems knew they couldn't depend on private investment to survive. But instead of scaling back their expenditure, they seem to have doubled down.

In May 2016, they lodged a **prospectus** with the Australian Securities Exchange (ASX) with the aim of becoming a publicly traded company. Ever the optimists, the founders aimed to list with a valuation of $1.3 billion. If you tuned in for our book's intro, you'll recall this valuation would have landed Guvera in unicorn terrain.

Alas, the prospectus read less like a unicorn, and more like a donkey in a party hat. While it touted the startup's music licensing rights, it also struggled to frame the figures in a flattering light. In fact, it suggested that Guvera couldn't keep the lights on (or pay its creditors) should the IPO fail. Without the $100 million it hoped to raise via an IPO, the doc implied, Guvera couldn't cover its liabilities. In other words, it was 'list or go bust'.

Perhaps Herft and Loberg knew they couldn't hide the bad news, so they might as well embrace it. Maybe they hoped the suits at the ASX would glance at the prospectus, peer over the rims of their glasses and say, 'Boys, being so frank with your numbers took courage ... The exact type of courage we're looking for in our next publicly listed company!'

Whatever fantasy the founders might have harboured, they can't have been too happy with the outcome. Come June, the ASX took the rare step of vetoing the listing — essentially damning Guvera's attempts to go public. Sure enough, less than two weeks later, Guvera's directors placed it into administration. After less than a year, in May 2017, Guvera quietly announced it had ceased all operations.

Of the 30 million tunes in their catalogue, we hope Aloe Blacc's 'I Need a Dollar' was one of them.

It didn't stop there, though. In late 2019, the Australian Securities & Investment Commission (ASIC) banned Herft from managing corporations for two years. Among its litany of reasons, ASIC found that Herft had 'improperly used the Guvera Group structure for his gain...in circumstances where there were significant conflicts of interest'.

In other words, it appears Herft's actions didn't only cost him his own startup, they also scuppered his chances of running any other company for the near future.

The next song in his defunct Guvera library? 'If I Could Turn Back Time' by Cher.

Key takeaways

- *Keep your **minimum viable product (MVP)** as minimal as you can.* Some of Guvera's costs lined the pockets of a co-founder. Others were essential for the music streaming business model. All of them drained the company's coffers. Choose an idea that, in its basic form, can function with as few funds as possible.

- *Don't spend money you don't have.* If you're launching an IPO because your startup has scaled, crack open the champagne. If you're doing it to pay off debts, you've taken a wrong turn.

- *Don't serve your own interests at the expense of your startup.* Meeting the needs of your investors and staff isn't just the right thing to do. It will also keep you out of regulatory trouble.

Milkrun

Launched: 2021

Closed: 2023

Location: Sydney, Australia

If you were a human with a pulse in 1999, you would have heard Lou Bega's 'Mambo No. 5'. A revamp of a 1949 Cuban track, 'Mambo No. 5' rocketed across Australia's airwaves from the unlikely launchpad of Munich. In a matter of weeks, it became the jazzy anthem to the Western world's Y2K fears.

Yes, Lou Bega sounded less like a *singer*, and more like a drunken frat boy yelling about his exploits. And sure, the 'buffet of available women' motif would have upset feminists and family values advocates alike. (Sidenote: Mr Bega later alleged in an interview with Fox News that the song was semi-autobiographical. Sandra, apparently, was his favourite — 'that's why she was the one in the sun'. Feel free to add that to your trivia arsenal.)

At the time, these problematic details didn't seem to matter. 'Mambo No. 5' was *everywhere.*

Go to a theme park? You'd find a fully dressed marching band belting it out down the main promenade. Turn on the TV? You'd find a 'Mambo No. 5'-inspired jingle promoting *Friends* on Channel 9. ('A little bit of Rachel drinkin' coffee…') For school dances across the country, it was pretty much the beginning and end of their playlist.

Seriously. It. Was. *Everywhere…*

…until it wasn't.

By the turn of the century, 'Mambo No. 5' had receded from our collective psyches. Bega's sophomore attempt, 'I Got a Girl', fell on deaf ears — despite his assertions that he 'even got a girl in Vatican Dome'. It was as if Y2K had erased Mr Bega from the charts, while still sparing our technology and infrastructure.

Looking back, it feels as if grocery delivery apps were the Lou Bega of the 2021 startup scene.

A chart-topping marketing campaign

Much like the German singer's mainstream maiden effort, these apps suddenly appeared all over Australia. Seemingly every other week, there'd be a new one vying for their place on the (app store) charts. However, one player banked on the gamble that 'a little bit of market saturation makes them our app'. And that player was Milkrun.

Like watching YouTube? Sooner or later, you were going to see a Milkrun commercial promising to bring you groceries in 10 minutes. Taking a stroll through an Aussie metro region? Those tongue-in-cheek Milkrun bus ads and billboards would find you eventually. Consider yourself a local meme connoisseur? It was only a matter of time before Instagram's algorithm served you a fresh, grocery-inspired meme from the Milkrun account. Famously, the startup even went viral for posting a sign in Bondi promising to 'get bags delivered in 10 minutes'. (For those of you who have made sensible life choices, 'bags' is a slang term for cocaine.) Milkrun, it appeared, were 1, 2, 3, 4, 5 steps ahead of the competition.

In the context of the era, the hype was understandable. By the third quarter of 2021, most of the country still hadn't fully emerged from COVID-19 lockdowns. Masks in supermarkets were a reality, and many Aussies were still confined to five-kilometre cells. The toilet paper shortages of 2020 still haunted many of us like a bad hangover. Suddenly, the prospect of having someone deliver our canned goods and laundry powder wasn't just a luxury. It was a buffer against future crises.

Alas, by 2023, most of the major delivery platforms had shipped their final bag of veggies. And rather than emerging as the last app standing, Milkrun joined the others in the delivery bike graveyard.

Milking the cash cow

Like our other two case studies, at its 2021 launch, Milkrun bore all the hallmarks of a winning prospect. Its founder and CEO, Dany Milham, had, in 2015, co-founded Koala: the rockstars of mattress and furniture e-commerce.

That may be a phrase you'd never expected to read, but Koala had earned the title. Their eco focus, smooth ordering platform and price-to-quality balance had set them apart from the sector's incumbents. They had also caught the eyes of consumers with unmatched branding and content marketing campaigns. These triumphs had rightly boosted the prospects of Milham, who, in 2019, became a non-executive director of innovation hub Fishburners. Put simply, his startup credentials were beyond reproach.

It also didn't hurt that he looked like a sun-kissed version of Henry Cavill's *Mission: Impossible* character. It's little wonder, then, that Milkrun raised $11 million in June 2021 — three months before its launch. When they first opened, Milkrun put their money to work; they made good on their 10-minute delivery vow, and their aforementioned ads seemed to blanket the suburbs in which they delivered. As 2021 drew to a close, Milkrun must have felt as if 2022 would be their year.

Sure enough, thanks to a successful Series A funding round in January 2022, Milkrun added $75 *million* to their coffers. In the Australian landscape, such an astronomical figure for such a young business was almost unheard of. However, despite forecasts of $7 billion in total revenue by 2026, they failed in their later 2022 attempts to fundraise. For such an early stage venture, this posed a major problem. Why did the milk curdle so quickly?

From running milk to running the gauntlet

There are a range of potential reasons why Milkrun couldn't wring more funds from investors. For starters, Milkrun faced an industry-wide problem: the 2022 'tech wreck'. Thanks to inflation, rising interest rates and a post-COVID-19 decline in tech product usage, tech companies saw a revenue slump.

Of course, the tech wreck didn't affect all tech companies equally, and many Aussie startups escaped its wrath. However, the collapse of Milkrun's grocery delivery rivals Send, Quicko and Voly would have likely sounded alarm bells for VCs.

In fairer weather, Milkrun may have been able to capitalise on this crisis. It could have proven that, in the world of delivery platforms, there could be only one. Sadly, Milkrun scored something of an own goal with their customer drop-off rate. At the point of launch, they'd offered a key selling point that set them apart: 'groceries delivered to your door in 10 minutes'. And, to the surprise of competitors and customers alike, they delivered on their promise during those early days.

However, Milkrun proved unable to sustain their efforts. In June 2022, Milkrun founder Milham sent a letter to customers conceding that delivery times had spiked. In the face of all those economic hurdles, they needed to extend their delivery window.

Milkrun had awoken from their 10-minute dream … and plunged into a nightmare of delays.

Indeed, it soon became clear that Milkrun wouldn't be able to fulfil their **unique selling proposition (USP)** any time soon. According to Milkrun, the time frame grew from 10 minutes to 30–40 minutes. Ask their customers, though, and you'll hear of even longer waiting times. As the couriers' pay decreased, and the customers' fees increased from $0 to between $2.60 and $7, the prospect became less appealing for all parties.

If you read the online reviews from mid 2022 onwards, you'll notice a recurring theme. A few feature spelling errors, and others opted for spicy language, but the essence was the same: 'Try UberEats instead. It's cheaper and faster'. In their ire, some (not all) customers were turning to a platform whose chief focus was restaurant delivery.

Whether these reviewers ran a dollar-for-dollar, minute-for-minute comparison is irrelevant. The mere *en masse* suggestion highlighted that Milkrun's grip on its niche was slipping. In these reviews, Milkrun had become the equivalent of a fast food outlet that only sells chicken nuggets. If customers say, 'Let's go to Maccas and buy their chicken nuggets instead', the Nugget Emporium — which *only sells nuggets* — will face a tough time ahead.

David vs Goliath: if David lost his sling

Milkrun's delivery time woes compounded further when larger players entered their market. In June, Woolworths — one of Australia's two biggest retail grocers — launched its own delivery app: Metro60. Unlike Woolworths' conventional online ordering systems, Metro60 could secure on-the-go delivery in 60 minutes or less. What's more, they offered delivery in Sydney and Melbourne suburbs, Milkrun's two key territories.

Had Milkrun maintained their '10 minutes or less' USP, they may have outmanoeuvred Metro60. However, a 40-minute-or-longer delivery window posed a much smaller threat to Woolworths' brand name recognition. The company had spent nearly a century building their **moat**, and Milkrun would need a robust USP to cross it. Investors would have known this — and it wouldn't have left them feeling bullish.

The fact that Milkrun was haemorrhaging money wouldn't have eased anyone's concerns, either. For every new customer they signed up, Milkrun would spend $57 on marketing costs.

'Okay,' a devil's advocate might say, 'that's not a great look, but you've got to spend money to make money. After all, most customers would probably make more than one order after signing up, right? Maybe Milkrun expected to recoup that $57 back over the customer's lifetime.'

That idea certainly reflects the business models of many startups. The problem was, after sign-up, Milkrun were still losing $10 *per order*. Put another way, they were spending money to spend more money.

A lactose-intolerant end

To be fair, Milkrun had lowered their overheads throughout 2022, with that $10 figure previously sitting at $40. Even so, with no profit horizon in sight, their growth forecasts may have felt too bombastic for their own good.

Remember their prediction of $7 billion in revenue by 2026? To put that figure into perspective, Amazon's yearly Australian revenue reached $1.75 billion in 2021. In other words, in their 2022 pitch, the shot callers at Milkrun were saying, 'Have you seen the latest Australian figures for Amazon? You know, the largest online retailer in the world? Yeah, we'll be bringing in four times as much within five years.'

In any event, their cash cows ran dry in 2022. That's why, in February 2023, amid a tense market climate, they cut one-fifth of their staff. Only two months later, they ran their last litre of milk. The startup ceased operations in April, and their entire employee base — riders and office workers alike — were made redundant.

Milham shared the news with Milkrun's 400-plus employees via email, citing 'economic and market capital conditions'. To Milkrun's credit, they didn't wait until they'd burned through the last of their capital before conceding defeat. As a result, they were able to pay what they owed to staff and suppliers. However, even this must have been cold comfort to the founders, investors and workers who rallied behind the idea.

In the weeks following Milkrun's closure, UberEats launched a new sequence of ads. They starred Kris and Kendall Jenner, and sought to remind everyone that Uber delivers on-demand groceries (as well as takeaway food, people, pets and carshare options). We haven't confirmed, but we suspect the Jenners' combined fee was more than Milkrun's payroll for an entire quarter.

Never one to waste a crisis, Woolworths bought the Milkrun brand in May 2023 for a reported $10 million. Anyone keeping score at home will note that such a figure pales next to the funds they raised from investors. Woolworths had essentially picked the carcass clean ... and then stripped that carcass' skin to fashion a new suit for Metro60.

In a move that would be perceived as cruel by cynics, and touching by romantics, Metro60 rebranded as Milkrun. The Joker had murdered Batman — only to then don his cowl and vow to keep fighting crime in his name. They used Woolworths' resources, and leveraged Woolworths' supply chain, but they flew Milkrun's flag. The zombie of Milkrun would keep shambling forth, cursed to serve the Woolworths necromancer to which it was bound.

Hopefully, while he awaits his Metro60-in-disguise order Milham can find solace in Lou Bega's back catalogue. Let's just hope he doesn't try streaming it via Guvera.

Key takeaways

- *Beware of basing your business on passing trends.* Ask yourself: does your proposed startup solve a constant problem, or a trending problem (like on-demand groceries during lockdowns)? If it's the latter, do you have reason to believe you'll survive a shift in market conditions?

- *Don't promise more than you can deliver.* Successful startups offer a unique selling proposition — that is, something that compels customers to use them over competitors. Once you stop meeting your USP, people may look elsewhere.

- *Make sure your MVP aligns with your USP.* You'll need a version of your USP that you can offer on a **bootstrapped** budget. When MVPs can't be minimum, they depend on funding to be viable.

Don't worry: there's a measure of silver lining here

Aside from Guvera and their shoddy fundraising tactics, none of these startups deserve our scorn. They delved into the forest to tame the mythical unicorn, and that's more than most people will ever attempt. Had circumstances favoured them, they may have survived to hustle another day.

As it stands, they've imparted lessons and warnings for other aspiring founders. Like fallen explorers whose journals warn travellers of the journey's perils, their experiences serve to guide us. What's more, one of these case studies gives us an even more crucial reminder: we *can* learn from our mistakes.

Reading this chapter, you might have noticed that our section on Roamz was shorter than the other two. That's because Roamz' story didn't end in July 2013. When Roamz founder Jonathan Barouch left those unsuccessful sales meetings, he didn't walk out empty-handed. With every 'no' he received, he pocketed something almost as valuable: insight into what clients *did* want.

The common thread in these meetings had been an aversion to another early twenty-tens social platform. However, many clients expressed an interest in the data that Roamz had extracted from its users. At the time, social media wasn't the only digital space seeing meteoric growth — third-party review platforms were having a moment as well.

TripAdvisor was on a global acquisition spree, buying travel sites great and small and assimilating them into the Hive Mind. Business review juggernaut Yelp were still coasting on a honeymoon period after their 2012 IPO. Public reviews had well and truly gone mainstream. Consumers could now expect to take their grievances to the masses, and Big Business had taken note. They wanted to seize and respond to feedback before it spiralled into the public domain.

Roamz saw the need, and they executed that most vaunted of startup verbs: they pivoted. With some MacGuyvering of the tech, a fresh coat of paint and (presumably) a warehouse worth of late night Red Bulls, Roamz relaunched as Local Measure. Their mission? To connect customer feedback with the companies that wanted to apply it — like market research at a Big Tech scale.

By the end of 2013, they'd found something that Roamz had always missed: paying customers. In 2017, they raised $4.5 million from **family offices** and private investors to expand overseas. And when COVID-19 closed the doors and emptied the pockets of many Local Measure clients, they pivoted again. Now, beyond customer data acquisition, Local Measure also provides a **SaaS** ('software as a service') product that lets contact centres operate via the cloud. During an era in which call centres needed to work from home, this was a game changer.

Today, Local Measure count their paying customers at over 2500. In 2023, they were named the AWS Marketplace Partner of the Year. And yes, it might sound condescending to say that Local Measure thrived because they learned from their mistakes. However, Local Measure aren't shy about saying it themselves. Visit their office, and you'll see 'We learn from our f***ups' scrawled on the wall in three different fonts.

So, please, learn from the mistakes of your predecessors. But, more importantly, learn from your own. You *will* make them, but if you heed their lessons, you'll take another step towards riding the one-horned horse.

CHAPTER 2
WHAT'S THE PROBLEM?

It's a question you've probably never asked yourself: 'What's the *problem*?'

'That's easy,' you might respond. 'The problem is the world doesn't have what I have to give!'

In fact, 'What's the problem?' is one of the most overlooked questions in business.

More than likely, you're solving a problem you encounter every day, in your work, life or study. It will be a bugbear that's personal to you: like Alinta Furnell, a biotech founder, who was unable to find any genuinely 0 per cent alcoholic beverages. Alongside lecturing fresh young minds in biotechnology and biomolecular science, Alinta is a co-founder of Synbiote, an award-winning biotechnology startup. Keen to solve the problem in front of her, Alinta brewed Sörzero, an Assam Ale with health benefits akin to kombucha, based on Assam tea, with absolutely no alcohol. This sets Sörzero apart from the low/'no' alcohol brews available, most of which are unable to eliminate alcohol and therefore can still cause a major reaction in those who are allergic.

Sörzero sold over 2000 cans within its first 60 days, with activations at over 20 events and a growing number of stockists. However, Alinta's overnight success — like many people's — is the kind you can't engineer without proper planning, patience, product testing, and most importantly, a *problem worth solving.*

So how do you know if you have a problem worth solving? To find your answer, you'll need to untangle this double-barrelled conundrum into two simpler questions:

- What *is* the problem?

- Is it *worth solving*?

The 'problem' is probably not what you think

Airbnb started as a response to the global financial crisis (GFC). Broke and struggling to make rent on their San Francisco apartment, Airbnb's founders noticed all the local hotels were booked out for a large design conference. Both unemployed, co-founders Brian Chesky and Joe Gebbia had just moved from New York. With a captive audience of temporarily homeless conference attendees, the pair mobilised to buy airbeds. They then advertised $80-a-night stays on their hastily published website, Air Bed and Breakfast, offering an airbed and breakfast per booking. They attracted three guests, and the start of a billion-dollar idea was born.

It wasn't smooth sailing from there, though. Many were wary of the shared accommodation model, with some raising safety concerns and claiming the idea would never succeed. However, to a founder a concern is simply a problem to solve. A refinement for the next iteration. It's what sets a founder apart: an obstinate willingness to find your way through more problems than most people would ever bother to fix. You simply won't give up.

Undeterred but still broke as ever, the founders targeted the 2008 Democratic National Convention, selling election-themed cereal (Obama O's and Cap'n McCain's) and raising $30 000 to fund their vision. In January 2009, Airbnb was accepted into Y Combinator, the Oxford of startup **accelerators**. Even so, much-feted VC fund Union Square Ventures passed on funding Airbnb. It's a decision that Union Square co-founder Fred Wilson would later describe as 'a classic mistake all investors make.'

Still, Airbnb had yet to hit the problem worth solving. At $200 a week, bookings remained sluggish. Something wasn't working. Rather than be disheartened, this was simply another problem to solve. Chesky and Gebbia headed to New York, their biggest market, to meet their users and figure out what was happening on the ground.

What they discovered was that poor photo quality was a major impediment to bookings. Ever the consummate hustlers, they bought a camera and headed door to door to take better photos of their listings. This helped, but Airbnb still didn't find traction — the bookings didn't flow — until, through more iteration and experimentation, they uncovered the true market opportunity: private listings of personal accommodation of all kinds, including standalone homes. By moving beyond shared accommodation, Airbnb truly rivalled the hotel/motel accommodation market, providing an alternative that was both cheaper and offered options previously rare or unavailable, like kitchen and laundry facilities.

This was the critically disruptive force behind Airbnb. A little like Uber, it introduced a multitude of homeowners eager to monetise more of their living space to compete against the behemoth chains. In doing so, they released profits from the domain of major operators and into the pockets of the homeowning middle class. Making money from your spare granny flats, renovated sheds and unused rooms became as easy as setting up a social media profile.

They'd hit upon a problem worth solving, matchmaking what the market wanted and a novel way to provide it. Funding followed in November 2010, as Airbnb raised $7.2 million. Airbnb is now worth over US$85 billion (nearly AU$130 billion). It's as far away from an overnight success as you can imagine, but its founders were inventive, patient and extremely open to market feedback. Arguably, they took at least two years to troubleshoot their problem: from 2007, when they first launched airbeds, to 2009, after visiting New York and expanding their accommodation offering. They never, ever gave up on solving each problem they encountered, seeing problems not as a setback but as an opportunity to find the right problem to solve.

Define and refine the problem

At a glance, the heading 'Define and refine the problem' might just feel like busywork. 'Why does this matter?' you might think. 'Shouldn't I just get started?'

So many early businesses fail because they don't solve the problem customers actually want solved. How do you avoid this? It's a little bit of a trial and error. It's a lot of customer research. And sometimes, it's just about being honest.

Resist the urge to make your passion profitable

Do what you love, and you'll never work a day in your life, right? True, but that doesn't mean a customer wants to pay you to do what you love.

Jenna Leo and Mathieu Bertrand loved fitness. Jenna taught yoga, and Mathieu, a college football player, had scored work as an underwear model for brands like Aussiebum, Nivea Men and Men's Health. Commercialising their passion felt like a natural corporate escape strategy. Together, they launched Lucky Lions Fitness — which offered couples training.

But like Airbnb's earliest days, it just didn't flow. They hadn't hit product–market fit.

'We realised that we'd gone about it the wrong way: we thought that because we liked the idea, other people would like it too,' Leo told us. 'But the reality was that we weren't solving a problem. When we spoke to people about it, they said, "I work out to get Me Time. I like to do it by myself, and it makes me a better partner when I go home to be with my other half".

'That's when we decided we should focus on the problem that we were facing,' said Leo. 'And the biggest problem we were facing — and why we were working out so much — is because we were stressed about Mat's parents.'

Mathieu was an only child, and at 26, didn't expect to become the primary carer for both of his Canadian-based parents. His dad, aged 75, had lung cancer. Six months later, his mother was diagnosed with herpes simplex encephalitis, damaging her cognitive abilities and impairing her ability to walk, talk and eat.

He returned to Quebec to care for his parents, and eventually moved both of them to Australia. However, here, in addition to their physical ailments, they faced an entirely new problem: Mat was the only person they knew.

Resuming a demanding job left little time for Mat to spend with his parents, who were both frail and ill-equipped to be independent.

'Every time they left the house they would get lost, and we would need to either leave work or spend time at work on Find My Friends trying to lead them back,' said Leo.

Neither Mat nor Jenna had time for a new venture that would take even more hours out of their days, and between full-time work and full-time care, they felt overwhelmed.

'When we thought about it, we realised that this was the big challenge in our lives. And we had a friend from the US — named Destiny, funnily enough — who was incredibly warm and extroverted. She said to us, "I miss my family back home. You two are both stressed. I'd love to help you out".'

True to her name, Destiny changed their lives. She took Mat's parents to the beach and coffee and helped with their groceries. Rather than a nurse, Destiny became a friend and companion, bonding with Mat's parents over their shared love of music.

'Mat's parents loved it, and we realised this was a really good solution to our problem and we should probably share this with more people. Then, when we started our research, we discovered that there were millions of people out there with the same problem.'

Rigorous customer research underpinned Jenna and Mat's second venture. They spoke to friends, who invited them to talk to their parents. Interviewing a slew of parents about their issues helped Jenna and Mat realise many encountered the same issues around social care: finding human connection, not just medical attention. In fact, one theme came up time and again: a lack of connection.

Recent studies conducted in the United States and the UK reveal that men, in particular, are experiencing a 'friendship recession', with 27 per cent saying they have at least six close friends, down from 55 per cent in 1990. During that same period, reports of having no close friends jumped from 3 per cent to 15 per cent. This problem compounds as men age, with men less likely to keep up friendships as the demands of work and family limit their social activities.

As people enter their senior years, they may find themselves far more socially isolated than ever before. It's not an issue our healthcare system addresses.

'We realised that there were lots of medical services in Australia, and we had a compelling solution for social care, so we wanted to focus on that niche,' explained Leo.

By their own reckoning, Like Family has since become Australia's fourth-fastest-growing tech startup. More important to them, however, is their status as the nation's largest community dedicated to addressing loneliness and social isolation. How did they earn these rankings? They ditched their egos and used customer research to uncover an unsolved problem significant enough to impact most Australians.

Practise 'suspicious listening'

Sometimes, however, it pays *not* to listen to your customers.

Forage started life as a mentoring startup. That's because its co-founders, Pasha Rayan and Thomas Brunskill, had interviewed countless students on the hunt for a good graduate job — and mentoring is what they said they wanted.

'We had thought that mentoring could be useful for helping students land amazing jobs,' Rayan explained. 'We had also heard the same thing from lots of students. They often said, "We want mentors!" So we built Forage as a mentoring platform.'

Once they had built their product, they began a charm offensive to attract students. But by their own admission, they learned a lot in a short time.

'We learned that students *said* they wanted mentoring, but a lot of students weren't prepared to *be mentored*,' said Rayan. 'On the flip side, we found that mentors didn't often know what to do when students didn't show up in the right way. The result was that we were giving out this product for free, but it didn't work! We realised that mentoring wasn't the solution. However, the problem of helping students land their next opportunity persisted.'

So what's the takeaway here? Practise *suspicious listening*. The truth is, your customers may not know what they want. After all, if they did, they might not need you. Focus on what they say, but also what they desire as their outcome.

'What we learned was that students saw mentoring as a way to figure out what a job was like, and get their names in front of employers,' explained Rayan. 'On the other side, employers wanted to reach out to students from more diverse backgrounds.'

What students weren't saying was that they wanted graduate jobs at prized organisations. Students assumed mentoring would help land these roles. However, what organisations look for is experience, usually in the form of an internship from a prized organisation. It's the classic student catch 22: if all you've ever been is a student, how can you have the relevant experience to get a graduate job? This is especially true when we concede that internships are only available to a select few. Forage's brilliance lay in resolving this absurdity.

'Almost as a joke, we started saying to each other that maybe we should just get everyone an internship at Goldman Sachs or Google,' Rayan said. 'We laughed about it at the time, but we came to realise there could be a deeper idea at play.'

Forage has since become a global provider of virtual work internships, partnering with prized organisations like JP Morgan, Electronic Arts and, yes, even Goldman Sachs.

Visualise your problem: introducing the Venn Diagram of Startup Opportunities

Still stuck? Try drawing a Venn diagram. It can help you visualise what you might be missing, where you should focus, who your competitors are and how you can challenge what they do. If you think of startup opportunities as a Venn diagram, the problem you're solving would ideally sit at the epicentre, between the problem and current solution (see figure 2.1).

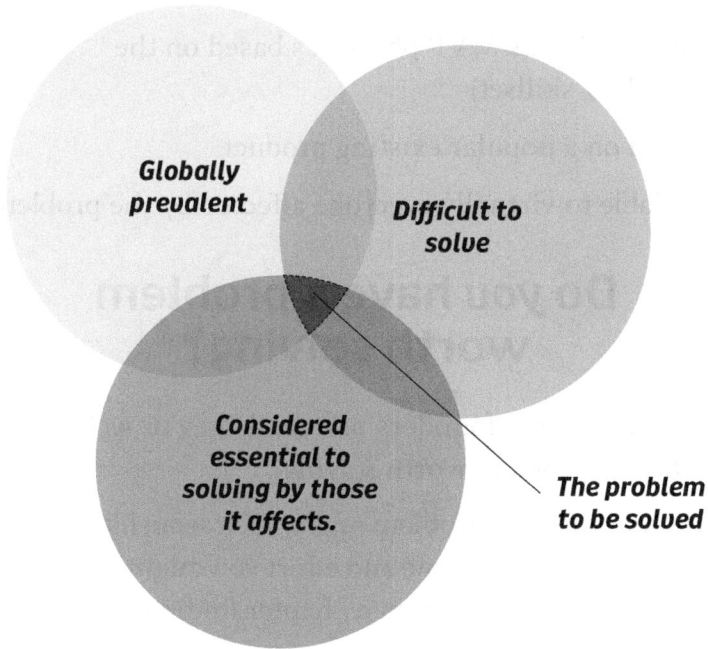

Figure 2.1: the Venn Diagram of Startup Opportunities

How does the diagram work?

In the Venn Diagram of Startup Opportunities, the problem sits at the epicentre.

The problem itself is:

- globally prevalent
- difficult to solve
- considered essential to solving by those it affects.

The current solution is:

- failing to fully address the problem of a proven business model
- only accessible to a fraction of those affected by the problem.

The solution proposed by the business is:

- low-cost (in its MVP phase, it's based on the founders' skillset)
- based on a popular existing product
- scalable to virtually everyone affected by the problem.

Do *you* have a problem worth solving?

It's the problem few founders ask until they're well underway: Do *you* have a problem worth solving?

Simply identifying a problem might itself seem like a significant task, and in terms of the time and effort you might invest in doing so, it is. After all, we just spent a chapter finding ways to identify your problem.

However, there are a few more factors to consider before you proceed.

First, does the problem matter to you? Is it within your wheelhouse of expertise and experience and do you deeply care about fixing it? Could you fix it better than most might? This may be due to your networks or knowledge. In other words:

- Are you the best person to solve this problem?
- Can you solve it better than anyone else?
- Is there profit to be made in solving this problem?

This last question is often not considered by novice entrepreneurs. Many problems exist but aren't profitable to solve. This is often where government intervenes to provide essential but unprofitable services, though social ventures or philanthropy can also play a role.

Mad Paws co-founder Alexis Soulopoulos had plenty of passion when it came to his startup problem.

'From the outset, we were convinced that the problem we wanted to solve was a problem that affected a large number of people,' said Soulopoulos. 'We also believed it was a problem worth solving. We all cared about our pets, and we knew lots of other people did as well. We thought we might be onto something.'

Some problems may have existed for a long time, but changes in consumer behaviour mean new solutions emerge. This is certainly what Lachlan McKnight, the lawyer turned CEO of LegalVision, discovered.

'When LegalVision launched in 2012, a small subset of business owners would go online to find a lawyer,' McKnight told us. 'Since then, the pool of potential customers has grown with digital adoption, particularly millennial business owners willing to go online to find legal solutions.'

This generational quirk wasn't just another example of *Boomers don't like solving problems with AI*, or *Millennials hate calling people*. Rather, it marked a seismic shift in how our society approached the engine of commerce.

'In the past, it was much more common for business owners to find a lawyer through, for example, their accountant,' explained McKnight. 'Now, if you're comfortable operating many aspects of your business online, you're likely to be comfortable with an alternative way of accessing legal services. More progressive business owners are also generally happier to deal with less traditional lawyers, so there's a heap of opportunity out there for different legal service models.'

Other problems, like providing social care or affordable pet sitting, required precise timing to make a **double-sided marketplace** work. Since a double-sided marketplace sells a supply of service providers, your business must focus on building supply before demand.

Co-founder Jenna Leo recognised this and onboarded social carers to Like Family first. Once they had 20 to 30, they started to onboard members.

Pets are a billion-dollar industry, with Australians spending $33.2 billion per year to keep their pets happy, healthy, fed, groomed, accessorised and insured. This comes as no surprise to Souloupoulos, who surveyed pet owners in dog parks alongside their research and found a real need for pet-sitting services. Like many founders, Alexis relied on his networks to launch his startup.

'When we first settled on the Mad Paws idea, I was a student at the University of Sydney,' said Souloupoulos. 'Through my uni networks, I'd connected with lots of veterinary science students, who we recruited as our first pet sitters. They were everything we wanted in Mad Paws pet sitters: passionate, knowledgeable about animals and flexible enough in their schedules to care for pets.'

However, they onboarded their pet sitters quite early, long before Mad Paws ever attracted any customers. At first, the pet sitters were excited about the prospect of caring for pets. Days passed, then weeks. By the time Mad Paws attracted customers, most of the sitters had forgotten all about Mad Paws. In the end, Alexis had no choice but to hit the phones and re-engage them.

'During those early months, I spent a lot of time on the phone,' said Soulopoulos.

'Calling pet owners, calling pet sitters, connecting the right booking to the right carer. It was a lot like sales: even if it was my hundredth call for the day, I needed to act as if it was my first.'

'It's not me, it's you': convince your consumers to change

Solving an unsolved problem is great. But if you're offering something for the first time, you'll need to convince people it's worth trying.

Vincent van Gogh famously didn't enjoy renown as an artist until he was dead. Singer Sixto Rodriguez needed to wait until the 21st century before his 1970s-penned music reached global acclaim. (He was also the subject of the 2012 documentary *Searching for Sugar Man*, which provides a pitch perfect case study in product–market fit.) A key premise of the New Testament Bible is that Jesus' teachings only widely took root *after* his crucifixion. Encouraging people to change their behaviour is no mean feat, especially when your art, word or product challenges the status quo.

Readers with a startup in their mind's eye might immediately connect with these case studies. After all, what is a startup if not a challenge to the status quo? However, the problem of changing consumer behaviour applies to any challenger brand, from crypto coins to corner stores.

According to Gerald Zaltman, Harvard professor and author of *How Customers Think: Essential insights into the mind of the market,* consumers make 95 per cent of all buying decisions subconsciously. In other words, you're fighting instinctive decision-making behaviours — and for the most part, you're fighting inertia. Consumers are looking at your product, and — sometimes without realising it — thinking, 'Why should I buy what you're selling? I've lived without it for this long, and I think I turned out all right'.

So, how do you change consumer behaviour?

Meeting this challenge has been at the core of Mad Paws' business model since they first paired pets with carers. According to Soulopoulos, their biggest rivals aren't kennels, pet hotels or other pet-sitting platforms. Rather, Mad Paws' stiffest competition comes from the friends and family of pet owners. For some people, the idea of asking a friend or loved one seems preferable to paying a stranger.

Mad Paws counters this challenge with four tactics:

- *They offer more certainty.* While friends can flake out, Mad Paws pet sitters are professionals. You can book a pet sitter months in advance, which enables pet owners to better schedule their plans. Mad Paws also convey that, if a sitter cancels, they will work with a customer to find a new one. This provides reassurance, and helps overcome a pet owner's uncertainty over trusting a relative stranger with their furry family member.

- *They offer more security.* If your pet injures themselves while in a friend's care, it's going to strain the friendship. Perhaps more distressingly, you're likely to argue over who will pay the vet bill. Mad Paws addresses this anxiety by providing insurance for all pet sitter bookings.

- *They promote their expertise.* Sure, every once in a while, you might find a friend who is blessed with the gift of dog whispering. In most cases, though, your mates will have no pet-sitting qualifications beyond 'is free' and 'will take your pet'. Mad Paws knows this — and they work it to their advantage. All Mad Paws sitters need to first pass a course, and only one in four are accepted onto the platform. Crucially, they share this figure with would-be customers as one of their USPs. In doing so, they're sending a clear message: 'We're a safer pair of hands than your stoner nephew.'

- *They work hard to build trust.* Of course, all the insurance and pet courses in the world can't change one simple fact: pet sitters are strangers. No online platform can compete with a lifetime of familial bonds, and Mad Paws doesn't try. Instead, they systematise trust through a series of in-app, codified steps. Feeling iffy about a certain pet sitter? Organise a free meet and greet before you book them. Worry how your furry friend will feel in your absence? You'll receive constant photo updates as part of your on-platform booking. Pet sitter police checks lend a legal credence to the process, and Qantas points on each booking lend the goodwill of Australia's biggest airline. In this way, Mad Paws aren't asking you to trust a stranger; they're asking you to trust a system.

Mad Paws' four-pronged approach may feel custom-designed for the pet-care industry. Even so, their example contains the following lessons for any business looking to change customer behaviour:

- Discover why consumers might be hesitant to embrace your idea. Is it an issue of trust, a matter of cost or simply a reluctance to change?

- Address their concerns, item by item. Don't trust our business? We've built a series of foolproof systems. Feel the product isn't worth paying for? Here's why it will save you money in the long run. Whatever their gripe may be, tackle it with the time and respect it deserves.

- (Gently) poke holes in the status quo. 'Friends can be flakey. Our professionals aren't.' 'DIY results can vary. Our results don't.'

- Show your would-be consumers that your business could give them a better quality of life.

Asking yourself 'What's the problem?' might feel like the Ringo Starr of your business journey. It's not as sexy as some of the other aspects, and when heard in isolation, it doesn't sound very interesting. But like Ringo Starr, it will give a rhythm to the rest of your efforts. Virtually every successful business founder in history has held a clear vision of the problem they're trying to solve, and with some planning, you can join their ranks.

Then, the world will be ready for what you have to give.

Key takeaways

- *When in doubt, ask your customers — but listen with a little suspicion. It's what helped Forage realise they weren't a mentoring startup, but instead in the business of facilitating virtual work experience.*

- *Visualise your problem with the Venn Diagram of Startup Opportunities.* Use this exercise to identify the problem, the current solution(s) and where your solution might fit.

- *Answer the question, 'Do you have a problem worth solving?'* Are you the best person to solve this problem? Can you solve it better than anyone else? Is there profit in solving this problem? These are the final sense-check questions to consider before proceeding.

- *Change the behaviour of your consumers.* Discover why they may be reluctant to embrace your offering, then systematically address their concerns.

CHAPTER 3
WHAT TO DO BEFORE YOU LAUNCH

'Just get started.'

You'll likely hear this time and again during your startup planning phase. Established founders will suggest it because they know that nothing prepared them for the startup like the startup did. Potential investors will insist on it because they want to see some proof of concept before they back you. Friends will yell it in frustration over Sunday brunch — because they're sick of hearing you drone on about your idea.

And we can't stress this enough: there's merit to this concept. As we'll explore in later chapters, the startup life requires you to run an endless gauntlet of unknown unknowns. No amount of planning, workshopping or Trello hacking can equip you for problems you haven't even discovered yet. The sooner you launch, the sooner you can unearth the alien crises you'll need to resolve before you can grow.

But for all the unasked questions in every startup's future, there are a few certainties. Problems that, regardless of their sector, every startup will need to confront. Meta and Amazon may leverage different business models; Canva and Atlassian may share few superficial traits beyond coming from the same country—and the obligatory ping-pong table. But for their myriad differences, their founders shared some common struggles in their earliest days. Those struggles are what this chapter is here to address.

Sure, you might not be able to solve them before you launch. But you *can* equip yourself with the tools to succeed when they do emerge.

In this chapter, you'll learn what you can do before you launch to set yourself up for success. This includes:

- padding your CV with the right accolades to woo investors

- building your Pyramid of Priorities (see figure 3.1 on page 48) ahead of launch

- being obsessive with your customer research

- avoiding the Capone Trap: a boring but crucial challenge that has sunk many founders (and crime bosses).

Are you ready? Let's stock up on rocket fuel!

Why your CV can give you a boost before launch

When many founders commit to launching, they assume their CV will land in the 'Trash' icon on their desktop. And, yes, they'll maintain a LinkedIn account—but it will serve as a networking tool and startup soapbox, not a resume. Surely, the CV belongs squarely in any founder's pre-startup past, along with performance reviews and office Christmas parties.

You don't need to delve too deep to find the origin of this myth. If you Google 'reasons to launch a startup', you'll find a series of listicles plugging the joys of startup life. In almost all of them, 'Be Your Own Boss' features in the top five. What use, then, would you have for an item designed to compel you into servitude?

In short, you'll need a CV because you *won't* be your own boss. The PM works for around 28 million Australian residents, Tim Cook works for Apple's shareholders and you'll work for your investors. Unless you self-fund, you'll always have someone to report to. We've devoted chapter 6 to funding, so we won't cover it here in too much depth. For now, all we'll say is that most founders will need to court funding at some stage. And when your startup is still just an idea in a **pitch deck**, investors can't back growth or revenue. They can't even invest in an idea, because what is an idea without the right team to execute it?

No. If they invest at all, they'll invest in the founder.

Richard D Harroch is the managing director at VantagePoint Capital Partners. Having emerged from California in 1996, VantagePoint rode the Silicon Valley tech boom after the turn of the century. According to Crunchbase, as of 2023, they hold more than US$4.5 billion in funds under management. In his article published on *Forbes*, '15 key questions venture capitalists will ask before investing in your startup', Harroch cites 'Is there a great management team?' as the first question. 'Many investors consider the team behind a startup more important than the idea or the product,' Harroch writes. 'The investors will want to know that the team has the right set of skills, drive, experience, and temperament to grow the business.'

Before you go and plaster your face over your business' mock-up website, we need to address the data. Based on a review of 320 pitch decks, TechCrunch found that there was only one slide that features in both failed and successful pitch decks. That slide? 'Team'.

What does this tell us? That VCs view founders as a make-or-break ingredient — but depending on how you present yourself, you can either make your pitch, or break it.

'Great,' you might say, throwing your hands in the air with exasperation. 'People with money will back me if they like me, and burn me if they don't. What a *hot take*. I could have told you that from every job interview I've ever been to. So, *how* do I get them to like me?'

Enter Mr Airtasker, Tim Fung.

Build a rocket ship, then brag about it

Beyond his guise as the co-founder and CEO of Airtasker, Tim Fung is also a sophisticated investor. Since his days as a founding team member of mobile-phone-plan provider amaysim, Fung has thrown money behind a slew of Aussie startups. In other words, he's sat on both sides of the pitch deck.

Whether he's gauging potential hires or startup prospects, Fung says he puts a high priority on a person's work experience. However, his key metric isn't where they worked, or even what type of title they held. Instead, he takes heed of the problems they solved, and the extent to which they sought responsibility.

'If you see on someone's resume that they helped **scale** Google, Facebook or Canva, you might think, *Oh, wow. This person scales rocket ships!* But you'd also ask, 'Do they know how to *make* rocket ships?' Fung told us.

'The person who knows how to do hard things is most valuable. We're looking for the person who can say, "I worked for a company that almost ran out of money and I figured out how to make it profitable". Or "I worked for a company that had a cost base of $100 million and a revenue of $10 million".'

Fung's advice sprouts from the same soil as 'just get started'. Most VCs and sophisticated investors know the score; they realise that the founders they back will need to solve brand new problems every day. Clearly, you can't solve problems that don't even exist yet. Even so, you *can* highlight the problems you've solved in your pre-launch life.

This doesn't mean you need to boast a Sheryl Sandberg-esque CV to impress investors. Instead, it suggests that you'll want to change the focus from 'What work have you done?' to 'What problems have you solved?' Ask yourself: When have your past environments faced wicked problems or existential threats? What role did you play in solving them? What did you learn from staring down the barrel of a crisis?

Notice how we said 'environments', not 'workplaces'? That's because you don't always need to prove your mettle on someone else's timesheet. Before he co-founded Mad Paws, Alexis Soulopoulos served as President of the CEMS Club Sydney. A student body, CEMS Club Sydney exists to enrich the lives of international students in the CEMS program. This mandate takes a range of shapes, from corporate partner activations, to raging harbour cruise parties. Or, put simply, it's an equal parts networking group, exchange student support service and party planner. Oh, and it's run by student volunteers. So, not the 'Head of Growth at Amazon' role you might expect for such a feted founder.

Did it prove to be a hurdle for Soulopoulos? Not at all. In fact, he rightly framed it as a perfect proving ground for any startup founder. Take a glance at his LinkedIn, and his CCS listing stresses two things VCs love to hear about: results and data.

Factoids like 'Led a team of 23 multicultural people' both highlight and quantify his leadership skills. He also notes that, under his guidance, his team 'brought the [Sydney] club to the official title of 3rd Best CEMS Club of 29 Clubs worldwide'.

For those of you who (like us) are unacquainted with inter-collegiate club rivalries, this figure might leave you saying 'Uh…great?' But this detail isn't a flex for a niche audience — it's a coded message for shot callers. Souloupoulos could have written something like 'became one of the top-ranked CEMS Clubs' and patted himself on the back. Instead, he realised that investors always crave more numbers. Metrics convey the depth of a problem (in this case, 28 other clubs to beat) and the extent of the solution (26 of them beaten). And when a would-be founder chooses raw data over self-flattery, they signal to investors that they recognise their priorities.

Whether you've managed a team, volunteered at a student body or waited tables, one thing is clear: you've solved problems. Use your CV as a canvas to paint a picture of what they were, and how you handled them. Use data and metrics as your paint, and you might end up with a painting of a rocket ship.

Key takeaways

- *Learn to promote your own USP.* In the early stages of a startup, investors will back people over ideas. Before you launch, build a CV for VCs.

- *Highlight problems, not promotions.* A series of title changes and top-tier employers might appeal to head hunters, but it won't always charm investors. Home in on the challenges you've tackled — and include the data to back it up.

- *No job? No worries.* Not everything in your resume needs to relate to a full-time role. If you've solved problems, surpassed hardship, or earned victories in a non-paid position, include it in your resume.

Are you focusing on the right thing?

Okay, you've polished yourself into a bauble that you'll be better able to market to investors. This will play a background role when you reach chapter 6. In the meantime, though, you have a much more pressing task: knowing what to focus on before you launch.

This might feel like an almost gratuitous suggestion, like 'Believe in yourself' or 'Get ready to hustle'. In reality, though, most founders don't know what to focus on before they launch ... so they focus on the wrong thing.

Admittedly, it isn't only would-be founder archetypes who face this problem. Established CEOs admit to having confronted it during their early days. In his conversations with us, Souloupoulos revealed Mad Paws lost early bookings by prioritising a speedy website launch to beat potential rivals vying to enter the market. However, this led to issues with the website. Beating their rivals meant they also needed to patch a leaky ship while it was at sea.

With a successful IPO now under his belt, Souloupoulos can look back on those nascent trials with clear eyes. He also sees a commonality in the challenges faced by many early-stage founders.

'I think for a lot of smart people creating startups, they may not be focusing on things that are entirely *un*important, but they may focus on things that are *less* important,' Souloupoulos said.

'And when you're such a small team, with limited resources, it matters a lot that you only focus on the most important details at the beginning.'

Build a Pyramid of Priorities

For anyone who's studied psychology (or marketing), this isn't some startup-savvy version of Maslow's Hierarchy of Needs. Instead, it offers a simple framework for knowing what to focus on before you launch your startup. And we don't mean 'first year of an MBA' simple; we mean 'able to recall it after a boozy lunch' simple.

Observe the Pyramid of Priorities (see figure 3.1).

Figure 3.1: the Pyramid of Priorities

What's the first thing you notice? The primary-school-level language? The crayon-esque design? Or the overriding sense of pessimism? These three details are features, not bugs. The aim of this pyramid is to stress two concepts:

- Keep it simple.
- Focus on the problems that will kill your business if left unchecked.

Before you launch, everything else is just window-dressing.

First, we'll stress that we explore the solution to many of these problems in chapter 5. For other challenges, we highlight the chapter in which you're most likely to find your answer. We mention this now so you don't feel dismayed by the impending roll call of issues.

Now, let's explore the three tiers of the pyramid, and what they mean for your startup.

WHAT WILL RUIN US ON LAUNCH DAY?

This tier sits at the top of the pyramid for a reason. As the name suggests, these are the problems that have the potential to sink your startup on launch day. In this context, by 'launch day', we mean the moment in which your startup begins operating as a business. This will look different for every founder, and no two launch days will look exactly the same. Even so, regardless of their sector, *no* founder wants to suffer a day one death.

Examples of problems that could ruin you on launch day include:

- *A fatal flaw in your product*

  Few founders' products are flawless when they first reach the market. However, if yours causes any manner of harm to its user, you will forevermore become a cautionary tale. Such are the perils of poor product testing.

- *A fatal flaw in your platform*

  If your business model depends on a website or app to earn its revenue, this could be a problem you'll face. Beyond common technical issues, a fatal flaw is something that would compromise your users' money or data. Some customers *may* forgive a few bugs or slow

49

load times on launch day — but none will forgive a loss to their assets or privacy. And, more grimly, the courts may not either.

- *Flagrantly false advertising*

  You've spent months hyping up the features of your product. Then, when it reaches its target market, it doesn't do what you said it would do. Yes, at times, marketers may stretch the surly bonds of objectivity. They may even exaggerate a product's efficacy. But if your offering clearly doesn't meet the standards that *you publicly set*, its demise will be swift and brutal.

- *No protections, no approvals*

  We explore this problem in greater depth later in this chapter. For now, we'll simply say this: you're going to need certain regulatory or liability frameworks in place. Depending on your industry, this could take the guise of insurance, licences, certifications or approvals from the relevant council or government department. Nobody becomes a founder because they enjoy bureaucracy. But to shirk your protections and approvals is to spell your own doom.

WHAT WILL RUIN US WITHIN THE FIRST SIX MONTHS?

These problems are the slow-acting poisons of your early-stage startup. They may not end your business on day one, but they'll gnaw away at your foundations until naught remains. In many respects, they're actually more formidable than the top of the pyramid; fatal flaws are often more obvious, whereas imperfections are easy to dismiss. Besides, if nothing else, a launch day failure will give you a quirky party story. A half-year demise, meanwhile, will spawn the same consequences (irate investors, litigious creditors, reputational damage) plus untold others (a pointless co-working space lease and boxes of branded merch, for instance).

These types of challenges could include:

- *a noticeable flaw in your product.* No-one will die, no-one will sue you ... and no-one will touch it again. While your product won't attract regulatory ire, or go viral for the wrong reasons, it also can't retain its users. These kinds of issues usually emerge during pre-launch product testing, which we discuss later in this chapter. For now, we'll say that if your product testers are largely reporting the same flaw, it's likely a six-month killer.

- *your product lagging behind its competitors.* Let's say you're looking to launch a shark-repellent e-commerce business aimed at middle-income masked heroes. You've researched your rivals, and you've priced your products similarly. The only problem: your range of products doesn't repel sharks as well as the incumbents. Without a clear USP, why would middle-income vigilantes take a chance on your product? The answer: they probably won't. Now, this doesn't need to undo you; your business could always pivot towards lower-income superheroes. However, unless you change strategies, your e-commerce platform will likely be BAM! BIFF! KAPOW!'ed out of the market within six months.

- *too little **runway**.* When you crunched the numbers and asked investors for capital, you either crunched too poorly, or asked for too little. Either way, you don't have enough runway to last until the end of the year. On launch day, this seemed like a problem for Future You. Six months later, Present You is scrambling to keep the power on with the change from your childhood money box.

- *too much spending.* Maybe you raised enough money for a more thrifty entrepreneur to survive the first half-year. But you? You calculated your burn rate while listening to The Trammps. You burned, baby, burned — and the inferno you stoked wasn't of the disco variety. No … it was of the bank-account-exhausting, startup-killing variety.

WHAT WILL RUIN US AT SOME POINT IN THE FUTURE?

By this point, you may be thinking, 'Why should I worry about these problems now? The list of immediate problems is already long enough. Besides, you began this chapter by talking about unknown unknowns. Aren't the problems of the future the mysteries of the present, or something like that?'

To which we would say, 'Beautifully put.' Then, we would say, 'Yes, some of tomorrow's problems are today's enigmas. Others are noxious weeds that take time to grow — but unfurl their roots before you ever launch.'

Those are the challenges we're interested in ripping from the soil before you plant your startup. They can include:

- *no clear route to breaking even.* Chapter 12 details the road to profitability, so we won't expend too many words on it here. In short, though, during the early years of your startup, your goal should be growth over profits. Even so, you should have a framework or roadmap for how you'll eventually break even. Without it, your backers will stop funding you, your funds will dwindle and you'll suffer death by a thousand invoices.

- *no product–market fit.* Like profitability, product–market fit requires its own chapter — which is why we wrote one (see chapter 9). For now, here's the haiku version of how its lack could destroy you:

Your product works well

but it hasn't found its tribe

so your startup wanes.

- *no unique selling proposition.* Sure, your product does what it says it does. Yes, it matches the performance and the pricepoint of its peers. But does it offer its users something that its rivals don't? Failing that, does your branding connect with your target market in a way that cultivates loyalty? (You'll find more on this in chapter 10.) If the answer to both is 'No', you'll forever be at the mercy of newer, more unique contenders.

- *no scalability.* Your revenue has increased — and that's great. Now for the bad news: for whatever reason, you've exhausted your growth. Perhaps you misjudged the size of your target market. Maybe you overestimated how much product you could create. In either instance, the result is the same: you can't grow any larger. Of course, you may feel perfectly content to eschew the startup route and embrace a typical small business model. Should this sound like you, head to chapter 8. But if you've built your business around a forecast of **scalability**, this growth ceiling will cause you trouble.

Tell me more

Congratulations! You've made it to the end of a very depressing list. However, you may still feel poorly equipped to pre-emptively resolve the threats to your startup. Terms like 'flaw in your product' and 'no unique selling proposition' do sound ominous.

Furthermore, your pyramid will look markedly distinct from another reader's. A fatal flaw in a dating app, for instance, will wreak a different kind of mayhem than fraudulently claiming you can run blood tests with just 'a single drop of blood.

For this reason, the best tool to help you fill your pyramid is customer research. Just ask Pasha Rayan, co-founder and CTO at Forage. During their early days, Rayan admits Forage (like many young startups) took a few missteps. However, while there are things he would do differently in hindsight, Rayan credits exhaustive customer research with Forage's success.

'When we first started out, we excessively talked to our customers — and that's one thing I wouldn't change,' Rayan told us.

In Forage's case, 'excessively talking to customers' involved hosting around 3000 users on their testing platform and then collecting their feedback. It also meant interviewing around 600 students — their target market — to learn what they wanted from a platform like Forage. As a result, they gathered the insights they needed to evolve their product and avoid the pyramid.

While your target market may differ, Rayan suggests that obsessive customer research will benefit any sector.

'For most people, I think excessive inputs will lead to extraordinary outcomes.'

Rayan's views aren't rare among founders. As you'll learn in the next chapter, Leo and her co-founder Bertrand learned from future users by attending disability expos. Before launching Mad Paws, Soulopoulos visited dog parks across Sydney to interview pet owners. His goal? Learn as much as possible about their needs, and create a platform that meets them.

In the next chapter, we'll explore how you can find and connect with your target market. For now, though, know that the process can be as simple as creating a survey. Populate it with the questions you *think* you need to ask, then adapt those questions in response to feedback. The more you learn before launch, the further you'll veer from the pitfalls of the pyramid.

Avoid the Capone Trap

Alphonse 'Scarface' Capone was arguably the most infamous North American gangster of the 20th century. From his throne in Prohibition Era Chicago, he allegedly presided over a conglomerate of crime, from protection rackets to bootlegging. So, how did the law finally topple his dark reign? Did it connect him to his web of gambling dens or narcotics supply chains? Was he caught at the scene of one of the many murders he allegedly sanctioned? No … old Scarface was convicted on tax evasion charges.

Before launching, many would-be founders focus on the sexy problems of a startup: capital, MVP and product–market fit. It scarcely needs to be said that these are crucial problems, and warrant the time and energy of any entrepreneur. However, in solely chasing these solutions, some founders neglect the more boring, admin-based demands of a business. In doing so, they risk falling into the Capone Trap: a snare in which a seemingly mundane problem proves to be their undoing. You also viewed this problem in the Pyramid of Priorities, in the section 'No protections, no approvals.'

If you view the Capone Trap literally, there's a pretty obvious lesson for any founder: don't swindle the tax office. To take it into a more abstract realm, the Capone Trap could involve any admin detail that threatens your business.

Uber almost crashed on several occasions after running afoul of various governments for sidestepping established taxi regulations.

DoorDash delivery drivers require two distinct insurance types: a personal auto policy and business use coverage. Regulatory distinctions between sharing and commercial letting continue to hamper Airbnb to this day. Compliance doesn't always make for exciting pitch fodder, but you don't want to be on its bad side. Having said that, by the very nature of their uniqueness, compliance can require different measures for each business.

Take the example of Like Family. Before they ever accepted their first booking, they sought insurance to protect themselves, their carers and their clients. However, since their concept was a rarity, they found the insurance sector didn't know how to classify them.

'From the very beginning, I decided we absolutely couldn't launch until we secured insurance that would cover the workers on our platform,' Leo told us.

'The problem was, at the time, insurers didn't know what to make of our type of business model. I spoke to at least six different insurers, and all six of them said, 'You shouldn't do this. It's a terrible idea, and we're not going to give you insurance'.'

Fortunately, after shopping around and further articulating their business model for an insurance-oriented audience, they finally found a provider.

'They understood the risks and challenges of our business, and they gave us a good deal on insurance,' Leo explained. 'It wasn't until we'd addressed that risk element that we were able to launch.'

Believe it or not, Like Family's commitment to caution is less common than you might expect. According to findings from the Australian Insurance Summit, around half of failed **small-to-medium enterprises (SMEs)** do so after suffering an insurable loss to their business. Or, put more simply, they could have insured against a problem, but they didn't, and it ended them.

Now, insurance is only one of the many forms your Capone Trap might assume. If you're looking to challenge an incumbent sector, as Uber did, you may need to contend with current industry regulations. Should you want to work with third-party freelancers, you may have labour laws to consider. Businesses that leverage physical space, meanwhile, may need to navigate council zoning rules. Like so much else, the prongs in a Capone Trap will differ depending on the nature of your business. Even so, ask yourself the following questions and you'll increase your chances of finding your Capone Trap:

- *'Could someone theoretically be at risk while engaging with my business, either directly or indirectly?'*

  Seek insurance coverage. Speak to different insurers, explain your business, and choose the provider who understands your needs.

- *'Am I working with employees, contractors or freelancers?'*

  Research the labour laws that apply to your industry — even (or especially) if you want to subvert it. Start with an internet search and go from there.

- *'Do I want to topple (or at least undercut) an established business model?'*

  Research the unions, government bodies and regulations that protect the sector. Again, you can begin with a simple search — for example, 'taxi regulations NSW' or 'food delivery legislation Vic.'.

- *'Am I planning on using property or public space in an unorthodox manner?'*

  Become familiar with the relevant council's requirements for zoning and public land use. This can range from speaking with a development and planning lawyer (which we detail in the next chapter) to contacting the council in question (although don't expect a speedy response). For projects that aim to span across multiple councils, opt for the former rather than the latter. It will cost you, but it will be worth it.

- *'Will I be working with [INSERT PRODUCT, FEATURE OR FUNCTION]?'*

  Scour the internet to find the relevant government body pertaining to [INSERT PRODUCT, FEATURE OR FUNCTION].

Key takeaways

- *Focus on the right thing by building a Pyramid of Priorities.* Address the problems that will destroy your startup on launch day, then within six months, then at some stage in the future. There's nothing more important.

- *Be obsessive about learning from your potential customers.* Talk to them. Note what they say. Survey your target market. Beyond shaping your knowledge of their wants, it will also help you identify the customer-facing problems on your pyramid.

- *Protect against compliance problems.* Whether it's specific insurance coverage or government approval, there will be compliance issues that pertain to your business. Avoid the Capone Trap and address them from the outset.

Don't forget to just get started

As the chapter title promised, we've spent the last several pages listing the problems you should confront before launching. Given your future will bristle with unknown unknowns, there is tremendous value in preparing for burdens you can identify today.

However, at some point, you'll need to return to that phrase you've heard time and again: just get started. For every problem you solve (or at least consider) before launch, another dozen will be lurking in wait post-launch. No level of planning, and no degree of brainstorming, will prepare you for on-the-job problem solving. Oh, and that customer research we spoke about earlier? There's only so much you can conduct without putting your MVP in front of users (which we explore in chapter 5).

To be fair, we're aware that 'just get started' seems easier to write on a page than to act on. Kakorrhaphiophobia isn't just a 10-dollar word — it's a persistent fear of failure, and it's something that haunts many founders. In their desire to create something perfect, they end up creating nothing at all.

For Lockpick Games founder Tash Jamieson, the answer to this quandary came to her during a talk she attended.

'I was listening to a presentation by Ajay Prakash, who is the founder of a company called EntryLevel,' Jamieson said to us.

'In his speech, he said something to the effect of, "There's no time in this industry to be sitting on your brilliant idea but not sharing it and getting feedback. If anyone can share their prototype with me by midnight tonight, I will personally review it and help you out".'

'So, from hearing that at 7 pm, I spent the rest of the night getting something ready, and then sent it to him. The prototype

I prepared was terrible, but it didn't matter — I sent it and got feedback.'

In addition to laying the foundations for an MVP, this experience set a precedent to always seek feedback. 'Right now, for example, we're running product trials in South Korea, and the feedback we're receiving is shocking,' Jamieson said. 'But getting negative user feedback and applying it is 20 times better than theorising what customers will and won't like.'

In the end, only you can know when you're ready to bring your startup to life. And before you do, there is an array of problems you can address. However, there comes a time in every founder's journey when they can plan no more. The prototypes have been sketched, the numbers have been crunched, the problems have been listed and the compliance has been met. When you reach that blessed day, let Tash's words ring in your ears: 'The best advice I ever received about running a startup was to just start. Just start doing stuff'.

CHAPTER 4
LET YOUR NETWORK BUILD YOUR STARTUP

Wait … come back.

We know when most people read the word 'network', alarms of cringe blare in their minds. But remember how we spent part of the previous chapter refining your CV and stressing customer research? Well, unless you can manifest would-be contacts into your LinkedIn account, that refined CV won't do you any good. And without a direct line to your target market, you'll have no prospective customers to research. However, before you shudder at the mere thought of networking, hear us out for a bit. Give us a few pages, and we'll aim to give you some peace of mind around the entire subject.

When you think of professional networking, what springs to mind? According to research published in *Administrative Science Quarterly*, many people feel 'dirty' at the mere thought of it. A slew of unwelcome images can waft into your head: clickbaity messages on LinkedIn. Conference rooms with no airflow. Bland, pre-rehearsed smiles. Limp handshakes. Overly forceful handshakes. Sub-standard canapes.

With online networking, you feel like a wifi version of a cold caller. At in-person events, you spend much of your time near the bathrooms in case you need to retreat from view. You want to look approachable without seeming desperate, so you settle on a vacant, deer-in-headlights type of smile.

You refresh your phone every 30 seconds, even though you're not expecting any important emails. Half the guests look as awkward as you feel; the other half are bounding around as if they're on a day pass at Disneyland. You don't want to impose on the former, and you haven't downed enough caffeine to contend with the latter. In short, you'd be forgiven for wanting to cast aside networking like an unwanted business card.

It's not who you know, it's when you know them

Here's the bad news: by networking *now*, you'll sidestep a barrage of obstacles later in your startup journey. For one thing, it can connect you with potential investors (which we'll discuss in chapter 6). But more pertinently to your pre-launch phase, your contact list can help you solve those unknown unknowns we mentioned earlier. The longer your contact list, the higher your likelihood of solving them. Hold onto that thought for now; we promise we'll return to it.

Now, we still haven't addressed your loathing of networking, have we? Well, here's where we get to the good news: by networking before launch, you'll avoid everything that makes networking loathsome. Think about it: most people network when they need something. If they fail to get it, they'll face some manner of consequence. The stakes create pressure, and the pressure can spawn resentment.

But you? You don't know the full extent of what you need yet. Your future problems are amorphous, so the consequences for not quashing them are, as of today, non-existent. Think of it like superannuation: start early when it counts for little, and your efforts might help you go far. Start late, and the stakes will be matched only by your stress.

Or, put differently, have you ever walked into a social function and felt no pressure to impress anyone? That's how you can feel when you network without a finite goal in mind.

How to win friends: a guide for introverts

If you're an introvert, the lack of stakes may not seem like much of a consolation prize. Luckily, other introverts have paved the way for you. They've suffered through countless conferences, meetups and corporate soirees so you can thrive in them.

Jevonya Allen is a networking coach and author of *The Introvert's Guide to Becoming a Master Networker*. Through her research and crystalised experience, she has distilled several networking tactics spanning from in-person events to online outreach. Unlike other networking protocols, which often feel like you need a baseline of Sigma Male energy, Allen custom-tailored these for introverts. From her teachings, these are the five that we believe are the most fitting for the conference-wary founder. May they apply a gentle poultice to the sting of networking.

CREATE AFFIRMATIONS AROUND NETWORKING

We know, we *know*. Thanks to the post-Goop self-help movement, 'affirmations' has become a loaded word. In this context, though, Allen simply wants you to acknowledge your feelings towards networking — then do it anyway. Confirm to yourself that you can dislike a thing and still excel at it. Remind yourself when the doubt slips past the guardrails in your mind. Write it in your phone if it helps. You've got this.

PRE-EMPT YOUR PAIN POINTS FOR EVERY EVENT YOU ATTEND

Neuroses have a habit of finding a problem for every win you score. Fortunately, they're also predictable creatures. With enough forethought, you can pre-empt the grievances they'll raise about your networking attempts.

Don't want to go to an event alone? That's fine; you can take a friend or colleague. Find the entire ordeal to be taxing? Schedule a buffer before the event so you can preload on energy. Don't know what to say? List the answers you seek, and the types of people you want to meet, before you arrive. Eventually, your neuroses will blow themselves out and leave your mind clear for meeting new people.

BE GOOD WITH NAMES

You know how most people claim they're bad with names? Don't be that person. To quote Dale Carnegie — the OG startup success story — 'A person's name is to him or her the sweetest sound in any language'. Jevonya Allen echoes these sentiments, and asserts that remembering someone's name is a shortcut to make a lasting impression.

Of course, this is hardly new information. Most of us know we *should* recall someone's name, but fumble to summon it under pressure. To this end, the New York School of Etiquette offers some tips for when a person's name evades you. As a first line of defence, repeat their name as soon as you hear it. If they're a peer, you might say, 'Sheryl, so nice to meet you'. If they're a senior, you might choose to say, 'Ms Sandberg, it's a pleasure'. Should you still have trouble committing their name to memory, you can always recruit your friend. Bring them into the conversation, then begin with 'Have you two met?' This way, they'll both need to repeat their names — and your brain will be ready to pounce on the moniker.

BOOK SOME FOLLOW-UP SIT-DOWNS — AND ARRIVE WITH A PLAN

Let's say you've gone to the trouble of planting a lemon tree. In this metaphor, you're not much of a gardener, but you want to make fresh lemon curd on the regular. You've researched backyard horticulture 101, bought a sapling from Bunnings, lugged it home, cleared the errant dirt and leaves from the backseat of your car, measured the angle at which the sunlight hits your backyard (if you're lucky enough to have one), dug a hole in a spot that receives at least six hours of daily sunlight, gingerly lowered the sapling into the hole and topped it with soil and mulch. In total, you've exhausted about a day's worth of labour and research. And keeping that tree alive? You'll need about 10 minutes a week to water it deeply. Now, let me ask you this: in what world would you decide to let the tree *wither and die*, rather than water it weekly?

You may have guessed where we're going with this: networking is much like planting a lemon tree. Once you've made a new contact at a function, you've finished your day's labour. Now, you need to water those roots. When you're parting ways from your new acquaintance, ask them how they prefer to communicate. Send them a follow-up message on their preferred platform the next day. This isn't the late 1990s — you don't need to play it cool and wait 48 hours. Propose that you meet for a coffee (or preferred beverage) over the next two weeks, and save them the admin toil by suggesting a few different times.

Now, let me ask you *this*: when you go to water your lemon tree, do you wander into your garden, hose in hand, *without* a list of pre-planned questions? No, of course you don't. The same applies to any function follow-up coffee. Write down the key talking points you want to cover before you meet, then use them to steer your conversation. But, much like the pirate code, you should view them more as guidelines than actual rules.

FIND THE SOCIAL MEDIA PLATFORMS WHERE YOUR NETWORKS CONGREGATE

We explore this concept in greater detail below, so we'll keep this concise. For now, all we'll say is this: different industries favour different platforms. Fitness professionals often flock to Instagram and TikTok; lawyers love LinkedIn like it's a client on retainer. Journalists, meanwhile, have historically gathered on the platform formerly known as Twitter. To find your tribe, find where they reside during their daily doomscrolls.

Key takeaways

- *Network today; solve problems tomorrow.* Building your network should be a focus for your pre-launch life. By growing your contact list now, you'll better equip yourself to solve your startup's future problems.

- *Low stakes = low pressure.* If you wait until you need something before you network, the looming spectre of failure may haunt your efforts. But if you make contacts before you launch? You're just a person, standing in front of another person, asking them to explain their industry to you.

- *Introverts can work a room as well.* Whether you love or loathe the limelight, you can thrive as a networker. It's okay if conferences aren't your thing; bring a friend, arrive with a plan, follow up and you'll still flourish.

Where to network when your startup isn't working yet

As liberating as this approach may be, it's worth little if you don't know *where* to network. But, at the risk of sounding like a startup Switzerland, we can't direct you towards the right events for you. Your ideal networking calendar will depend on a range of factors tailored to you and your proposed startup. With that caveat out of the way, your networking targets will generally fall into four clusters:

1. Your target market

2. The sector that will bring your business to life

3. The Australia and New Zealand startup community

4. Your force multipliers.

Let's make like a conference panel and deep dive into each one.

1. Your target market

During Like Family's nascent days, its co-founders Jenna Leo and Mathieu Bertrand made themselves a frequent presence at disability expos. There, they met would-be customers, assessed could-be competitors and formed relevant partnerships within the sector. They also learned from their target market in real time, which offered insights that most market research couldn't buy. In fact, in her conversations with us, Jenna credited those expos with some of Like Family's most crucial early learnings.

Similarly, when Airtasker was a two-person operation, co-founders Tim Fung and Jonathan Lui wanted to meet residents in specific areas. To this end, they attended community meetups, where they would promote Airtasker to anyone with a task that needed doing. As with Like Family, it gave them the opportunity to conduct customer research (which we discuss later in the chapter).

Whatever your startup's focus, it will aim to reach a specific target market. And, chances are, that target market will attract events designed to meet their needs. Attend those before you launch, and you'll learn more than hours of online research can unveil.

'Okay, *fine*,' you might mutter under your breath, possibly while stretching some Blu Tack with your hands. 'Target market events, and whatnot. But I'm not some expo bounty hunter, you know. How am I supposed to just sniff out industry events?'

Simple: act like a member of your future target market. Scour Google for the types of answers your target market would seek. Head to social media and follow the accounts that your would-be customers would follow. Subscribe to email newsletters, listen to podcasts, watch YouTube content that someone designed for your target market.

Why? Several reasons. First, you'll start to tacitly learn about the industry in which you want to function. Second, you'll, sooner or later, discover the right roadshows, expos and festivals. For one thing, you'll likely hear about them from the plethora of sources you now follow. For another, your online behaviour will train the algorithm to feed you similar content.

Last, your data will begin to align with the target ads that event promoters will run. You know, those infuriating online ads that follow you around, seeming to know you better than you know yourself? In this rare instance, they'll serve *you* in the name of market research.

Once you've found an event, you won't need to prepare an **elevator pitch** for your unborn startup. In fact, you may prefer to attend the function incognito. This way, you can extend your target market roleplay into the real world. Approach prospective competitors, and ask them the kinds of questions their customers would. Chat with other attendees, and learn of their pain points without the pressure to make a sale. Listen to would-be partners, and focus on what they *do*, rather than what they can do *for you*. In all three cases, you'll learn more as a buyer who doesn't purchase than a vendor with no product.

Once you've returned home, note down your key learnings. Follow the competitors you met. Send follow-up emails or LinkedIn requests to any provider who might tessdelate with your future startup. Like compound interest, your efforts now will pay outsized dividends in the coming months — and years.

2. The sector that will bring your business to life

There's an old joke among jaded metal fans: 'Where are you most likely to find a Metallica fan? At a Metallica concert. Where are you most likely to find a Metallica member? At an Armani store.'

When networking, always distinguish between the people who will use your product and the people who will build it. If you're looking to, for example, launch an on-demand massage service for orangutans, then your target market will be orangutans. But who will build the app that connects tense orangutans with massage therapists? Who will administer the much-needed messages to the stressed apes? Who will steer the finances, handle marketing and create a smooth on-platform experience for your simian target market?

In almost all cases, the answer will be 'not orangutans'.

While startups differ, they all share one inalienable fact: no founder can do it alone. To launch, you'll require skills and labour beyond your own. To scale, you'll need even more of it. (In chapter 7, we'll explore this concept in greater depth.) At this stage, though, we would suggest you take the following steps:

- Identify the gap between the skills you possess and the skills you'll need to grow your startup.

- Find the industries in which these skills are common.

- Attend those industries' events with that same 'no stakes, no pressure' attitude.

In Australia, just about every industry hosts conferences, panels, meetups and expos. They're also not shy about promoting them; simply follow your sector's leading bodies on LinkedIn, or register for their newsletter, and you'll hear of their upcoming events.

Not sure where to begin? Start by asking yourself which industry will bring the most essential skillsets to your startup. For example, if your startup is likely to require ample financial savvy, follow *Chartered Accountants Australia and New Zealand*. If it's engineers you'll need, watch *Engineers Australia*'s movements on LinkedIn. Beyond drawing your eye to their events, these groups can also connect you with currently practising professionals.

The longer you follow these groups, the more prepared you'll be to approach the right people when you need them.

3. The Australia and New Zealand startup community

There's a (slightly) newer joke among stalwarts of the startup community:

'For most founders, launching a startup is pretty much the opposite of *Fight Club* ... because the first rule of their startup seems to be never shutting the hell up about their startup.'

As an early founder, your startup idea will likely feel like a freshly blooming romance. You'll want to shout about it from the rooftops — or, most likely, shout it at your friends over lattes. For reasons we discuss later in this chapter, there's a benefit to discussing your startup with your loved ones. However, unless you already fraternise with founders, your loved ones won't grasp the full emotional nuance of your journey. Fret not, dear reader, for help is at hand.

As we mentioned at the start of this book, Australia and New Zealand's startup culture is enjoying a growth spurt right now. As a result, startup **incubators** and accelerators are sprouting from our urban landscapes like Easyways in the mid 2000s.

Names like Fishburners, Startmate, Muru-D, UNSW Founders, Lightning Labs and Founder Institute have become bylines for ANZ innovation. Some of them are government supported, while others hail from the private sector. Some earn their coin as startup-centric co-working spaces, while others build a business model around entrepreneurial crash courses. In one, you might attract mentors; in another, investors (we'll cover the latter in chapter 6). However, for all of their variety, they all share a crucial common denominator: they're loud, they're online and they *love* hosting networking functions.

From mixers to lunch and learns, from pitch nights to meet and greets, Aussie accelerators run functions of every flavour. Sure, many of them serve as veiled soft sells for the space's courses or co-working spaces. Even so, you can extract tangible value from these events without spending a cent.

First, you'll learn from people who are facing the same challenges you are. Whatever the theme of the event, they invariably attract past, present and future founders. That's not to mention the investors, mentors and other pillars of support you'll be likely to meet.

Sometimes, the guests at these functions will share solutions to problems that you're currently grappling with. In other moments, they'll spout the same complaints you often heap onto your glassy-eyed friends. At best, you'll leave with actionable answers to your problems; at worst, you'll meet people who know your struggle. There's a subtle power in community, even if greenwashing corporations have given the word a saccharine aftertaste. You may recognise that your challenges aren't unique, but when you spend time with other founders, you'll *feel* it.

As with points 1 and 2 in this section, you'll find the trail to these events online. Simply Google 'startup incubators near me' or 'startup accelerators [INSERT CITY CLOSEST TO YOU]', and you'll find some of the key players. From there, visit their websites, subscribe to their newsletters and follow them on social media. With time, the algorithm will suggest other local startup enclaves for you to watch. In a matter of weeks, you'll be abreast of the leading accelerators in your area. Before you know it, you'll be hearing of startup events faster than you can update your iCloud calendar.

Yes, we're exaggerating... but only very, very slightly. Seriously — these. Accelerators. *Love.* Hosting. Events.

Whether you choose to join an accelerator or hire a hot desk is a choice only you can make. But for a founder in the dawning hours of their startup's lifespan, these events offer a bounty of riches. They're low cost (or often free). They offer ingestible insights into aspects of startup life. They put you in the same room as the people who can guide or support your startup's growth.

And if nothing else, it isn't *Fight Club*. No-one will ask you to shut the hell up about your startup.

4. Your force multipliers

Admittedly, this title channels more testosterone than it needs to, but we stand by it.

Sometimes, the best networking you can do will occur through your *existing* contacts. McCarthyFinch co-founder Nick Whitehouse discovered this hack early in his business journey.

'There's that old adage: surround yourself with people who are smarter than you,' Whitehouse shared with us. 'I've flipped that and said: surround yourself with people who network better than you. I keep a small group of people who know a lot of people, and I lean on them for networking.'

In business, it's common practice to partner with people who plug your skills gaps. Money minds often find technical co-founders to steer all things engineering; tech whizzes frequently hire finance gurus to sharpen their business models. For those among us who fear the office water cooler, should networking be any different?

To be clear, we're not suggesting you spend money you don't yet have on a business that doesn't yet exist, to hire people who *may* build your network. But by finding the networkers in your existing network, you can leverage their contacts for some easy wins.

Key takeaways

■ *Go where your buyers are.* Events that cater to your target market are a treasure trove for both networking and research. You'll meet would-be customers, scope out someday rivals and forge potential alliances within the industry.

- *Meet Metallica in Armani.* Consider the skills you'll need to build your startup. Make a list of the ones you don't possess. Find the industries in which those skills are common and become fluent in their language.

- *Join the Anti-Fight Club.* All across Australia, you'll find startup accelerators and working spaces that host social functions. Here, you can learn from other founders, discuss startup-specific problems and bond with people living the same experience as you.

Do the hard work before you ever show up

Still can't shake that feeling of smalltalk-induced dread? Nick Whitehouse has lived that life. A self-professed introvert, Whitehouse's relationship with networking hasn't always been a rosy one.

'I think I'm terrible at networking,' he told us. 'I don't socialise much, and I don't go to events. I could count my friends on one finger. I always thought, "Well, this means I'll never be able to be a good founder because I'll never be able to build these relationships". But that hasn't been the case.'

From McCarthyFinch's early days, Nick managed to sidestep these networking hurdles with a simple formula:

- Find the unique angle in his product.
- Refine the messaging around his brand.
- Let the product make the introductions.

'We had a cheat code, and our cheat code was that nobody was thinking about or doing what we were doing, when we were doing it,' Whitehouse said.

'People would take my calls and set up time because we were doing something new. Nobody had presented the solutions in the way that we presented them. I think if you're that new and you can put your message together coherently, people will be interested in hearing about it.'

Nick acknowledges that it didn't begin and end with product messaging; he also ensured his personal online presence was job-huntworthy.

'I had some credentials behind me, which helped,' Whitehouse said.

'If somebody checks me out, they'll see: "Oh, this person's not a complete nobody. They actually exist, and have done things". I think there's an element of that, which helps. If you've got credibility and you've got a unique message and you've articulated it in a good way, then you can get those meetings.'

With the gift of hindsight, it's easy to see why tech titans and corporate czars clamoured to speak with McCarthyFinch. After all, they were building machine learning and proto-generative AI back in the twenty tens, before it had gone mainstream. Even so, you don't need to create the next ChatGPT to replicate Whitehouse's success.

Leverage your CV revamp from chapter 3. Distil the essence of your idea and highlight how it differs from the status quo. Find who you want to contact, then be ready to explain it in a sentence. Do this, and at the least, you can forego those awkward intros that begin with, 'So, what do you do?'

Look in your own backyard before you open your (or your investors') wallet

By now, you might have wondered why we've devoted so much time to networking. After all, at this stage of your journey, you don't have problems that require a network yet. To many, networking before launching might feel like getting your hair done for a night of binge streaming.

Now is the time when we echo a sentence we promised we'd return to:

The longer your contact list, the higher your likelihood of solving tomorrow's unknown problems.

Part of this concept implies that you should invest in networking, which is why… *gestures at the last several pages*. But the other, more exciting, part suggests that you may already have some of the future's solutions at your fingertips. Today, the careers of your friends and relatives may seemingly have little bearing on your startup idea. A year from now, though, their skills or resources may be able to plug a crisis-shaped hole in your business. All you need to do is regularly ask yourself, 'How can the people I know help me solve this problem?'

Of all our interviewees, no-one embodies this talent better than Like Family's Jenna Leo. If enthusiasm is infectious, Leo is a veritable bubonic plague. Like any good storyteller, she wraps her rhetoric in anecdotes; and like any good networker, she always recalls details about the people she's meeting. When you walk away from a coffee with Leo, it's hard not to find yourself thinking, 'Well, shucks. We must have really made an impression!'

It's no surprise, then, that Leo has built a network that serves her like a superpower. The result? Less money squandered during Like Family's launch, and more staff secured during Like Family's growth. In the first instance, Leo's network offered a DIY alternative to spending money they didn't have yet.

'When we first launched, we wanted to create a bit of a splash, but — like most young startups — we didn't want to spend a fortune,' Leo told us.

'Luckily, I have a friend who works in media, and she helped me prepare a press release. I sent that to the *North Shore Times*, and they wrote about us, which is how we first drew attention to what we were doing.'

Leo acknowledged that those early days were awash with new and unforeseen problems. However, contacts like her friend in the media helped to give them the tools to nimbly address them.

'We just took a scrappy approach to getting off the ground, and when something worked, we'd do it again.'

When your friend solves your problem, everybody wins

True to her word, when Leo found that seeking answers from her contacts had worked, she did it again. In later years, Leo and her co-founder Mathieu Bertrand came to face a problem familiar to many startup founders: a shortage of developers. That's why, before they paid a recruitment firm, Leo turned to her social circle for support.

'My best friend works in the immigration department at a consulting firm, and she organised our visa process for new employees,' Leo said.

'Now, whenever we need to sponsor a new team member, we just go through them. They take care of everything — all the documentation, the liaising with the employee, everything. It makes my life much easier, because I don't need to worry about it, and it makes life much easier for international employees who want to stay in the country.'

Of course, the moral of the story isn't to treat your friends as free labour. In Leo's case, she didn't cash in favours from people who owed her something; she sought mutually beneficial collaborations with people she trusted. Yes, Like Family found a competitive hiring advantage over other tech players. But at the same time, Leo's friend landed a stable client for her employer. The rising tide, as they say, lifted all boats.

At the dawn of their friendship, Leo didn't dream of sourcing future staff visas. In fact, back then, the concept of Like Family hadn't even taken shape in Leo's mind. Likewise, her friend in media? When they met, Leo wasn't silently counting her blessings, safe in the knowledge she would soon need a press release. No, in both cases, she did what most people do: she focused on the friendship. Bonded over common interests. Enjoyed brunches or nights out or weekends away together. Then, when Like Family confronted an unforeseen problem, Leo could turn to her friends for answers.

Beware the hidden blade

We found ourselves following Leo's example when we launched Catmosphere, Sydney's first dedicated cat cafe. Before we opened our doors to the public, we had never owned or run a hospitality business. In fact, between the two of us, we *may* have totalled three months of serving experience from our uni days. There was also the fact that we were welcoming 15 rescue cats into our care ... and one of us was allergic. And setup costs? We'd tucked a few thousand dollars into a savings account, and even we knew that wouldn't take us far. Suffice to say, our pre-launch challenges were legion.

But because we knew about these problems, we could address them in advance. To offset our hospitality shortcomings, we hired a veteran café owner to guide the venue setup process. We knew that rescue cat care was a serious responsibility, so we partnered with a registered animal rescue group. For capital, we launched a crowdfunding campaign on Facebook that exceeded our target of $40000 — certainly not enough to fund the fit-out, but enough to convince investors that the concept might warrant their backing. We even stocked up on cat allergy meds to keep the sneezing to a minimum.

However, as so often happens in early business, it was the hidden blade that almost ended us. Without giving you a short course in council approvals, there was an issue with one of our rooms. We'd thought we'd obtained approval to host guests there, but the room wasn't zoned for hospitality. As a result, we could use it to store kitty litter, but not to introduce coffee-sipping guests to rescue cats.

At the same time, the local council had come to doubt our very business model. In their eyes, the concept of a cat café didn't fit into any pre-existing, council-approved mould. It wasn't a regular café. It wasn't a cattery. It was a bureaucratic aberration. Until we had recertified the room in question, and until the council had ruled on our chimaera of a business model, we would need to close.

The coffee would go unsipped; the cats would need to remain stoic in the absence of their admirers. And, as small business owners, our bills would go unpaid.

Is your drinking buddy a legal genius?

On the day the council broke the news to us, we'd planned to visit a brewery with our friend Joe. A beer connoisseur of the highest calibre, Joe often invited us to pubs and paddle tastings. He was also a lawyer at a boutique firm — but that fact had never borne any relevance to our friendship. It always felt like something he did offscreen, something that would never tie into the narrative thread of our connection.

When we called Joe to explain that we needed to cancel our brewery visit, we expected him to make some sympathetic noises. Perhaps he'd say, 'Bloody council', or 'You'll get through this', or 'But you don't mind if I still go to the brewery, do you?' Instead, he said, 'Why don't you call a planning lawyer?'

One of us worked as an admin law lecturer, but had no experience with planning law. The other didn't even know that planning lawyers were a thing. Collectively, our response was, '... wha?'

'A planning lawyer,' Joe repeated. 'They might be able to liaise with the council for you. Get you permission to keep trading while you sort out this certification problem. They could also probably help with the council's questions around how to classify your business.'

Instead of going to the brewery by himself, Joe called the managing partner at his law firm. The partner, in turn, referred us to Vasili Conomos, a former colleague who now ran a planning law firm. Within a day, Vasili had compelled the council to allow us to keep trading while we addressed their concerns. Within a month, he had helped us resolve the zoning issue that haunted our café hosting area. And within a quarter, he had convinced the council that our business model was perfectly acceptable within the parameters of their judgement.

Catmosphere wasn't anything new, he argued; it was merely a café, and the cats were ancillary to the business' main function. People didn't pay $20 to spend an hour with the cats — they paid $20 for a cup of coffee. The cats just happened to be there, a part of the ambience, like elevator music in a Starbucks.

For the council, this sleight-of-hand legalese was exactly what they needed to hear. They revoked their issue, the caffeine kept pouring and the cats kept basking indifferently in the admiration of our guests. Had we not complained to our friend Joe, Catmosphere would have choked in a noose of red tape. But by sharing our problems with our friends, we found a solution that never would have occurred to us. Yes, we still paid for the legal services, and for a small business, they *weren't cheap*. Because a trusted party had given us a framework, though, we only paid for what we needed. Joe also earned kudos in his firm for passing a referral to someone who would repay the favour. Everybody won (especially the cats).

And in case you're wondering, after our council hijinks, we did finally make it to the brewery with Joe. No paddle has ever tasted so sweet.

The unknown problems in your startup's future will likely look different from Catmosphere's or Like Family's. Even so, the solutions will lie *somewhere* — and the best place to search first is your social network. As was the case with us, you may not even know that your friends hold the answers you need. But when you share your burdens with the people you trust, you'll find answers where you least suspected.

Key takeaways

- *Where you can, spend less.* You'll face problems that invite you to spend your way out of them. Before you dip into your (or your investors') money, ask yourself whether your network can provide a cheaper option.

- *Your friends are secret superheroes.* Share your startup burdens with the people you trust. You'll be surprised at the solutions they can offer.

- *Make sure that everyone wins.* Ask your loved ones for free labour when you're getting married or moving homes — not when you're launching a startup. Instead, ensure that your friends' assistance benefits both of you. Not only is this good karma, it will also ensure they'll be more likely to assist you again.

CHAPTER 5

FIND YOUR MVP

For a term that only sprang to life in 2001, 'minimum viable product' has become a mainstay in business circles. Since its creation, it's become a catch-all phrase to encompass any number of meanings. It's also inspired a flurry of alternatives, from 'minimum marketable product' to 'maximum awesome product'. Perhaps because of its widespread use, many fail to grasp its true meaning and — more importantly — its key commercial function.

From Slack to Dropbox, countless world-renowned startups have built their success off the back of their MVPs. However, for every success story, there's a cautionary tale. Some founders focus more on the 'product' than the 'minimum', and overcook their MVP. As a result, they invest more time and money than they need to, and commit to a less agile product. At the other end of the spectrum, some founders inadvertently skip the 'viable' part of the phrase. These are the startups that crash into the Pyramid of Priorities we introduced in chapter 3.

In this chapter, we explore how to find (and build) an MVP that can set up your startup for success. This will include:

● what to do before you launch your MVP

● how to keep your MVP as 'M' as possible

- making your life easier by launching your MVP close to home
- avoiding the dangers of not making your MVP 'V' enough
- creating an MVP that can scale
- striking a balance between overcooking and undercooking your MVP.

But first, what is an MVP — *really*?

At its core, an MVP is like fingerprint evidence in a police investigation: it can prove (or disprove) an entire case, and no two fingerprints are the same. The term was first coined by SyncDev co-founder Frank Robinson in 2001, and later popularised by Eric Ries. A serial entrepreneur, Ries tallied a series of startup wins and losses before founding the Lean Startup methodology. As the name suggests, this methodology offers an approach that strips needless expenses and encourages adaptive planning.

The MVP embodied a low-cost means to both test a product and learn from users. To quote Ries from his website, Startup Lessons Learned:

> ... the minimum viable product is that version of a new product which allows a team to collect the maximum amount of validated learning about customers with the least effort.

Note those key words: 'validated learning'. Put differently, the chief aim of an MVP is to collect insights into the product and the customer. Sure, you're testing whether your product works, but you're also testing a hypothesis: *Does it work for our target market?* From there, a founding team can apply their findings, improve their product and generate revenue.

To begin, you'll want a deep understanding of, and rapport with, your future customer base. This is where you'll be grateful for the market research of chapter 3, and the networking of chapter 4. For a textbook example, we can look at Forage's market-research-to-MVP transition. By attending student events, networking through universities and (to quote Rayan) 'hustling nonstop', they compiled an email list of university students. They also learned the flaws in their proposed mentor program. Initially, students had responded well to the idea of pairing with an industry mentor. However, after speaking with more students, Rayan and his co-founder Brunskill learned something interesting: most users simply saw mentorships as a route to internships.

Armed with this insight, Rayan and Brunskill pivoted their MVP concept from a mentor program to a virtual internship. They then emailed their student list and asked them to register their interest in this new idea. Within minutes, they were swamped by applications.

The only hurdle? The internship program didn't exist yet.

Building a(n intern)ship while you're sailing

'We only had a rough idea of what these virtual internships would look like,' Rayan told us.

'We knew they wouldn't just be remote work. We also knew it would require a bit of effort to convince big corporates to create these internship programs. At the same time, we could see that our database really seemed to love this idea. We realised we could be onto something.'

Suddenly, they had a demand for an MVP without a supply. By stoking interest in a virtual internship program, they had set themselves a ticking time bomb. If they didn't deliver their internship soon, they may have lost their window of opportunity. On the other hand, if they had provided a sub-standard experience, they may have squandered the goodwill they had accrued. So, they did what entrepreneurs have been doing since BCE: they set a daunting deadline and they activated their networks.

Since an internship program needs a place at which to intern, they began by speaking with their investors, H2 Ventures. As a VC behind the startup, H2 wanted Forage to succeed, and the demand for the internship concept was apparent. They agreed to partner with Forage for their first virtual internship, which focused on life at a VC fund. Because H2 and Forage already worked together, Rayan and Brunskill were able to create an MVP in a short time frame.

'No joke — we literally made the first program within two or three days,' Rayan told us.

'We asked our VCs for an analysis of what happens day to day; put that analysis into a program; briefed the students about the program itself; created a page through which students could pre-enrol into the program; and shared the pre-enrolment page with our mailing list and on the internet.

'We attracted around 900 signups within the first few days, which blew my mind. We were getting signups from Harvard, Oxford and Egypt — from people who had just discovered the program on Reddit.'

Ask questions first, shoot later

Such a tight turnaround would be the envy of any founder. Even so, it pays to remember that Forage's goal with their MVP was validated learning, not market penetration.

'After we launched this virtual job simulation, we received really positive feedback,' Rayan said.

'Mind you, the platform wasn't perfect back then — it was quite ugly, and, for some reason, very purple. Regardless, people genuinely seemed to love the fact that they could find out what work was like.'

When considering MVP's like Forage's, heed the words of David Allen, creator of the 'Getting Things Done' time management system: 'You can do anything, but not everything'.

The team at Forage knew they needed to deploy their time wisely. That's why, instead of investing in website **UX** or branding, they focused on affirming their product hypothesis. Or, in layperson's terms:

- 'Will our target market like this product as much as we think they will?'
- 'Is there a business case for building it further?'
- 'Before we start building it, does our target market have any feedback that can help us?'

Learn the answers to these questions, and two to three days of hustling feels like a fair exchange.

Key takeaways

- *Let your target market lead the way.* When shaping your MVP, listen to your customer research, not your gut. Be prepared to kill your darlings if your vision and your target market's desires don't align.

- *Be disciplined with time and resources.* Once you have the data you need, waste no time in applying it. Set yourself an accountable deadline, and extract what you need from your team and your network.

> ■ *Treat your learning like your parking* ... and validate it. Never lose sight of your MVP's true purpose: to learn whether your product is right for your target market. If and once you've affirmed that, focus on improving it for them.

Put the 'M' in 'MVP'

Looking at Forage, we can see how minimal a minimum viable product can be. Instead of waiting until they had partnered with a range of companies, they launched an internship program through their investor. In doing so, they proved their hypothesis, and armed themselves with ammo to approach other providers. In saying this, we recognise that Forage's story is a tad specific. For a more homespun MVP, we need not look beyond Airtasker.

Remember how, in chapter 4, we learned that Airtasker's founders would attend community meetups before launch? They put them to good use during their MVP launch.

'[My co-founder] Jono and I were pretty hands-on,' Airtasker co-founder Tim Fung told us. 'We attended a lot of community meet-ups to [promote Airtasker and] get the thing going, and we did a lot of the jobs ourselves.'

This involved completing tasks that freelancers on the platform would eventually accept, from moving furniture to conducting end-of-lease cleans. As a result, they didn't need to wait until they hosted freelancers on their platform to launch their MVP.

Of course, if you're savvy with the concept of scaling, you might say, 'Hang on — this approach couldn't have been sustainable. Airtasker currently has over 2 million users, which means it scaled effectively. At some point, the demand must have outstripped Tim and Jono's ability to paint walls and carry lounges.'

In response, we would simply refer to those two words from Eric Ries: 'validated learning'. When Tim and Jono had secured paying users, they proved their hypothesis. At that point, they had something to offer freelancers, meaning they could sustainably build out a double-sided marketplace. In other words, by being as minimal as possible on launch, they were able to scale.

Now, we should mention that not every MVP starts life as cleanly as it ends it. With the virtue of hindsight, it can seem like every founder finished preschool with a crystal-clear vision for their MVP. In reality, though, many would-be founders struggle to connect their idea with an MVP. This often occurs when they can only envisage their concept in a fully-formed guise: a 'VP' without an 'M'. If this sounds like you, don't worry. Recent history offers a simple roadmap for you to follow.

When your tech actually works, your MVP might be your market

McCarthyFinch began life as an internal innovation project at major New Zealand law firm, MinterEllisonRuddWatts. Back then, Nick Whitehouse served as the firm's Chief Digital Officer, charged with transforming the firm's technology operations to be more efficient, serve clients better and be more cost effective — that is, to work smarter, not harder. During his tenure, he established an innovation fund and process that allowed the firm to experiment with disruptive ideas. One of the ideas was Artificial Intelligence. It proved the ideal incubator for McCarthyFinch, which spun out in February 2017, bringing together PhDs, Software Engineers and Lawyers to build legal Artificial Intelligence from the ground up.

Fast-forward 15 months, and the startup was one of only 21 selected to compete for the highly coveted $100 000 equity-free Disrupt Cup at the 2018 TechCrunch Disrupt Battlefield in San Francisco.

'We'd been running really, really hard at problems for 15 months,' said Whitehouse. 'Our user base was lawyers. What I didn't realise at the time was that I was so focused on making lawyers happy and providing exactly the right answer for them that I failed to recognise that lawyers could be the most pedantic, risk-averse and nitpicky user you could possibly have.

'When I finally got to the Valley in 2018 and started meeting with VCs, I found our technology was way ahead of everybody else's. I found that our contemporaries talked more than we did — that is, talk to create FOMO and attract investment. I talked to a corporate investor and they mentioned that they'd just given $100 million to an "AI" company. So I asked, "What are they doing?" The corporate investor said, "Oh well, they're not really doing anything with AI yet. They're just trying to collect the data to do something with that". To which I asked, "But how do you know that their AI is ever going to be able to use that data?"'

This kind of freeflow of funding felt baffling to Whitehouse, given the sparse VC landscape to which he'd grown accustomed.

'What the hell was going on? What have I been doing for 16 months, trying to build this AI that *actually works*? There were so many people at TechCrunch Disrupt where the products weren't necessarily super real. We had this technology that actually did what we said it could do.'

This contrast between McCarthyFinch's product-led development and Silicon Valley's FOMO-fuelled funding-first mentality spurred Whitehouse to reconsider his strategy.

'Money is the lifeblood of a startup, and with it, you'll try to get your minimum viable product,' said Whitehouse. 'But what I recognised was that this is not how the process works in the Valley. Their process is more about how you create FOMO and interest so your next investment dollar is actually your minimum viable product, not necessarily your next user.'

What McCarthyFinch learned from their foray into Silicon Valley is that their challenges differed from those of their North American peers. It was less around having a working product, and more around finding the broader market.

'We asked ourselves, "Do we go to the consumer level? Do we go B2B? Do we work with law firms?" This was a big challenge that we went back and forth over for a good year. Where is our actual market? We know that nobody likes working with lawyers. We know everyone thinks lawyers are too expensive — corporate clients think this, and so do individuals on the street. Even law firms talk this way. So we knew this was a common problem, but where were we going to get our money from? For us, that's what really fit into this minimum viable product challenge.'

The turning point came when McCarthyFinch decided to leverage Microsoft Marketplace to reach potential users directly. Rather than debating over who the market might be, they essentially found a way to let the market decide.

'Once we put our product on Microsoft Appsource, we had thousands of people downloading it. We didn't have to spend any money on marketing. We saw people using it and started collecting data. That was our minimum viable product. It was so much more visceral because you saw people interacting with our product.'

Key takeaways

- *Focus on building tech that works, not just tech that talks.* What works in Silicon Valley may not translate to other markets, and vice versa. Understand the funding and growth expectations specific to your ecosystem. If you're building outside of cash-rich innovation hubs, differentiate yourself by creating technology that delivers on its promises.

- *Let the market decide through direct engagement.* When struggling to identify your target market, find ways to put your product in front of diverse users and let their adoption patterns guide your strategy.

- *Choose your initial users carefully.* Highly specialised or demanding early users (like lawyers) may set unrealistic expectations for your MVP that delay broader market validation.

- *Be prepared to pivot your MVP strategy after market exposure.* Your initial assumptions about users and markets might change dramatically once you venture beyond your comfort zone and familiar territory.

Don't forget the 'V' in 'MVP'

Launching an MVP is very much a 'Goldilocks and the Three Bears' scenario. In this time-tested allegory, overengineering your MVP is akin to eating the cold bowl of porridge. Every moment you dither, that bowl of porridge cools a fraction more. By the time you finally sit down to eat, the porridge has lost its tepid lustre. Now, all you can do is yearn for the breakfast that could have been.

That's a wistful image, right? No-one likes cold porridge. It's dense and slimy and sports a texture like cement. But do you know what's worse than cold porridge? Really, really hot porridge. Ingest a mouthful of this, and you'll think you've swallowed lava. Your mouth and throat and stomach will all shriek in protest, and little sores will fester on your tongue. Cold porridge is a missed opportunity — but hot porridge is an emergency.

In case this wasn't already obvious, an undercooked MVP is the hot porridge of our tale.

After reading the past several pages, this idea might make you rub your temples in frustration. What happened to keeping an MVP minimal, to building a ship while you're sailing? At the risk of sounding like a LinkedIn meme, an MVP needs to be minimal, but also viable. Or, to frame it in a less cringe-inducing way: the product itself should be simple and scrappy. How your target market uses it needs to be rock solid.

For a cautionary tale from the co-founder himself, let's look at Mad Paws. These days, Mad Paws is Australia's largest online pet care marketplace. As a publicly listed company, Mad Paws has nurtured a complete ecosystem for animal care, spanning everything from dog sitting to pet insurance. To maintain their leading mantle, Mad Paws runs a best practice website and app that fulfils an array of functions. It may surprise you, then, to know that the website for their MVP was closer to a dog's breakfast.

'Back then, there were a number of potential competitors who were looking to provide the same service as us,' Mad Paws co-founder Alexis Soulopoulos told us.

'We wanted to beat them to market, so we launched our website as quickly as we could. The problem was that our first website was very, very MVP — so MVP that it didn't do what it was supposed to do.'

The premise for their MVP was simple: create an account via the website, and book a pet sitter near you. It was, in essence, Airbnb for pet care. The only issue? In those first few weeks, the account signup process via the website didn't function properly. Whenever someone tried to create an account, they would face a barrage of errors. In their exasperation, many users simply gave up. Those who persevered to create an account would receive a confirmation email … which landed in their spam folder.

People were reacting positively to the MVP's concept, but, due to technical issues, few could actually use it. Pet owners didn't book the services they needed, and — with few bookings to accept — many pet sitters became disengaged.

'Because of these problems, we lost a lot of potential pet sitter bookings during those early weeks,' Soulopoulos said.

'Those that we did receive were the result of manual effort; since our platform wasn't working, I would need to call potential customers and complete the bookings for them over the phone.'

Looking back, we know that Mad Paws cleared these hurdles. Much like any origin story, we can view Mad Paws' early hurdles through the lens of the end result.

'We always knew this method wasn't scalable but it was good to start and learn. Once it was validated, we implemented a tech solution,' Soulopolous said.

'Firstly, we re-engaged those pet sitters [who had become inactive], then we implemented an SMS system to connect bookings. This, combined with an upgrade to our website, allowed us to start scaling properly.'

A pragmatist might argue that these problems served an important purpose. Mad Paws learned from these technical errors, and created a much smoother signup experience in the future.

The devil's advocate has something to say

Okay, then. A clear moral has emerged from this gaggle of case studies: don't overthink the product, but don't *under*think the platform. That's the key takeaway here … right?

At the risk of furrowing more brows in confusion, Like Family's Jenna Leo has shared a contrasting view. In fact, Leo's experience led her to conclude that underthinking their platform was an unsung blessing.

What makes this finding more interesting is that Mad Paws and Like Family share many similarities. They both run double-sided marketplaces. They both connect carers with people (or pets) who require care. They launched within a year of each other — in the mid-twenty tens, to be precise. So why did their founders reach such divergent conclusions around MVP tech?

To hear Leo's take, it had nothing to do with any tech expertise in Like Family's founding team. 'Back in 2015, the Australian startup community wasn't what it is today,' Leo told us.

'We didn't know much about it, we didn't know any developers and we sure weren't developers ourselves. Just finding someone to build an MVP for a website was hard. We had to go through a friend of a friend of a friend to find somebody who could build the website cheaply.'

With so many degrees of separation involved, Leo and her co-founder Bertrand set themselves clear parameters for the website. That way, they could ensure the unknown aspects of their MVP didn't spiral beyond their control.

'We agreed that we were only going to build an MVP, and that we'd invest no more than $10 000,' Leo said. 'If it didn't work, we would scrap [the idea for Like Family] and find something else.'

The story of their website build will ring familiar for many founders. They hired a project manager who ran a team in Bangladesh, and worked with him to build a bare bones MVP website. Since Leo and Bertrand were at the start of their founders' journey, there was much they didn't know about UX. According to Jenna, this actually fast-tracked their MVP launch.

'If we'd known more about development, we probably would have spent much longer working on it,' Leo said.

'I remember I was shopping in Costco during those early days, and the dev called to ask: "What's the flow of how someone should make a booking?" Because I didn't know much about UX, I just said: "Why don't we make it A, B, C, D, E?" It wasn't this complex thing that I spent months mapping out — but it could have been if I'd known what I know now.'

Fortunately, Like Family didn't encounter major tech issues in their first days of operation. Their simplified approach to their platform paid off, and gave them the space to smoothly transition from their MVP. So, what's the difference between the two? How did two startups, with similar business models, launching in the same era, with similar budgets and time frames, have such divergent experiences with their tech?

Test, test, one-two, one-two

Soulopoulos himself highlighted a key factor: pre-launch testing. As he mentioned in his conversations with us, Mad Paws were in a rush to beat their rivals to launch. In their haste to leave the first paw print on the market, they didn't exhaustively test their MVP signup flow. By contrast, while Like Family didn't overthink their tech, they *did* invest time in testing it. Not only did they confirm every angle of the signup process themselves, they also asked test audiences to do so. While their MVP website may have been a shoestring offering, they knew it was as tight as a constrictor knot.

For Mad Paws, their early experience served as a blessing in disguise. Because of this experience, they set a company culture for extensive testing. Moving forward, whenever they planned to introduce a product or feature, they would always recruit a highly engaged segment of customers and pet sitters to test a beta version. Using this approach, they were able to expand from pet sitting into dog food, pet health, pet insurance, dog grooming, pet accessories — and, in 2021, an **initial public offering (IPO)** on the ASX. Even so, you can learn from their teachings and avoid those maiden testing issues altogether.

It's for learning, not earning

Ahead of their MVP, both startups set themselves rigid targets. For Mad Paws, this involved being the first dogs to get to the market. In Like Family's case, they applied a budgetary constraint: no more than $10 000 on their MVP. However, of the two, Like Family burdened themselves with less pressure. Yes, in the scheme of global startup launches, 10 grand is a meagre amount. No doubt, a more anxious founding team would have lost sleep over the prospect. But despite these limitations, Like Family didn't feel the need to launch quickly and earn it back. Instead, to re-quote Leo, 'If it didn't work, we would scrap the idea and find something else.'

Or, from a very meta perspective, they saw their MVP as a chance for validated learning.

The moral to the story is this: keep yourself accountable, but don't lose sight of an MVP's true purpose. The moment you view it as a means of revenue or competition, you'll undermine the reason you're keeping it minimal. Keep the target on learning—not earning—and you'll make better choices for a bare-bones product.

Key takeaways

- *Minimal product, viable tech.* Your product can—and should—only be a rough version of your ultimate vision. However, the tech that hosts it can't fail the demands of use. If it doesn't dependably connect your users to your product, you may lose business before you ever start.

- *Test, test, test.* Looking to distinguish between 'shoestring tech' and 'broken tech'? Rigorously test your product before you launch. Better yet, find a test group of your target market to test it as well. In doing so, you'll find any UX flaws that would deter the people you care about: your target market.

- *Treat it as a learning tool, not a revenue raiser.* To once again quote Lean Startup godfather Eric Ries, your MVP's purpose is to accrue 'validated learning'. Once you've sourced those learnings from your MVP, you'll know where to apply your resources to improve your product. With a sharper product in your hands, you can *then* turn your sights on reaping that revenue.

In the end, you're starting at the beginning

Many would-be founders have a grand vision of a perfect product, but struggle to envisage an MVP. They want to begin at the finish line, but forget that the start line exists for a reason.

'The idea that your product needs to meet your long-term vision from the start is so flawed,' Lockpick Games co-founder Tash Jamieson said to us.

'I don't care if you have a deep-tech problem that requires $200 million in R&D. I guarantee you there will be a no-code website-type form that can allow you to validate the problem. I've yet to see a problem that can't be at least tested first with something really simple.

'Even if it's just an Excel sheet, you need to get something out there.'

Despite the tug of war we've run between the M and the V, it really can be as simple as Jamieson suggests. Create the most basic version of your product. Ensure the platform through which you provide it works properly. Share it with your target market. Apply their learnings to refine your product.

Do this, and you'll take a crucial step towards your perfect product.

CHAPTER 6
HOW TO SECURE FUNDING

'Show me the money!' If you're old, like we elder millennials are, you'll probably recall Tom Cruise screaming this down a telephone in *Jerry Maguire*. If you're not so aged, it's probably still a sentiment you wouldn't mind screaming down a telephone. Preferably followed by *squillions*, yacht parties and an IPO, right? It's on the vision board. It's in the five-year plan.

But before anyone can show you some money, ask yourself: What have I actually done?

Why would anyone give you money?

No, really. Why would anyone give you money? It's the first question you should ask yourself. The answer can't just be, 'Because of my big, beautiful idea!' Or even your 'concepts of a plan'.

Even though your idea may have taken what felt like an eon to squeeze out of your imagination, it's only the beginning. Those in charge of funding—from venture capitalists to equity crowdfunders, or even potential pre-sale customers — usually want to see evidence of two things: traction and potential.

Traction could be in the form of a working prototype. Or an MVP. Or, even better, a mailing list of potential customers interested in your product — as Forage had when they launched their first virtual internship. Perhaps you even have pre-launch sales: a crowdfunding campaign is an excellent place to start, as we found when we used a viral PR campaign to raise $40 000 in pre-sales for Catmosphere. In fact, pre-sales allowed us to raise the remaining $60 000 we needed for a razor-thin budget to launch — and it was still a scramble to do so within our promised five-month deadline.

Potential is usually down to the people involved in your founding team. For example, can you prove your founders have experience bridging the distance between a wild idea and a revenue-generating, **scalable** commercial venture? Or do you have a complementary skillset, often regarded as 'one to build it, and one to sell it'? Or do you even get along?

Don't forget the red flags too. Are you doing anything illegal? We've met founders who are two years into building their product before they've questioned whether it's legal to re-use content without crediting its author. This is particularly an issue in highly regulated industries, such as fintechs.

In short, having the idea is probably the least important part of founding a startup. Executing the idea is where you prove your ingenuity. There are few better forums for feedback than the free market.

However, every investor will tell you that the founders matter the most.

Founders are a strange breed of human. Eschewing the highly accessible comforts of an easier life, founders are willing to take the pain to try new things, push through failure, learn and try again — often for far less pay or recognition than they would ever get in a regular job.

Green flags for investors

So what are investors looking for in founders?

A tolerance for pain — and a little bit of magic

'It's probably a cliche, but the founder or founding team needs to have some magic,' Tim Fung told us. 'Who is that person who will keep going when things are really crap? That resilience, and that tolerance for pain? The ability to gather resources — to raise money and hire people — is important.'

Tim would know. In addition to starting Airtasker, he is an angel investor, having backed Mad Paws, as well as sneaker and streetwear marketplace Pushas.

In many ways, being a founder is much like being a fighter. To quote the iconic Rocky Balboa: 'It ain't about how hard you're hit. It's about how you can get hit and keep moving forward.'

What does this look like for you? After all, setbacks and pain are a guaranteed part of your startup life. How will you take the pain? Can you push through and learn a thing or two, round after round? That's the kind of tenacity — the true grit — investors want to see.

It's rarer than you think. And it can't be taught, only endured.

Winning teams, not individual superstars

Beste Onay is an investor, co-founder of 361 Angel Club, and New Ventures Manager at UNSW. Not only does she invest, but she has, for years, taught others the fundamentals of picking winners through UNSW Founders' popular Angel Investors Program.

For Onay, it's all about the team dynamic.

'The biggest factor is the team,' Onay told us. 'At the end of the day, they're the ones who will execute and make it all happen. I look for how obsessed they are with the problem, and how deeply connected they are to it. They need to be committed and resilient, because building a successful company is really hard.'

Onay also looks for any insider knowledge founders may have: anything that gives them an edge in understanding and solving the problem.

'Do they have any industry expertise? A unique background? What makes them the right people to do this? What evidence do they have that they can actually deliver?'

Someone to build, and someone to sell

What you don't want is a team that thinks the same way. The best teams never share the same skillsets or even the same personality types.

'In general, you need someone to build it, and someone to sell it,' explained Onay. 'You need the skillsets to be complementary.'

Think about how this applies to you. Right now, you might lack the skills to do either. If so, what does your personality lean towards, and what are you willing to learn? Where do you think you can win the most? As a builder, or as a seller?

Scientist Alinta Furnell, co-founder and CEO of Synbiote, would never have considered herself a salesperson when she first started out. But she went towards what the business required. She became more comfortable presenting at conferences and roundtables, featuring in interviews and doing the outreach needed for an investment-heavy biotech startup. In this way, she started as a person to build it, then grew into a person who could sell it.

Red flags for investors: what they are and how to avoid them

Just as investors look for green flags to signal a promising unicorn, they also watch for the signs of dysfunction or distraction that are so common to the 90 per cent of failed startups. Here are the top six.

They're too in love with the product or technology

'A common issue is founders who are very obsessed with the product or technology but not working closely enough with their customers,' explained Onay. 'Potential customers might seem interested, but unless they're paying for it, it can be hard to know if the startup is solving a big enough problem. It sounds obvious, but if people don't truly want or need the solution, the startup is going to fail.'

They won't survive without enough funding

While many startups can **bootstrap** their way to recurring revenue, some require extensive investment before they can hope to bring their product to market. This is why so many research-intensive startups expire during the valley of death, their unfinished prototypes littering the landscape of what might have been.

'Money can be a challenge,' observed Onay. 'Will they be able to raise enough capital to commercialise what they're building? Some ideas are really capital-intensive. Many first-time founders also struggle to clearly communicate their business model and how their company will make a lot of money, which is critical, because investors want to know how you are going to make *them* a lot of money.'

There's too much competition

'Another factor to consider is the competitive landscape,' said Onay. 'Is it a saturated market?'

'And then there can be a technology risk from being ambitious and trying to do something that hasn't been done before, especially with deep tech.'

It's a complex regulatory environment

How regulated is your industry? Fintechs are a good example of a highly regulated market. Team dynamics may also be a risk factor. A team that have just met, versus a team that have known each other for years, might be poorly placed to navigate stress and setbacks.

They're in a relationship

Some investors may be wary of founding teams who know each other before their startup, either as friends or romantic partners.

'I have the privilege of getting to hang out with a lot of founders who launched startups in the last 10 years in Sydney,' said Fung. 'There are so many amazing people.'

It doesn't need to be a dealbreaker, though. Indeed, some of our most successful startups are helmed by married couples: from Melanie Perkins and Cliff Obrecht's USD$49 billion Canva unicorn to Justin Truong and Sandy Li's sneaker reselling marketplace Pushas.

'It's a mistake to say that friend pairings and husband and wife pairings can't really work,' said Fung. 'It seems to make sense to me, and many are incredibly successful — you just have trust in each other and say things directly.'

They're not sure who's in charge

For Tim Fung, a common red flag can be unclear ownership or leadership structures. You might recall the co-CEOs of HBO show *Succession,* where unclear succession planning led to rival brothers Kendall and Roman Roy sharing power as CE-*Bros.* This arrangement indicates an underlying leadership struggle and a lack of clarity over who has the final say.

'It's not a no-go,' said Fung. 'It can just sometimes flag that we haven't yet made a hard decision about who is best positioned to be the final dealbreaker.'

Interestingly, a recent analysis published by the *Harvard Business Review* revealed that 87 companies led by co-CEOs produced more value than their sole-CEO peer companies. Indeed, companies led by co-CEOs produced an average annual shareholder return of 9.5 per cent — well above the 6.9 per cent average for each company's relevant index. This result wasn't due to a handful of outliers either: close to 60 per cent of companies led by co-CEOs outperformed their sole CEO peers.

Harvard Business Review suggested several benefits of a power-sharing model, one of which was a sense-check, which kept 'egos in check'. Among the companies featuring co-CEOs were Goldman Sachs, Oracle, SAP and Unilever. However, organisations led by two leaders often opt for a president and CEO title rather than co-CEO.

For joint leadership to work, the *Harvard Business Review* suggested nine key factors must be present:

1. They must be willing participants in joint leadership. The arrangement can't work when, as Insight Partners Managing Director Jeff Horing put it, 'one wants to run the whole thing'.

2. They must have complementary skillsets that allow each leader to play to their strengths.

3. There must be clear responsibilities and decision rights, demarcating each leader's turf. 'The key to success is complementary domains of recognised competence,' explained Bill Janeway, Former Vice Chairman of Warburg Pincus. This proved a potent recipe for success for PIMCO CEO Manny Roman and PIMCO's Chief Investment Officer Dan Ivascyn. The former led marketing, sales and operations while the latter led investing.

4. Mechanisms for conflict resolution are necessary to allow for disagreements to be resolved behind closed doors. This may be through private conversations or a board member or executive chairman who can intervene.

5. They must maintain an appearance of unity. Speaking to one leader must be considered the same as speaking to both. Public disagreements can lead to confusion and indecision throughout the organisation.

6. Fully shared accountability for the company's overall performance must be evident, which can be reflected by both leaders signing quarterly financial statements and equal compensation.

7. The board must demonstrate support for both leaders, with minimal intrusion.

8. The joint leaders must share values of honesty, respect, trust and compromise.

9. There must be an exit strategy in place to shift back to a sole-CEO model if needed.

Do you even want their money?

Funding can mean relinquishing control over your startup, at least to some extent. This can be beneficial: smart money comes with intelligent investors who may bring the experience and expertise you need to succeed. However, a poor investor fit can cause issues, especially if they intend to be actively involved in daily decision making.

In the case of Catmosphere, this led to an investor commissioning murals and OH&S services without communicating these expenses. It was a well-meaning move, and showed a commitment to the business. However, it occurred during the crucial lean-launch period when every expense mattered. In the end, it highlighted our need to set parameters on what investor input we required and when.

It's important to establish early on how investors will be involved, and what the money they've invested means to them. Is it throwaway cash they can afford to lose? When will they expect to see a return? What kind of return are they expecting? Failing to manage these expectations, or air out these issues early on, can impede the time and space you need to test revenue-generating ideas, experiment with marketing, and take your time to fail and learn.

A case study feat. Wenee

My first startup, Survive Law, launched with no-strings-attached **seed funding** from UTS: Law, where I was a final-year student. While it wasn't much ($4000), I didn't need much. At 20 years old, I was half-heartedly applying for graduate roles, painfully aware I lacked the drinking ability to last multiple rounds of clerkship mixers.

Past midnight, I flicked through *Lawyer 2B* magazine, a student edition of *Lawyers Weekly*, and scoffed at the cover story: 'Inside the Mind of the Ideal Graduate Lawyer'. It showed a brain carved in parts to reflect traits desirable for a future employer. I wrote over every trait with my own observations: raging cocaine addiction; dad owns the firm; probably non-ironically reads *The Game/The Secret*.

Nine months later, I'd written a 10-part guide to surviving law school featuring interviews with senior lawyers, judges and academics. It was lean enough to launch as co-branded content at law school orientation weeks, and it grew from there. However, having no major pressure from investors meant we also had the time to experiment. Two years later, it replaced *Lawyer 2B*, and we made $12 000 (which, at that age, felt like a fortune). Four years later, we'd attracted most major firms and legal training providers as advertisers. Six years later, we sold it.

What made it work? Recruiting an editor-in-chief (a law student herself) who helped break up the guide into bite-sized, 300-word blogs. These were posted to socials, creating a feedback loop of engagement between social media and our website. We grew to over 70 000 Facebook fans and more than 50 writers without scaling our expenses. Embracing a hybrid model — part digital magazine, part student community — we attracted advertisers and event sponsorships, which provided funding to turn out new products. All this without the pressure of rent, staff or overheads.

What kind of money do you want?

'I'm not a money discriminator!' we hear you say. 'I'll take any kind of money. I'm super open-minded like that.'

Counterintuitive as it might sound, it can pay to discriminate when it comes to funding. As we explore the following six categories of funding for early-stage startups, you'll soon see why:

1. Self-funding (aka **bootstrapping**)

2. Friends and family

3. Prizes (industry grants)

4. Angel investing

5. Venture capital (VC) funding

6. NFTs (non-fungible tokens).

Many founders opt for a mix of these categories to keep their startup going, and these represent most, but not all, funding methods available.

1. Self-funding (aka bootstrapping)

'Pull yourself up by your bootstraps!' It's not just what your comfortably retired elders implore you to do when you're facing a cost-of-living crisis. It's also a term for the most common form of startup funding, especially at the start.

Raised without the blank cheques of investment hubs like Silicon Valley, Australian innovators rarely have the funds to burn. Certainly, there's no room for frauds like Theranos.

However, bootstrapping, or self-funding, can prove much easier for the independently wealthy. At a minimum, it requires a degree of middle-class privilege.

Soul Burger's founder, Amit Tewari, is a notable exception. Growing up in Sydney's west, Tewari started vegan burger chain Soul Burger while studying medicine at UNSW. Now with four outlets, he's branched into fast-casual Mexican vegan Plantas

Taqueria and Zaynas Lebanese. Together, his operations have generated more than $20 million. Born to a single-income migrant family of five, Tewari had no choice but to bootstrap. His success speaks to the benefits of bootstrapping and that it can be done without — to quote a two-term US president — a 'small loan of $1 million.'

The benefits of bootstrapping

Bootstrapping can provide some sizeable benefits, especially for those able to launch a business without expensive R&D investment. Here are a few.

YOU RETAIN FULL CONTROL AND OWNERSHIP

Asking for funds means diluting your equity as you part with a share in your company. In the long run, retaining 100 per cent ownership may turn out to be far more financially rewarding than diluting your equity through multiple funding rounds, even if you raise money to achieve a billion-dollar valuation.

Accepting external funding can also mean compromising your vision and expediting your timeline to commercialise. While legal safeguards, such as super-voting rights, can be put in place, if you want to retain control over the direction of your venture, you may want to self-fund.

YOU AVOID AN UNWANTED EXIT

If you are building a business to sustain you throughout your life, self-funding may be a better option. Investors want to see a return, and this can only occur with a significant exit event, generally within a decade. If your business is acquired, your new owners may not want a founder to stay on. Often, they prefer to install their own leadership. An IPO can be a more attractive option in this regard.

YOU ONLY HIRE WHO YOU NEED

Bootstrapped startups hire only who they truly need. They can't afford to do more, so every person they hire needs to be essential for their product, operations and growth. Richly funded ventures, by contrast, might be distracted by 'MBA-goggles' — that is, a desire to hire an expert consultant, often ex-corporate, to 'get everything right'. Think of a C-Suite stacked with ex-McKinsey, ex-Google corporate stars who expect corporate salaries, but may lack the startup experience and resilience to build a business from the ground up.

YOU BUILD AN EFFECTIVE BUSINESS MODEL

Highly valued startups can still be losing money. Uber took 15 years to hit profitability. Self-funded startups have no such luxury. Founders work to build a business model that hits positive cashflow as soon as possible. You can scale what works.

When self-funding can limit your growth

Conversely, self-funding can limit both your growth and your shot at survival. Here's why you might want to reconsider bootstrapping your business.

YOU CAN'T OUTLAST DEATH VALLEY

Lack of financing or investors was listed as the top reason why 47 per cent of startups failed in 2022, with 44 per cent failing because they ran out of money. This can particularly be a problem for R&D-intensive startups that need funding to create their prototype, much less bring an MVP to market.

YOU'RE POISED FOR RAPID GROWTH

Funding can drive significant growth by improving your visibility, the breadth of multi-channel marketing you can pursue and how you can serve your customers. Failing to fund any aspect of this can hinder your growth.

YOU'LL GAIN INSIGHTS FROM EXPERIENCED ADVISORS

Seeking 'smart money' can make a major difference in the success of your startup. It's why legal tech startups like Josef would prefer funding from a legal tech fund over a non-specialist investor. Informed investors can make for excellent board members and shareholders who can provide influence and introductions to drive your growth.

2. Friends and family

It can be daunting asking your friends and family for funding, but it's one of the most common sources of early-stage funding. According to a survey published by Silicon Valley Bank, 38 per cent of startup funding comes from friends and family, contributing $38 billion per year to startups.

Indeed, some of the world's most well-known startups had a friendly cash injection from a loved one. According to *The Guardian*, Mark Zuckerberg reportedly received a $100000 loan from his father to start Facebook, while Jeff Bezos' parents were early investors in Amazon. Bill Gates' mother introduced him to senior executives at IBM, facilitating one of his earliest deals for MS-DOS, his first operating system. Phil McKnight, founder of Nike, credits his parents with helping him start his company, while Michael Dell's parents provided seed funds for his first computer startup. Elon Musk comes from intergenerational South African wealth.

Innovation benefits from both privilege and a minimum degree of middle-class stability. As Shira Greenberg, chief economist of Israel's Ministry of Finance, observed in an agency report:

There is a strong connection between your parents' income and your chances of becoming a startup entrepreneur, with those from a strong financial background having a higher chance of becoming entrepreneurs.

This chance increases if your parents come from a science or technology background. However, given that one in five startups fail within their first year — and about half fail within five years — it's important to be upfront about the risks to friends and family.

Consider a service like Pigeon Loans to help formalise your investments from friends and family. If you want to open funding to a larger pool of investors, try WeFunder, which can allow investments of as little as $100 and open funding to hundreds.

3. Prizes (industry grants)

Prizes or industry grants can be appealing because they provide funds without parting with equity. They also deliver credibility to customers and potential future investors.

'In 2017, [we took part in] Remarkable['s] Accelerator [program],' said Jenna Leo, co-founder of Like Family. 'It was run by the Cerebral Palsy Alliance, and as part of it, they gave us a $20 000 grant.

'Mat and I were still doing yoga and PT to pay the bills, and the entrepreneur-in-residence, Ben, said, 'What are you two doing? You're leaving early and coming in late because you're teaching yoga and PT? We've given you $20 000 because you have a really good business. You're making $20 000 in (gross merchandise value) GMV right now.'

However, not all support needs to be financial. Participating in accelerators and competitions can make a major difference to your startup trajectory. Tash Jamieson completed a program with the South Korean government called the K Startup Grand Challenge. 'We were also one of the Australian finalists in She Loves Tech, which is a global competition for women in technology,' said Jamieson.

For Synbiote co-founder Alinta Furnell, their inflection point came through an accelerator. 'I think our point of no return moment happened after the UNSW Founders 10× program,' said Furnell.

'Until that point, our attention was on proving the concept and pivoting when we needed to. It was challenging, but there was also a freedom to it; no-one expected anything from Synbiote.

'Then, once we started speaking to customers, we started hearing, "This is an excellent idea. This will be useful for us, and make a real difference in our labs". Believe it or not, that's when things became a lot more difficult for us.'

For her co-founder, Ismat Kabbara, it wasn't funding but lab space that proved transformative.

'Having the lab space made a big difference,' Kabbara told us. 'For me, that was the real milestone. It was when I felt that this was something feasible, you know? We had a dedicated space where we could conduct the experiments we needed to conduct.

'I think, especially for deep tech, if you don't have a certified facility, you can't bring your product to life. It isn't something you can do in your backyard or your garage. That's why the lab felt like my point of no return.'

Of course, Synbiote's needs won't reflect those of every early-stage startup. Even so, their experiences can provide a rubric for the kinds of requirements other businesses might face.

'The main thing for us is access to equipment and facilities,' Kabbara said. 'A lot of machinery that we needed to build our MVP costs millions of dollars. Being associated with the university allows us to piggyback, so we don't have to buy these multimillion-dollar machines. Here, we can establish these research collaborations to get to the point that we need to be.

'And sure, it might take a contractual agreement, through which we pay for their time. However, being part of the university makes that accessibility piece a lot easier. If we were to approach it as externals without an established name, it'd be harder to get into those spaces.'

4. Angel investing

Beste Onay is an experienced angel investor and co-founder of 361 Angel Club. She has invested in over 20 companies, and recently enjoyed a partial exit.

'Angel investing involves funding a startup in return for equity,' Onay told us. 'It occurs at a very early stage, before VCs typically get involved. Founders might start with friends and family or bootstrap, then approach angel investors at the pre-seed, seed or sometimes Series A stage.'

The timing of the capital isn't the only distinguishing feature of angel investment.

'Cheque sizes are usually smaller than VC investments,' said Onay. 'Angels can make a direct investment, or invest as part of an angel syndicate, starting with as little as $1000. In Australia, cap tables are limited, so direct investments tend to be larger.'

Given the high risk of failure, what compels angel investors to bestow their funds on a startup? Unlike friends and family, they are not obliged by personal ties. So what are they looking for?

'It's very risky because you are coming in so early,' agreed Onay. 'Usually these startups don't have a huge amount of traction. You're really betting on the team and the market opportunity.'

Ideally, a startup at this stage will still demonstrate some form of early validation and a bit of customer traction.

'You don't have as many **proof points** as a VC coming in later would,' said Onay. 'It's a numbers game. You need 20 or 30 to hit a few big ones. The 'power law' means your top 10 per cent will return most of the value of your portfolio.'

The power law to which Onay refers is explained in depth in *The Power Law: Venture capital and the art of disruption* by Sebastian Mallaby. In short, it refers to the fact that a handful of investments drive the majority of returns for VCs.

As Peter Thiel, billionaire co-founder of PayPal, explained in *Zero to One: Notes on startups, or how to build the future*: '[W]e don't live in a normal world, we live under a power law.'

"The biggest secret in venture capital is that the best investment in a successful fund equals or outperforms the entire rest of the fund combined,' observed Thiel.

It is a law reflected in nature. In 1906, Italian economist Vilfredo Pareto noticed that 20 per cent of people owned 80 per cent of the land in Italy. Similarly, 20 per cent of his garden's pea pods produced 80 per cent of his peas. Investors seek outliers.

This is what can make startups a compelling **value proposition** for early-stage investors. However, as Onay explains, it is not one without risks.

'Compared to other assets, it's very illiquid,' said Onay. 'By the time that a startup exits — through an IPO or acquisition — you can wait, on average, four-and-a-half years. In medtech or life sciences, you can wait 10+ years.

'But the returns can be huge. An average internal rate of return is 20 per cent, which is a lot higher than real estate or the stock market. The upside is big, but it's incredibly risky and you have to be okay with losing all of it.'

Onay has applied this approach across a range of investments.

'I invested in an NFT startup a while ago, and had to look up what NFTs were,' laughed Onay. 'The platform is a marketplace for digital art.'

She also invested in a cancer therapeutics company using mRNA.

'mRNA was a really hot space after COVID-19 vaccines,' said Onay.

5. Venture capital (VC) funding

The main difference between an angel investor and a venture capital (VC) fund is where the money is coming from.

While angel investors provide their personal funds, venture capitalists invest capital controlled by a fund or a firm. VC funds tend to invest in later-stage startups, and often contribute far more substantial investments. It's why many startups regard the VC fund stage as hitting the big leagues.

According to the Australian Investment Council, venture capital can provide a range of benefits, including:

- *long-term equity finance,* providing a solid base for growth. VCs can also provide subsequent rounds of funding when required

- *mentoring in the form of strategic, operational and financial advice* informed by the successes and missteps of other companies in its portfolio

- *strategic alliances* that may assist in recruiting key personnel, contacts in international markets, introductions to partners, and where necessary, co-investments with other VC funds

- *facilitating an exit* for your startup, either through an IPO or a trade sale.

VCs seek capital gains over dividends and can derive their funding from superannuation funds or banks. Like angel investors, they subscribe to the power law and hunt for startups that might deliver outsized returns and exponential growth.

Stages of VC investment

There are three key stages of VC investment.

1. *Preliminary screening* involves a preliminary review of the startup proposal to ensure it falls within the firm's investment criteria. If it does, an initial meeting will be organised to allow the venture capitalist to meet the entrepreneur and key members of the management team. During this meeting, a review of the business plan and due diligence will be conducted; the venture capitalist will consider the team's skills and backgrounds.

2. *Negotiating investment* involves agreement over the MOU (memorandum of understanding). The venture capitalist will estimate the size and growth rates of the markets, barriers to entry, competitors and the opportunity to exploit niches, product life cycles, distribution channels and any export potential. This process is assisted by reports from accountants, industry experts and other consultants.

3. *Approvals and investment completed* involves an exhaustive due diligence process alongside disclosure of any relevant business information. Terms are negotiated, and an investment proposal is sent to the board. Should this be approved, legal documents are prepared, including a shareholders' agreement. This could involve veto rights by the investor on executive remuneration or loans; acquisition or asset sales; audit; IPOs; right of co-sale; and warranties regarding the accuracy of information. This can take up to three months, or even longer.

It is crucial to select a venture capitalist with whom you are likely to have a good working relationship, as investment horizons can last 4–6 years.

Explore the Australian Investment Council's (AIC) Directory of Members on their website. Simply search for your postcode or area, and the directory will list the closest VC funds, along with their investing preferences. The AIC is home to the lion's share of VC funds in Australia, so you're likely to find the most relevant results.

6. NFTs (non-fungible tokens)

You probably don't know Wendy Huang, the accountant. However, you might know Wengie. With 13.3 million followers, she is one of Australia's most popular YouTubers. In fact, she's such a big deal, Google named a room after her.

'When I started YouTube, my one goal was to get one million subscribers and win the "gold button" from YouTube,' Wengie said to us. 'I thought this would take a lifetime; I didn't expect to reach it in two years.'

Not bad for an accountant YouTubing in secret. (Asian parents, amirite?)

How did she get there? Right time, right platform, right content, right work ethic.

'I started creating tutorials around Ulzzang makeup, a popular Korean influencer style of makeup which I really enjoyed,' said Wengie. My viewers asked for advice, so I created organically useful content. I grew my channel into a niche and need for information.

'We had no idea people were actually making money from YouTube, which is probably the best time to get into something.'

Until then she had been a blogger, which was the only proven way to monetise user-generated content at the time.

'I built a very engaged fanbase, started exploring 'general makeup', and made my first ever viral video — over 1 million views — comparing Western vs Korean makeup, and how the styles differ,' Wengie said. 'My second viral video was a five-minute makeup routine.'

At her height, her videos regularly hit a million views within the first day or two of going live, and her channel grew by over 100 000 subscribers per day.

So what does any of this have to do with NFTs?

'Raising money via NFTs was very much based on community building, which my co-founder and I had a lot of experience doing from building the YouTube channel,' said Wengie.

Her crypto gaming startup, NYAN Heroes, raised $4 million from NFT sales of 'Genesis Nyans', which represented game characters (cats and their Guardian Robots).

'Some are legendary, some are basic, and it's a lucky draw', explained Wengie. You pay one amount, and it randomly generates an NFT for you. If you get a legendary, it could be worth a lot. We sold a set of these when we first launched.'

On top of NFT funding — which is considered funding from the community — NYAN Heroes raised an additional $13 million from investors and $70 000 from an initial coin offering (ICO) at a valuation of $200 million. But at this point, you might be saying, 'Wait, wait ... *crypto gaming? NFTs?*'

Let's rewind. What do you do after you've built Australia's largest YouTube channel? Cats in mech suits, of course!

Wengie's YouTube success took her to Los Angeles, where her agent landed her brand partnerships. While there, she decided to learn about crypto.

'I became aware of crypto in 2016', said Wengie. 'My friend told me to "buy some ETH". This was back when ethereum was valued at $13. You'd think I'm rich now, but my friend didn't tell me how to buy the coin, and to be honest, I was swamped making YouTube content. I looked up ETH on CommSec, realised it wasn't ethereum, and gave up.'

As you may have suspected, though, this didn't mark the end of Wengie's crypto journey.

'When I heard ETH was valued at $300, I started taking crypto a bit more seriously', said Wengie.

She and her partner decided to pivot from making content to learning about crypto, and started trading alt coins and other items.

'Fast-forward to the pandemic, and my friend invited me into the Axie Infinity guild he was building,' said Wengie. 'They needed a marketing strategy, and my background was in digital marketing. I started researching the Axie Infinity phenomenon, which was gaining a lot of traction at the time.'

Did your mind go blank when you read the words 'Axie Infinity phenomenon'? So did ours when we first heard them. To condense a worldwide craze into one sentence: imagine a hybrid between a mobile game, a cryptocurrency and Pokemon-style trading.

'There was a vertical within the crypto called 'play-to-earn' gaming, which involved making real money because you can sell the tokens on the open market by spending time playing the game and breeding your characters,' Wengie said.

'Essentially, it's like having a gaming economy [that] you can transfer into real-life currency. This is possible because there [is] a market for it.'

Deep in pandemic boredom, Wengie ended up on a Discord chat with a top Axie Infinity influencer, who gifted her an 'Axie', a little character NFT from the game. An Axie could be very valuable, depending on its traits, and you could earn money breeding and playing them in the game.

'There was so much money floating around this game,' said Wengie. As an avid gamer — think Warcraft and Dota League — she found herself unimpressed with Axie Infinity's quality and gameplay.

'My company was building a different game at the time, and we decided to build a crypto game, because we believed we could do it so much better.'

They kicked around a few ideas, and settled on NYAN Heroes.

'We took a popular game format as yet unseen in crypto — a shooter — and threw in a fun theme: cats piloting mech robots,' Wengie said. 'It's a combination of my favourite things: cats, and the anime, Neon Genesis Evangelion.'

She self-funded initial artwork prototypes and marketing, but to build a triple-A quality game, she needed serious funding.

She shortlisted investors based on who was generally investing in crypto games, got a few pointers from her Axie guild friend and cold outreached.

'I contacted a hedge fund in Singapore via Twitter, and in a weird coincidence, I noticed he followed an account that was literally a cat in a mech robot,' said Wengie.

'So, he loved cats and mechs, and I told him we were building cats in mechs as a crypto game, and would love to chat. It helped that I had a Twitter following so I wasn't just some random account. From here, he introduced us to his sister fund.'

Through her LA connections, Wengie scored a meeting with the fund-backing blockchain platform Solana.

'Once we got our initial funding, it was easier to get funding from others. It was a kind of seal of approval,' said Wengie.

It wasn't her first time pitching, as she'd done it for other startups, but it was the first time she had successfully raised money for a company.

'What was really beautiful was being involved in an industry that's growing quite rapidly,' she said.

'When it's still quite small, it's easy to get to know everyone in the space. Our advantage was my large YouTube audience. It showed we could grow a following and gave us a good base.'

Like so many ventures, founder differences caused Wengie to leave NYAN Heroes. She's since returned to making music: did we mention her song, 'Empire', debuted at number 22 on the Billboard World Digital Song Sales Chart? In unrelated news, NYAN Heroes burned its runway after her departure, and at the time of publication, is offline.

Long story short: what is NFT fundraising?

Startups can raise funds by offering unique digital assets — or non-fungible tokens (NFTs) — often to a loyal following. Fungible items (in other words, cash) differ from non-fungible items, which are by definition unique and not interchangeable.

Buying NFTs means purchasing something no-one else has — like VIP access, digital art, membership perks or in this case, playable game avatars imbued with various attributes, strengths and weaknesses. NFTs are recorded on a blockchain, reflecting their ownership and uniqueness. Sales of NFTs then fund the startup.

For a bonafide influencer like Wengie, NFT fundraising allowed her to unlock its unusual benefits: a broader investor base that you can access directly at lower cost, without an existing investor network. In addition, it played the role of engaging early players in the game. Whenever they pre-purchased their characters, they helped fund the build of the game.

Much like cats in mech suits, NFT funding options may not make sense to everyone. But for those who grasp them, they can offer countless hours of fascination.

So, how do you secure funding?

Now that you're across all the kinds of funding you might receive, how do you go about securing funding?

For Mad Paws' co-founder Alexis Soulopoulos, it was all about preparing a killer pitch that would capture their story. His initial VC conversations occurred through introductions, and he had to ensure what he delivered was impressive.

'When the first draft of the pitch deck was ready, I practised, practised, practised,' said Soulopoulos. 'I practised on my own, and I practised in front of the founding team at Mad Paws. I knew I would only have a limited time to pitch, so I wanted to be highly energised and memorable. It was also important to get the right content across in the limited time frame, and allow a lot of time for questions.'

So what are investors looking for during your pitch?

'Consider the value proposition,' advised Onay. 'Are they creating something people actually want? Do they understand the problem and the customer? Do they have evidence — metrics, traction — that show people actually want this?'

'If they have a little revenue, that's great. Customer acquisition, adoption and retention are even better.'

What distinguishes a startup from a regular business is growth. In your pitch, consider market opportunities: you need to demonstrate a venture-scale startup. Investors are searching for strong rates of return from a large market opportunity, and a good pricepoint.

'Try to identify the main risks,' advised Onay. 'What could kill the business? Some will have a big competitor risk, technology risk, business model risk, all kinds of things.'

Investors who understand your industry are best placed to support you. H2 Ventures, an investor in Forage, has also supported EdStart and Spriggy, showing an interest and understanding of the EdTech space.

'We got our first boost because H2 Ventures seeded us to start a company in that space,' said Forage co-founder Pasha Rayan. 'It was really lucky — we had some investors who believed in us, which felt crazy at the time.'

CHAPTER 7

HOW TO FIND (AND KEEP) THE RIGHT PEOPLE

Just as the One Ring required a Fellowship, or as the Avengers assembled, so, too, do you need a crack team to realise your big idea. Without a unique set of complementary skills possessed by people eager to work far harder than their salaried contemporaries, it is unlikely your startup will ever fire up to a trot, much less a unicorn's gallop.

First off, employment has changed a *lot* within the startup scene. Ten years ago, aggressive staff growth was a key metric of startup success. Now, AI heralds such as Sam Altman claim we are mere years (or months) away from seeing our first AI-powered one-person unicorn. However, until AI can steer itself towards an IPO, you'll still want to involve the right people.

So how do you attract the right talent to your startup, particularly in the absence of competitive salaries… or any salary at all?

Become a top startup employer

Like Family was recognised as a verified top startup employer, based on an employee survey of over 70 startups. This reflected their approach to employee recognition and retention, training and development, workplace flexibility and benefits, as well as a clearly articulated commitment to how they improve diversity and inclusion.

'Like Family was founded to make Australians of all ages and abilities feel supported and included,' the company said in a public statement. 'This extends to our own team! So it's an honour to be recognised for our efforts to foster an inclusive, collaborative and innovative company culture.

'Every person at Like Family plays a role in shaping our culture — we couldn't have done it without you!'

Receiving recognition as a preferred place to work is a major way startups can attract and retain talent. Jenna Leo thinks Like Family's appeal comes from the fact it is a growing, socially focused startup.

'They can see the social impact of their work, and enjoy that feel-good element of helping people,' said Leo. 'They also get more responsibility than they would in a large company, which is a motivator for many people.'

For some employees, this kind of upward mobility and exposure to a broad range of experiences can provide a point of distinction that larger and long-established organisations cannot offer. Startups are by nature ambitious, and so can often deliver employees more responsibility and growth opportunities than other employers. Many are run by younger founders and are more willing to be flexible in terms of how, when and where people complete their work.

'We've always been very flexible with our work arrangements, which I think is a plus for our team,' said Leo. 'This wasn't so common pre-COVID-19, but parents would arrive at 9.30 am and leave at 3 pm. We've never been clock watchers; it's always been more about outcomes. We've increased that level of flexibility since COVID-19 because that's what everyone has become accustomed to.'

Indeed, recent studies show that after COVID-19, half of Australians reported working mostly from home: 59 per cent of Victorians and 47 per cent in the rest of Australia. With return to office mandates underway, flexible work has proved a major drawcard for one of Like Family's developers.

When a new developer started in 2017, hybrid work had yet to mainstream. Like Family offered him workplace flexibility: two days in the office, and the other three remote.

'It's crazy, after COVID-19, to think of flexibility as a perk because most workplaces offer it now. But back in 2017, when this developer started, it was a relatively rare thing,' said Leo.

Becoming an employer of choice can help a scrappy young startup scale while retaining the strong culture that made it so initially successful.

As Jeff Bezos maintains, 'Your brand is what other people say when you're not in the room.' This is just as true for potential talent considering your startup. Much of what attracts driven, intelligent people comes down to culture. Notably, none of this pertains to remuneration. Rather, it's about building a culture that attracts people to do their best work.

Use equity to attract talent

Startups often can't out-pay their rivals to attract talent. In any case, what makes people choose startups over established organisations is frequently their vision — and the potential upside of gaining valuable equity as an early-stage employee.

For many startups, selling a slice of the pie — or parting with a little bit of equity (usually 10–15 per cent) — can be well worth it in return for employees feeling as invested in your company as you are. Equity often vests over time, allowing startups to conserve precious capital while keeping team members committed to ensuring the startup's valuation grows and scales effectively. It's a strategy that can prove very successful. Many of Mad Paws' first employees worked for sweat equity to earn a stake in the company's success.

So how do you go about creating equity compensation that's attractive to potential employees and beneficial to your business?

Here is a three-step guide.

1. Set up an employee stock option pool (ESOP)

Most startups set aside 10–15 per cent of their equity for ESOP towards future employees. If you assign half your stock options in your first 18 months, you're left with only 5 per cent for future employees. Funding rounds can help replenish employee equity pools, and you could dilute existing shareholders to top up your ESOP.

Decide whether you want to offer stock options (a right to buy/ sell a specific number of shares from the founders at a specific price, which can be exercised between a vesting and expiration date), stock warrants (similar to stock options, usually with a longer expiration date) or stock grants (bestowing a specific amount of stocks without a vesting date, so employees don't need to 'earn' the stocks). Stock options are the most common.

2. See my vest!

No, it's not hit Simpsons song, 'See my vest', but the equally important concept of 'vesting periods'. That is, how long will it take for employees to earn a share of your company. Often, this includes a 'cliff period' — a minimum time employees must work before vesting can begin. If your vesting period is four years, employees receive 25 per cent of their equity with each year. Some startups even increase equity with each year served. If an employee leaves early, they may have a 90 day window to exercise their stock options — fail to do so may mean losing their stock options, which revert to the original ESOP.

3. Track equity in a cap table

Allocate equity according to experience, or relative risk — so early employees may receive more equity. Don't forget to track all equity in a capitalisation table ('cap table'). This reflects stock options already exercised, and those still available.

Make your employees millionaires

Equity isn't just some ploy to make people work for lower than market rate. Exit via acquisition or IPO can make employees millionaires, especially when founders opt to reward employees over and above what their stock options require.

Creative networking site Behance was bootstrapped for five years by co-founders Scott Belsky and Matias Corea before Adobe offered them $150 million for an acquisition.

In response, the co-founders created a spreadsheet listing every employee in one of two columns: what they were owed in vested stock options, and what the founders felt they deserved to make.

Acquisition funds were set aside to distribute to employees, both as cash and RSU (restricted stock unit).

Two years post acquisition, no Behance employees had resigned, and about a dozen experienced a 'very material life change' following the sale.

'You have to ground yourself with the realisation that you did not make this [exit] happen,' Belsky told *Business Insider*. 'You got the team together and maybe initially you took the most risk, but you did not make this happen.'

Belsky calls this approach 'long-term greedy'.

Behance wasn't alone in this approach. MoPub founder Jim Payne had been through a few startup exits and was all too familiar with being an employee who missed out when a company went bust or was acquired.

Payne provided performance-based stock options grants, available through company-issued loans to allow employees to buy options at low prices without taking major personal financial risks. Stock options were reviewed regularly, with new options issued in line with performance.

Payne turned down three acquisitions before accepting Twitter's $350 million buyout. This made 36 of MoPub's 100 employees millionaires.

'You can hoard the whole pie for yourself, but it's a team sport you're playing,' Payne told *Business Insider*. 'If you're doing [a startup] for ego ... I don't think you're going to be a great CEO.

I think you can make money ... by being mercenary, but you'll never truly be great.'

When Wiley Cerilli sold SinglePlatform for $100 million in cash and stock to Constant Contact, half his employees became millionaires, even though their stock options hadn't fully vested. Some didn't even have options. Despite this, Cerilli vested employees with additional stock options and provided cash bonuses to brand new employees.

Forage co-founder Tom Brunskill is a corporate lawyer, a skillset that saw him prioritise the company's equity structure.

'We organised everything quite evenly and fairly based on people going fulltime into the company early on,' said co-founder Pasha Rayan.

'Most of our equity structure was geared towards making sure everyone went fulltime to make the company work. It was a balancing act. On one side, we wanted the stock to be fair and even across the team. On the flip side, an even split only worked if everyone went all in at the same time.'

Master people management

Learning how to manage people is one of the most critical skills founders need, along with constant and creative problem solving, and a certain tolerance for pain and setbacks.

'The only thing that's really hard in business is people management,' said Airtasker founder Tim Fung. 'The rest is maths. The hardest stuff is disciplining people, and taking away the resources from a project that people are passionate about.

And, of course, firing people. Those are really the only things that as a founder, you kind of dread having to do.'

Like Family co-founder Jenna Leo agreed. Before her startup, she had never managed people. She finds people management to be one of the biggest challenges — and delights — of running a startup.

'I've now realised that every time you double a team, you need to change everything you do,' said Leo. 'I probably didn't understand enough of that as we grew. I also don't think I tried hard enough to develop myself as a manager. In the past, I'd focus on growing the business or chasing some exciting opportunity. If I had my time again, I would have channelled some of that attention into growing myself as a leader.'

Early-stage employees were attracted by Like Family's mission and vision. As such, it was easy to work closely with them to achieve significant results. Leo cautioned against expecting the same output from later-stage employees; as the company grows, their outlook might differ.

'When you push the newer employees to generate the same results, they say, "You're too tough, Jenna. You're too demanding". The company was growing, but I didn't know how to bring out the best in these new employees,' admitted Leo.

'When Like Family was early stage, I could be 100 per cent me all the time. Because I worked so closely with those first team members, I could do that and still be an effective manager. But, as the team grew, I should have been more people oriented, instead of goal oriented all the time.'

Once the team grew to 15, Leo switched her focus to how she could improve as a founder and a CEO. People management is always changing, which spurs Leo to keep learning and improving.

Find people driven by your vision

Like Family was able to attract such committed early-stage employees because of its vision, which was to provide personalised care that felt 'like family'.

Mad Paws, as a pet care venture, was similarly positioned to find people passionate about its cause.

'The factor that worked in our favour was the goal behind Mad Paws,' explained co-founder Alexis Soulopoulos. 'Pet care is a topic which brings out a lot of passion in certain people. More than adaptability, or a risk tolerance, we needed team members who believed in our vision.'

Mad Paws identified a lack of personalised pet care options as a real problem in Australia. To solve it, they needed a team of people who loved pets and were committed to their welfare.

'Luckily, these were the exact type of people we attracted as our first employees,' said Soulopoulos. 'If they hadn't been so willing to take a risk on a startup, and so excited by the industry, we wouldn't have been able to scale the way we did. Many of those early employees stayed with Mad Paws as we grew, and came to manage new employees themselves.'

Attracting the right talent can also mean knowing when a person might not be right for your business.

'We've needed to accept that our business isn't the right fit for every lawyer,' said LegalVision co-founder Lachlan McKnight.

Some lawyers will always be better suited to working in traditional law firms, or as in-house lawyers, or not working as lawyers at all.

'Our core employee value proposition is for our people to progress their careers during their time at LegalVision. It doesn't mean we expect them to be here for their entire careers. If someone is here for a couple of years, they grow really quickly as a professional, and the business gets value from them being here, then we've delivered a heap of value to both the employee and the business.

'If that's the mindset you have, you can be accepting of the fact that people are going to leave. This is the reality of the modern portfolio career. You've got to have an employee value proposition that works for your business — and therefore works for the people in the business.'

This is a sensible approach. According to the Australian Bureau of Statistics, fewer than 10 per cent of Australians stay in their job for more than 20 years, with 56 per cent staying for less than five years. Twenty-one per cent of the population came in at less than one year. Job mobility sits at 9.4 per cent, the highest in a decade, with 24 per cent of professionals changing jobs in the previous year.

Recruit people at the right stage in their lives

Finding the right people can also come down to finding them at the right stage in their lives. Younger employees are more open to the risks and rewards startups present, unburdened by mortgage, lifestyle or family commitments.

'When we first launched, we weren't anyone's idea of a big company,' said Mad Paws co-founder Alexis Soulopoulos. 'We hadn't raised any money beyond what the co-founders had invested, which meant we couldn't outbid other companies for staff. We knew this ruled out the possibility of cold recruiting experienced professionals from the outset. I also couldn't reach out to workplace veterans in my network and try to woo them with our vision — because I didn't really know any!'

Alexis started Mad Paws in his 20s, shortly after finishing university. While this left him short on contacts with impressive professional track records, he did know many young people at the start of their careers, hungry for new experiences and excited to adapt.

With relatively few life commitments, they were also willing to take a risk on an early-stage startup. They didn't need to consider how such a risky venture would impact their mortgages or families. As it turns out, these people were — in the case of Mad Paws — the perfect employees to join during its first days.

People are what make or break a business, and those first few years taught Alexis a lot about what can attract amazing people to a workplace.

'Maybe even more importantly, it taught me about what can keep those people at your workplace, and what motivates them,' explained Soulopoulos. This led to Mad Paws' emphasis on culture, enabling transparency by removing gatekeepers of data; democratically choosing company values and incorporating them into **business as usual** (**BAU**); and attracting pet lovers through initiatives such as 'pawternity leave'.

'I feel as if I got lucky with some key management team members who joined pretty early,' said LegalVision's Lachlan McKnight. 'By early, I mean both in terms of their careers and in the story of our business. They've really helped to drive the growth of the business from day one.'

Alongside his co-founders, McKnight's early team members were crucial to his success. LegalVision's core management team has remained relatively stable from the beginning, which McKnight credits with their success.

Sometimes the best place to look for motivated employees is among your earliest users. This was certainly true for Like Family.

'The first people we had working with us were [Like Family] social carers because I would call every single one before we approved them on the platform,' said Jenna Leo. This helped her get to know people who understood care and were committed to their mission.

Like so many new businesses, Like Family's staff also held multiple roles.

'We had a couple of social carers who did more,' recalled Leo. 'There was one person, for instance, who called prospective clients on their phones. I could tell that we were all very mission aligned, which was important during those early times. It was also a really exciting sensation because we were all building something from scratch together. Those first team members enjoyed the work because they'd all bought in as social carers.'

Think 'out of the box' incentives

High-value employees can be worth an entire team, so it's worth thinking a little out of the box to attract them. This is exactly what Like Family's Jenna Leo did to find a developer with exactly the skills they needed.

'After [the initial carers], the first employee we hired was a developer, and we'd been trying to convince him for about nine months before he joined us,' explained Leo. 'He came from another marketplace, and he really believed in what we were doing — but he was also really talented. That meant he could command a higher salary than we could afford to pay him at that point.'

They worked around this issue by agreeing to pay him a sliding salary.

'In his first year, we would pay him $X. In his second year, we would increase it to $Y. By his third year, he would be on $Z,' said Leo.

The developer wasn't after equity, just a salary. This 'sliding salary' approach allowed Like Family to reward his skillset without paying more than they could afford during his first year.

They also offered him the opportunity to own the tech and product departments, which is exactly what he was after.

'Mat [Bertrand] was working on the member side, and I was working on the social carer side, so we were just focused on growing the business. Everything tech and product-related fell to our developer, and I think that was a strong motivator for him. He made a big impact on the business, and he was involved in every single decision.'

Embracing this level of responsibility was on par with him being a founder, and made a major difference in the growth of Like Family.

Not every employee will be after sweat equity, flexible work or more responsibility. Some may seek migration assistance and sponsorship.

As Like Family's team grew, many of their developers became international employees.

'We'd bring them into the company by paying for their visas and sponsoring them to stay in the country,' said Leo. 'That's how we've gotten some of our really good developers because there are a lot of companies who won't organise visas for their employees.'

CHAPTER 8

BE HONEST: ARE YOU RUNNING A STARTUP, A SIDE HUSTLE OR A REGULAR BUSINESS?

In 2017, Like Family were having a moment. Having joined the Cerebral Palsy Alliance-backed Remarkable Accelerator, the startup had grown fivefold in four months. At the end of the accelerator, they won the Telstra People's Choice Award, and earned a $20 000 grant. Outside the program, they were similarly winning pitch comps and wooing carers and clients alike.

While they were only a year into their quest, they were already finding their rhythm. They were Barack Obama in late 2007; they were Taylor Swift in the days after her first album dropped. Everyone could see they were going places.

In short, it was a startup worthy of full-time effort. But Like Family's two founders, Jenna Leo and Mathieu Bertrand? They were still working other jobs to pay the bills.

Jenna's and Mat's career juggling didn't stem from their passion for personal training and yoga (although both look as if they've stepped out of an Under Armour ad). Rather, their crossroads in 2017 reflects one of the most common conundrums faced by founders: 'When should I quit my day job and commit to my business?'

Attend a pitch night, startup social or founder fireside chat, and you're likely to hear some version of this question. And, like most common questions, it's a fair thing to ask. Quit too early, and you risk missing a rental payment before your business proves itself. Cling to the safety blanket of a job for too long, and you may squander the potential of your business.

With the gift of hindsight, it seems obvious that Jenna and Mat were ready to take the plunge. But when you're living minute to minute in an early-stage business, doubt can sometimes be a more persuasive mentor than hope.

Of course, no-one *wants* their idea to languish in an innovation purgatory. If you've committed to bringing a concept to life, you don't want it subsisting on life support. But before we explore the next step of growing your business, we'd like you to ask yourself a question: Are you running startup, a side hustle or a regular business?

And it's very, *very* important that you're honest with yourself... because your answer determines how you approach literally everything that comes next.

Side hustles: the 'food coma' of business jargon

At the risk of sounding like a bad wedding speech, we're going to quote the *Oxford English Dictionary*. According to the dictionary, the term 'side hustle' first appeared in a 1950s issue of the US newspaper *The Chicago Defender*. Fast forward several decades, and it has become a widely accepted term, like 'food coma', or 'adulting'. However, unlike those terms (which are universally embraced and reviled, respectively), 'side hustle' means different things to different people.

Across the street from the *Oxford English Dictionary*, at Merriam-Webster, you'll find the definition of 'side hustle' as 'work performed for income supplementary to one's primary job'.

A bit...flat, no? For a more perky definition, let's leave Dictionary Road and visit Self-Help Boulevard. Chris Guillebeau, an entrepreneur and author of *Side Hustle: From idea to income in 27 days*, cheerily proclaims:

A side hustle is like a hobby, with one big difference: most hobbies cost money. A side hustle makes money. It's like playing entrepreneurially, getting paid to try something new and learn different skills.

This is a brighter lens through which to view side hustles, I'm sure we can all agree. However, in both definitions, the parameters are clear: *This is something you pursue on your own time.* The moment it eclipses your job and becomes a full-time pursuit, it ceases to be a side hustle.

'Yes, that's what I want to do,' you might say, with a hint of exasperation in your voice. 'Take my idea, begin it as a side hustle, then transition into a full-time startup when it's ready. Can you stop throwing dictionaries at me and give me something useful?'

At the risk of irking you more, we're going to reply to a question with another question: 'Are you sure that it's a startup you want to run?'

No, seriously.

Small business vs startup: earn and grow, or spend and scale?

Ask Google, an AI chatbot or your annoying bitcoin-buying friend for a 'startup versus small business' breakdown. Go on, ask — we'll wait.

...

...

...Welcome back! Now, chances are, whatever you read (or heard from your bitcoin-buying friend) would have focused on the shinier aspects of startups. Sure, your source may have told you that 'Startups can be higher risk' or 'They require more investment'. However, we're willing to bet that the spotlight lingered on actors like 'Startups Disrupt the Market' and 'Startups Can Scale, Small Businesses Can't'. Or — and this is usually the star of the show — 'Startups Have a Clearer Exit Strategy Than Small Businesses'.

It would be easy, then, to decide that you want to run a startup over a small business. Yes, yes, higher risk, yadda yadda yadda — but aren't *all* businesses high-risk? If you're going to assume the pressure of starting a business, you might as well go *all the way*. Why not chase the business model that lets you be a maverick, grow like weeds and exit for more?

You likely saw this coming from a paragraph away, but the differences don't only centre on risk and reward. They also involve money — and, crucially, when you can expect to earn it.

Jared Hecht is a venture partner at New York–based VC fund Union Square Ventures. Perhaps more dazzlingly, he also founded two startups that progressed to acquisition; he fulfilled the founder's dream of exiting not once, but twice. Despite his startup success, Hecht was clear-eyed in marking the differences between startups and small businesses. On startups, Hecht said in *Forbes*:

> *... they're better defined as organizations [sic] formed to search for a repeatable and scalable business model.*

> *A small business isn't in search of a business model that works down the line — they're looking for a business model that works from day one.*

Part of this distinction centres on how (and when) you generate revenue; in a small business, you earn what you can, when you can. But an equally crucial aspect is how (and when) you *spend* what you've earned.

LegalVision CEO and co-founder Lachlan McKnight has watched this issue play out in recent years within the legal profession. The concept of NewLaw — which we introduced in chapter 2 — has grown in popularity of late. However, to McKnight's eyes, most self-styled NewLaw firms are in fact living the lives of a small business.

'These days, anyone who starts a law firm seems to call themselves a NewLaw firm,' McKnight told us.

'In truth, a lot of these businesses are simply pretty traditional. And that isn't a bad thing, but there are still few businesses trying to do what we're trying to do. By that, I mean really investing in product and technology, and driving for outsized growth.'

On its own, 'outsized growth' sounds like something every business owner would want, like 'constant revenue' or 'company culture'. However, McKnight asserts that it's an outcome of investment, rather than a goal.

'When you want to really grow and scale, you have a different mindset in terms of how much you're prepared to invest in technology, how much you're prepared to invest in new sales channels and the time horizon that you'll invest in terms of **customer acquisition cost (CAC)** to **customer lifetime value (CLV)**,' he said.

Or, put as plainly as possible: small businesses aim to earn and grow. Startups plan to spend and scale.

Startups are weeds, small businesses are trees

Ask NewsCorp, a financial adviser or your annoying real estate-buying uncle, and you'll read (or hear) small business horror stories. Stats around café closures make effective clickbait, and everyone knows someone who was brought to ruin by small business. Even so, unlike startups, the *aim* in small business is to turn a profit as soon as you can. This means that, also unlike (most) startups, your business model doesn't demand VC funding to stay afloat. Provided you cover your expenses, you keep what you earn — unfettered by the shackles of investor returns or growth expectations. For anyone with rigid lifestyle costs, like a mortgage or school fees, this business model might paint a prettier picture.

There's also the fact that small businesses don't need to stay small. When we compare business models, it's easy to equate startups with Amazon, and small businesses with Mum & Pop's

Local Grocer. One lands you on a *Forbes* list, while the other roots you to a neighbourhood plot for 40 years. However, while they aren't designed to scale, small businesses can certainly grow. After all, most fast-food franchises, laundromat chains and multinational consultancies began life as small businesses.

Rather than growing like weeds, the small business model is much more like a tree. Under poor conditions (or sometimes through bad luck), they'll die as saplings. Others may grow large enough to cast a shadow, but lack the space or nutrients to reach any higher. Some, though, keep growing until their canopy becomes its own ecosystem, and their roots become one with the earth. These are the trees that host elaborate cubby houses or appear in those nature-themed coffee table books. Sure, they'll never scale like weeds, but there's no mistaking their presence.

By now, you may have noticed that our assessment of these three business models has lacked something crucial. It doesn't involve data, and there won't be a dollar sign in sight. No — it involves what each business model will *require you to do all day*. Depending on your reason for wanting to launch a business, this could be the single most vital factor you face. And before we delve into why, we'd like to pose yet another question for you to consider: 'Are you sure that it isn't a side hustle you want to run?'

Please read on.

Must love dogs (?): how to choose the right business type for your goals

We've thrown a lot of quotes and metaphors at you recently, so let's use a simple example. If you love dogs, the idea of launching a pet-sitting startup like Mad Paws might appeal to you. However, a startup may not be the best way to feed that passion. Should your startup become successful, you'll spend your days grappling with finance, marketing, tech, HR, spreadsheets, board reports and the litany of other demands that encroach on a CEO's time.

You know how you *won't* spend your day? Caring for pets. This is because, as Like Family's Jenna Leo told us earlier, founders should be delegating tasks as soon as they're systematised. In fact, your goal as a startup founder should be to decentralise the service. This means you need to empower freelance workers around the country (or beyond) to care for pets via your platform. While this grants you the power to scale, it also deprives you of a big doggy daycare centre filled with furbabies. Instead, you'll need to find solace in the fact that pets are receiving care in your startup's name.

'Well, that doggy daycare centre you mentioned sounds nice,' you may reply, the fire of hope still burning in your eyes.

'Maybe I'll open one of those instead. I get that I might not grow into the next Mad Paws, but I can live with that. I'd rather have a dog-filled space to call my own.'

Okay — let's say you have a canine care centre to call your own. How much time are you willing to invest into accounting? Marketing? Managing your stock and juggling your invoices? Placating council workers who want to ensure you're not breaching the zoning rules set for your property? Fielding baseless one-star reviews from clients who expected their dog to return home with a Cambridge diploma? Finding and hiring new staff when current staff leave? (Side note: this last issue is so common and time-consuming in small business that it warrants its own book).

As dour as these last few paragraphs have been, we haven't raised these problems to deter you from your dream. Rather, we simply want to highlight the joys and drawbacks of all three business types. The right choice for you can depend on a range of factors, but four of the most integral are:

- What problem do you want to solve?
- What appeals to you the most about running your own business?
- What would you struggle to do on a stressful day?
- Can you manage your current obligations under your chosen business model?

To show you a few archetypes in action, here are three case studies: Eliza's, Andres' and Chihiro's.

Eliza

By her own admission, Eliza is obsessed with dogs. The only problem: she can't keep one herself thanks to her draconian landlord. While she wants to make new furry friends, she's in the early stages of a fulfilling career. Eliza is also saving for her first home, so she's looking to make every dollar she can.

SOLUTION: ELIZA BEGINS A SIDE HUSTLE AS A DOG WALKER

By creating a profile with an existing dog-walking platform, Eliza can lower the barrier to entry. She'll also benefit from their marketing, meaning she'll need to spend minimal time promoting herself. Since the dog-walking platform provides legal and technical infrastructure, she won't need to invest any of her own money. Finally, she'll be able to choose her own dog-walking hours, so she can fit it in around her career.

In short, low risk + extra money + 100 per cent focus on the dogs = one happy Eliza.

Andres

Like Eliza, Andres would spend all day with dogs if he could. He currently works as an accountant, but he yearns to cast aside the manacles of his worker drone life. He's done the books for countless small businesses, so he knows how volatile the market can be. However, his desire to spend his time with fur babies compels him to accept the risk. Over the past several years, Andres has accrued some savings, and wants to invest it into his dream.

Having assessed small businesses before, he also knows that any full-time pet enterprise wouldn't only involve playing fetch. If it allows him to spend his days in the company of canines, he's willing to accept the more stressful — and sometimes boring — aspects of business management. Even so, because he has two young children, Andres wants a business model that empowers him to *earn*.

SOLUTION: ANDRES OPENS A PET-GROOMING SMALL BUSINESS

Andres understands the risk of small business and feels ready to accept them. Moreover, he is determined to build a career around his passion. Sure, he'll need to master an array of new skills and spend much of his time solving business problems. However, he'll be able to spend the rest of the day caring for dogs. In Andres' mind, that's a worthy exchange.

Chihiro

Chihiro is sick and tired of hunting for the cheapest dog food, toys and health supplies across multiple websites. Luckily, Chihiro's dual career as an eCommerce marketer and dog walker has uniquely qualified her to create a scalable answer.

Similarly to Andres, Chihiro has a young family. As such, Chihiro wants to cap their personal investment. She understands this means seeking funding from VCs, angel investors and other sources earlier in her journey, and possibly giving up more equity.

SOLUTION: CHIHIRO LAUNCHES AN ECOMMERCE PET SUPPLIES SITE

Beyond the typical risks of small business, Chihiro will face many of the unique challenges we've explored in this book. On a personal note, she'll also spend little to no time actually interacting with dogs. This will be especially true if the startup scales and she needs to channel her focus into new and larger problems. However, Chihiro isn't looking to spend her day with dogs. Instead, she wants to make dog ownership more affordable by way of a website that lists the cheapest price for any dog product, initially gaining revenue as an affiliate, and earning referral fees from pet product providers. Her long-term plan: to be the Bunnings of pet supplies, directly selling the most affordable pet products to a mass market.

• • •

These case studies have been rather dog-centric, but the principles apply to any pursuit. Find the problem you want to solve, choose how you want to spend your work hours and your business model will reveal itself to you.

Key takeaways

■ *Side hustles can be a journey... but they can also be a destination.* For many would-be founders, the side-hustle approach can provide a testing ground for a business concept before going fulltime. However, depending on your goals, it can also offer a 'final form' for your business.

If you're looking to earn money from a particular pastime, a side hustle can offer you more than a startup.

■ *Small businesses want to earn and grow, but startups want to spend and scale.* A small business isn't simply a startup with less tech, fewer new ideas and a lower growth ceiling. Instead, it's a business model that aims to grow more organically and put money in your pocket sooner. This isn't automatically an inferior way of growing a business, but a preferred method for many founders.

■ *Is a startup* really *what you want?* Do you want to spend more time pursuing your passion? Or do you want to solve a problem that many people with a certain passion often face? Your answer may dictate whether the startup model is right for you.

Does passion need to die for growth to come alive?

If you're old enough (or a nostalgia bug), you might remember those police procedural TV shows from the 1990s. The protagonist — usually a poorly dressed detective — was *married to the job*. They also often grappled with alcoholism, and they were almost always men.

At some point in the series, the detective's *other* spouse — a human — would stomp their feet, fold their arms and incite a B-plot.

'You listen to me, McKracken,' they would huff. 'This job of yours will be the end of our marriage, d'you hear? You've got to make yourself a choice: me, or the Force.'

In the above case studies, you may have seen a shadow of old Detective McKracken and their spouse. It may have felt as if the sliding scales of business models reflect a choice between passion and growth. After all, to build a startup, most founders need to gravitate away from their startup's core business offering. Much like Chihiro in the case study, Alexis Soulopoulos seldom dog sits these days because he's busy ensuring other people can. And Jenna Leo doesn't find much time to care for Like Family's clients because she's growing the community at scale (and she certainly has no time to teach yoga anymore, either).

Similarly, few successful founders stumbled onto their growth by mistake. Before he committed proper resources, Forage co-founder Pasha Rayan spent countless hours finding a concept that would scale. And as we just saw, Lachlan McKnight ensured that outsized growth drove LegalVision's strategy from its dawning days.

These examples can lead to the assumption that, to create a profitable business, you need to:

- kill your darlings
- choose growth over passion.

However, our next interviewee is living proof that you can prove this rule wrong. This real-life Detective McKracken sidestepped the 'spouse or the Force' ultimatum entirely. In their case, 'the Force' was a love of animation. And the 'spouse' was business growth on a global scale. And instead of 'McKracken', their name is McQuinn — Nellie McQuinn, more specifically.

You have the right to remain silent … as you learn how she grew her passion into a 10-figure children's entertainment empire.

I'm in love with the CoCo(melon)

At a glance, you may not recognise the name 'Moonbug Entertainment'. But if you've spent more than 15 minutes in the presence of toddlers (or their parents) in the past several years, you've probably heard of CoComelon.

A YouTube channel for children, CoComelon is currently the world's largest preschool brand. As of March 2025, CoComelon sits in the top three most subscribed channels on YouTube *in the world*. Through merchandising, Netflix deals and a brand that would put The Wiggles to shame, CoComelon has become a worldwide behemoth. It was also one of the first to display the power of short-form children's YouTube content on a global scale. It's a disrupter in the classic sense of the word — and it has the numbers to back it up.

In mid 2020, Moonbug Entertainment acquired CoComelon, before shepherding the brand to an even broader global audience. However, Moonbug's resume stretches well beyond 'buyer and custodian of CoComelon'. Since their inception in 2018, Moonbug have shown an eye for acquiring short-form web content aimed at kids. Series like *Blippi*, *Little Angel*, *Little Baby Bum* and many other YouTube staples have all joined the Moonbug fold.

It was little surprise, then, that in November 2021, Blackstone-backed US company Candle Media bought Moonbug for US$3 billion. The moral to the story? Moonbug's founding management team committed to Chihiro's approach to business, and they were rewarded with an acquisition. While they weren't running a tech startup per se, they focused on spending and scaling rather than earning and saving. They aced the assignment, and they received full marks.

Nellie McQuinn was a member of this founding management team. Her own production company, Grass Roots Media, was acquired by Moonbug at its launch in 2018. Since, for Moonbug, it was an equal parts acquisition and inception, Grass Roots formed part of their founding DNA. In other words, Nellie found the Holy Grail of hustle culture: not one, but two exit events. Surely, then, she had spent her career as a bona fide Chihiro, forsaking passion for the promise of growth.

… yeah, nah. In fact, if any of the three case studies described her, she'd be Andres with a dash of Eliza. When she first ventured into production in London, she did so to fuel another passion: acting.

'I started my production company when I was 19, and that was sort of an accident,' McQuinn told us.

'I was acting at the time, and I'd gone to London to perform. I was in a show, and when I met the director, I said I thought the show was being produced really badly … in a way that only a 19-year-old Australian who has no experience in producing can do.'

Like with so many young founders, Nellie's mixture of vision, candour and professional inexperience served her well. In this case, it was the catalyst for what would become a market-leading foray into children's entertainment.

'He replied that he actually needed a producer, and asked if I wanted to come onboard in a production capacity,' she said.

'That's how I got started in production.'

Listening to her humble account, it would be easy to see Nellie's story as a case of 'right place, right time'. However, over the course of nearly two decades, she made countless pivots — both to her business plan and to her goals. The result was that her passion evolved alongside her value proposition.

'At first, [my reason for entering production] was mainly because I wanted to create jobs for myself as an actress,' McQuinn said.

'I thought: "If I can make the jobs, then I can cast myself". Before long, though, I fell in love with the producing aspect of the work. That was 19 years ago, and it just went from there.'

Any parent who has sat through hours (and hours) of Moonbug content will know that Nellie is a unique success. Nellie herself is quick to acknowledge that she benefitted from privileges that others don't enjoy; for instance, she grew up in a family of working creatives. She also lived with her father when she first moved to London, temporarily freeing her from the burden of rent.

Even so, her success isn't a product of nepotism, nor good timing. While there are many factors responsible, the one that interests us is her capacity to mould her passion. At first, her passion revolved around acting. Then, as opportunities emerged to make short-form children's content, she discovered what *fuelled* her passion: an urge to create. Once she grasped this truth, she could reshape her passion into whatever the business required: animation, editing — even acquisitions. Beyond stoking her motivation, this ensured she kept evolving her skills as both a founder and business owner.

As we'll explore in later chapters, McQuinn doesn't spend as much time in the creator's chair these days. However, for most of her company's lifespan, she was able to make a happy marriage out of growth and passion. By doing so, she's grown from a side-hustle outlook to a startup mindset.

'If you can make your passion your career,' she said, 'it doesn't feel like a career.'

Key takeaways

- *They're more like guidelines, anyway.* While side hustle, small business, and startup business models do differ, they're not set in stone. Just because you pursue one doesn't mean you can't borrow from the others.

- *It's a maze, not a straight line.* Whether it's user feedback, external factors or your own motivation, your business' focus can change for a plethora of reasons. So long as it happens for considered and intentional reasons, there's nothing wrong with a nonlinear route.

- *Spare your darlings... provided they're adaptable.* Often, founders need to forsake the things they enjoy for the things the business needs. However, the things they enjoy can evolve over time. Find the root cause, rather than the symptom, of your passion, and you can remain in love with your work as your business evolves.

The great leap sideways: transitioning from a side hustle to a full-time business

If you take anything away from the prior section, let it be this: you don't need to commit fulltime to fulfil your dreams.

But let's say you *want* to commit fulltime. You've pondered the three different business models, cross-sectioned them over your own hopes and found your truth. For you, a side hustle isn't the destination, it's a stop on your journey. No, your true target is a full-time business, one that can absorb your every working moment. Your side hustle is merely a pitstop, a roadhouse, one of those highway motels that Airbnb destroyed.

The only issue? You're not quite sure when you should leave the side hustle and arrive at the full-time business.

You wouldn't be alone in this feeling. Since co-founding Mad Paws, Alexis Soulopoulos has spoken at countless startup events. In that time, one of the most common questions he has received is some version of, 'How do I know when to stop side hustling and commit to my business fulltime?'

It's a common feeling for would-be founders and thriving entrepreneurs alike. As you'll recall from the first page of this chapter, it was a key conundrum for Like Family back in 2017. But while their success in the Remarkable Accelerator galvanised them to commit, it wasn't the only factor that informed them. According to Jenna Leo, they began to note signs of promise as early as 2016 — a mere year after launch.

'Mat and I got married in March 2016, and we thought, 'You know what? We're only going to get married once, so let's take the week and properly enjoy it,' Leo told us.

'After we came back from our 'mini-moon', we logged onto the platform and found that we'd made $800.

'That was huge for us at that point — because it was money the company had made without us doing anything. We took it as a sign that the idea had legs.'

For a product such as Like Family, which offers an online marketplace, $800 wasn't simply a dollop of revenue. Indeed, it served as product validation: a murmur that the business might have the bones to scale. For founders who wanted to create a scalable social support network, this served as a vital sign.

It's also telling that Mat and Jenna didn't refer to **vanity metrics**. They could have swooned at the media coverage they'd earned or the extent to which their mailing list had grown.

However, they recognised that such figures, while encouraging, didn't validate their business model. It was only once they'd seen scalable revenue that they started to consider going fulltime.

Now, your markers will depend on the goals of your business. In your case, earning money in a scalable format might not align with your goals. Perhaps, for instance, you'll book more clients than you fit into your spare hours. Regardless, if your business shows signs of life — and it's the life you want to lead — you may find yourself ready to commit.

Part time to fulltime: what's the vibe?

Of course, performance metrics can be a useful guide, but they alone don't possess the power to uproot your life. To embark on a full-time journey, only one light source can illuminate your path: your own mindset.

If you cringed at that last sentence, we wouldn't blame you. But your working style, appetite for risk and relationship with multitasking play an equal role to any growth figures.

Tash Jamieson knew herself well when she founded Lockpick Games — and this knowledge steered her transition into full-time business.

'When I committed fulltime, it was more for my personal wellbeing as opposed to any market indicators,' Jamieson told us.

'At first, I tried really hard to be measured about it. I started by going down to part time, but found I couldn't fully focus on Lockpick and my personal life. I knew that, to be the best I could be at this, I needed to give it my full attention.

'The urge to be safe made sense, but was only keeping me from committing 100 per cent.'

Jamieson acknowledges that the decision of when and how to transition to fulltime is a deeply personal choice; others, for example, may have felt the urge to mitigate risk by first sourcing an income from Lockpick Games. However, in Jamieson's case, her preferred framework for productivity trumped any concerns around risk.

'For my personality, it's not feasible for me to be trying to focus on too many things,' she said.

'Once I got the idea in my head, it was really difficult to switch off.'

Put yourself in Jamieson's shoes for a moment. Imagine your user base is demanding more than you can give them on a part-time schedule. Surely that's a cause to quit your day job, no? Now, superimpose that thought over a mortgage to pay. Or rent to cover. Or a savings account that will dwindle to zero in six months if this business doesn't justify you an income. How do you feel about that day job now? At the risk of sounding like a startup Switzerland, these are crossroads that no-one else can walk for you.

Can I pay myself with other people's money?

Perhaps you've landed somewhere between Tash Jamieson and some risk-averse alternative. (Let's call him Greg. He owns several pot plants, tracks his expenses in a spreadsheet and brings a thermos of soup to café lunches.) While the Tash in you wants to take the plunge, your inner Greg is already fretting about your budget.

'I know what,' exclaims your inner Grash (an unholy hybrid between Greg and Tash).

'We'll take on some pre-seed funding! That way, we can pay ourselves a salary during that first rocky year of full-time business. The side hustle part of our business has already shown some promising growth. Once we go fulltime, we'll be able to pin an investor down easily. Cowabunga!'

After reading chapter 6, you may think that Grash has just spouted some profound wisdom. (Except for that 'Cowabunga' line. Neither Tash nor Greg say that, so we have no idea where it came from.) However, as experts in the Australian startup sector will confirm, accepting early-stage funding can sometimes be a poisoned chalice.

David Burt serves as Director of Entrepreneurship at the University of New South Wales (UNSW). As the leader of UNSW Founders — the university's startup accelerator — he has guided hundreds of Australian startups through their early days. Pertinent to Grash's idea, Burt has most commonly worked with founders during their part-time-to-full-time transition phase.

Outside of UNSW, he also serves as a non-executive director for Cicada Innovations (a deep-tech startup incubator) as well as other startups and charities. As such, his knowledge of startup problems extends beyond the start line of the race.

When it comes to taking on early funding, Burt offers words of encouragement — and words of caution: 'What you need to keep in mind is that taking funding comes with expectations from a new group of stakeholders, your investors,' he told us.

'Every business is concerned with serving their customers. If you take on investment, you'll need to consider how you manage the expectations of this group as well.'

That's not to say that seeking early funding is automatically a bad idea. In his career, Burt says he has watched some startups accept funding from day one — and progress to thrive.

At the same time, he has watched other businesses scale to earn millions without ever taking a dollar in funding. With this in mind, ask yourself: are you willing to accept the strings that accompany funding? And if not, do you have the funds, resources and peace of mind to commit to a full-time business?

Should your answer be 'no', there's no shame in running a side-hustle business model for a while longer. You may disappoint Grash, but they'll get over it.

Key takeaways

- *Search for (the right) signs of life.* What would your business need to thrive? Engaged users? Revenue that it earned while you were asleep? Whatever it may be, seek to prove it in your side hustle before you plunge into a full-time business. Focus on your business' core prospects for growth, and don't distract yourself with vanity metrics.

- *You are your greatest resource.* Regardless of what the numbers suggest, there's only one real factor that can influence when you switch to fulltime. Ask yourself: can you multitask, or do you prefer to throw yourself into one pursuit at a time? Does the unknown excite you, or do you prefer to remove as much risk as possible before you commit? Only by knowing yourself can you know when to make the leap.

- *Don't replace a shoestring with shackles.* The idea of finding an early-stage investor to bankroll your full-time transition may sound appealing. However, any investor will expect their dollars to buy them something. Before you search for backers, consider whether you can accept the expectations (and the influence) that an early-stage investment entails.

A weed in a world of trees: how to run a startup business model

Now that we've laid it all out, let's say you've made up your mind. You're determined to cast aside the surly bonds of the side hustle when the time is right. You also know you want to run a startup and scale to the distant corners of the earth. So how can you avoid the slow growth of a small business?

To stress the point once more: startups scale, whereas conventional businesses grow. And according to Forage co-founder Pasha Rayan, a core aspect of scaling involves offering a product rather than a service.

'It's easy to forget, but products can scale, whereas services don't,' Rayan told us.

'I think a lot of Australian startups make the mistake of beginning with a service first. And it's kind of understandable: products are usually harder to get off the ground in Australia. Meanwhile, you can accidentally think you're doing well with a service.'

The data backs up Rayan's hypothesis. Per figures collated by industry research firm IBISWorld, the Australian professional services industry employed around 953 000 people in 2023. In terms of revenue, it cleared $263.2 billion from the domestic market within the same time frame. It's easy to see, then, how it might offer a tempting target for a new entrepreneur — especially one with experience.

'Ex-professional services people are often really good at selling services to different corporates and companies in Australia,' Rayan said.

'Because of this, a lot of startups can forget to make a good product because they're able to make a sale based on their reputation or experience.'

Rayan credits this distinction with Forage's status as a startup. 'What I believe made a difference is that we tried to build a product, instead of a service,' he said.

By 'product', we're not exclusively talking about a smartphone or a Stanley Cup. A product doesn't need to be something you can hold in your hand, or forget about in your cupboard. However, it does need to exist without your hands-on input — even if it depends on someone else's.

For example, Airtasker connects people who need services with people who provide them. So, is it a service? No, it's a product that offers services. Mad Paws does the same thing for pet sitting, and Like Family for social care. Crafting a product, even if it's service-centric, will let you scale because your output won't depend on your own limitations.

Find your product, and a future of scaling will unveil itself to you.

Remember: your business journey is a philosophy class

... because there is no wrong answer. If you've spent years daydreaming about a thriving business, a side hustle may feel like a betrayal of your vision. Similarly, you may see a conventional small business model as an insult to the tech-centric, cloud-dwelling startup future you'd envisaged. Even so, what you choose to do is what you'll need to live with.

Failing to meet a self-imposed Melanie Perkins ideal may be worth the loss if you're doing what you love. And we don't only say that to promote self-care; without enduring passion for what you do, you'll struggle to commit. And without commitment, your business will suffer.

Still not certain where you land on the issue? Look at your business, then look at yourself, then answer: which of these best describes you?

- 'I want to spend more time pursuing my passion.'
- 'I want to create a livelihood out of my passion.'
- 'I want to solve problems that people with a particular passion often face.'

Once you can reply to this honestly, you'll know where your tomorrow lies.

CHAPTER 9
FIND YOUR PRODUCT-MARKET FIT

Finding product–market fit is a strange alchemy. As angel investor Beste Onay explained, 'You have to feel your way to product–market fit. You'll know it when you see it. Instead of pushing a boulder up a hill, trying to convince everyone it's a great idea, it starts rolling down on its own, and you're scrambling to meet demand.'

In other words, it's when you leave that Sisyphian feeling of constantly pushing a boulder uphill. When everything stops being hard — when your product just works, your customers love what you do and orders flow in.

Product–market fit is essentially what happens when your product sells itself. It's a thrilling inflection point. It's what makes exponential growth possible. It is this exponential growth — the ability to '10×', to scale, grow and disrupt a market — that distinguishes a startup from a traditional business.

'All startups are businesses, but not all businesses are startups,' explained lecturer Joel Mier to *The Conversation*.

In the pursuit of exponential growth, startups seek to invent something new — often with a new kind of technology, innovative business model or some other way of approaching a problem. This new approach aims, over the long run, to cost less than existing alternatives.

As Joel notes, a sushi restaurant is a business. But Uber is a startup. What sets them apart is an ambitious goal to disrupt the market leader or consumer behaviour. This may be achieved through innovation — a new product/service, technology, brand, process, or business model.

How does product–market fit distinguish a startup from a business?

A business can be incredibly successful but can still be largely similar to other businesses in its industry. Good examples of this would be accounting firms and law firms, where your point of difference might be in the client service you provide or the specific expertise you have in applying your knowledge to a particular field. For example, you might be an accountant or lawyer with an expertise in agribusiness, primarily serving clients in regional Australia.

What sets apart a startup is its ability to innovate in ways previously unseen or thought impossible. New technology, as we've seen with artificial intelligence, can be applied to vastly expedite research, automate workflows and provide assistance in ways previously considered impossible. How this could apply to specific industries is where a startup can create value.

Startups can also disrupt by finding markets previously under-serviced or untapped. Pearler, which entered the top

1 per cent of Australia's fastest growing startups in 2024, does this well. While competitor trading platforms prioritised day-traders, Pearler embraced a 'get rich slow' mindset. Their message of steady, progressive investment through ETFs set them apart in a market dominated by finance dudebros eager to 'beat the market' with a few hot stocks.

This approach allowed them to unlock something unseen in the industry: an almost 50:50 split of investors across genders. Pearler also attracted a younger group of new investors who felt locked out of the expensive Australian property market. Their friendly optimism encouraged novice investors to try investing for the first time. Much of their marketing focuses on user-friendly financial education on the fundamentals of investing, in all its forms. In other words, Pearler targeted what its rivals neglected: first-time and cautious investors who wanted to build wealth without watching the markets every day.

So how is Pearler a startup, and not a business? we hear you ask. *Business, schmizness, startups, whatever! How do I make money?* All you need to know here is that finding product–market fit is essential to scaling a startup.

For Pearler, finding a totally different market for a fairly familiar product — a trading app, essentially — was how they found product–market fit. It's how they've scaled to over two billion dollars of funds under management. If you are after this kind of growth, ask yourself: *What can I do differently from everyone else? How will I do it? Why will it be different?* A business, by contrast, might not bother asking itself any of these questions. You simply need to know you can offer your product or service to a clientele who will buy it. It's a living, but it's not a living likely to grow exponentially.

What is product–market fit? (It's the only thing that matters)

'Product–market fit means being in a good market with a product that can satisfy that market,' explained Marc Andreessen, co-founder of Netscape. According to Marc, *the only thing that matters is getting to product–market fit.*

'You can always feel when product–market fit isn't happening,' Marc explained.

Customers don't understand the value. Usage is flatlining, word of mouth is tanking, press reviews are mediocre, and deals never close. Equally, you can also feel when you hit product–market fit. Customers are buying as fast as you can sell. You're hiring sales and customer support. Journalists are calling. Investment bankers are staking out your house. You start getting Entrepreneur of the Year awards.

Right, we hear you say. *I like the sound of this. So… how do I get this brilliant 'product–market fit'?*

When Airtasker started and nobody knew who they were, co-founders Tim Fung and Jonathan Lui were running all over town doing tasks themselves. At this stage, they decidedly didn't have product–market fit. But when Airtasker turned up in detective-noir comedy *Deadloch* — in the form of a mother–son team whom Airtaskers hired, against their knowledge, to dispose of a body — the show assumed audiences would know what Airtaskers did. It was a pop-cultural signal that by 2023, when the show aired, Airtasker had hit the mainstream. Everyone knew who they were. Users had shared their positive experiences with others, spurring more activity on the platform. In short: product–market fit.

Don't be deterred if you already have a competitor. Uber existed for years before Grab came to seize market share in

South-east Asia. Founded by Malaysian Anthony Tan, Grab operates in eight countries throughout South-east Asia, and listed on the Nasdaq in 2021. One of its key points of difference is local knowledge: its drivers include Tuk Tuks, a common and cheap form of transport in the region. By including Tuk Tuks on Grab, the app solved a problem for those wary of getting scammed by unscrupulous drivers: the app provided price certainty for passengers and business for drivers.

Grab, is an example of a product that fits a particular regional market.

Don't aim for the whole market: serve only your market

'I think [finding product–market fit] is always a series of smaller wins,' said Pearler co-founder Hayden Smith.

'You never really notice when you're doing it, because as a startup, the question is always around the market. If you define your market as the first 10 people who use your product, it can be very easy to achieve product–market fit.

'But similarly, if we said "Our market is all Australians between 18 and 50", we wouldn't have found product–market fit. The vast majority of Australians wouldn't be able to use our platform, because they might lack the requisite assumed knowledge or it might be too complicated for non-tech natives to use.

'In a sense, that feeling of product–market fit changes as your target market grows,' explained Smith. 'When you have 10 customers, you obviously don't feel like it's reflective of the whole market. Once you reach around 10000 customers, it's a little bit different. And the journey between 10 and 10000 customers is certainly quite gradual.

As a founder, you must resist the urge to think of your target market as *the entire world*. Nothing successful ever aimed at the entire world. Or even 'all Australians between 18 and 50.'

Such ambition is impressive, but even the biggest film franchises — from *Mission Impossible* to *Bridget Jones* to *James Bond*, — never aimed for the entire world.

Each found a niche. Broad enough to please a crowd, small enough to make it feel like a film made only for *that crowd*. Each delivers exactly what that crowd wants: Tom Cruise spectacularly not dying, Bridget Jones spectacularly love-triangling, James Bond spectacularly *doing the dying ... of others ...* in a designer suit (preferably while driving a convertible en route to an invite-only poker game).

Like some of the most successful brands in the world, these film franchises often expand to wider audiences. However, it's their core target markets that keep the franchises going strong.

This is what Pearler has done so well. By leading with a philosophy of long-term investing, they created a highly engaged, incredibly loyal community of long-term investors — the target market critical to sustaining their growth. In response to customer feedback, Pearler built features specific to a long-term investing community, such as auto-investing and goal-setting tools. Thus, Pearler's product and the market grew in tandem, achieving product–market fit over time.

'For me, the realest moments of product–market validation were when we started seeing ourselves appear in investment trends surveys, and other competitors' product surveys,' said Smith. 'There was a real acknowledgement that people were aware that we were a key player in the space.

'Honestly, it was quite comforting. Everyone who starts a company is a human, and it's difficult to process that something you do is relevant. We're almost wired by nature to feel irrelevant in such a big world, so there was an overwhelming sense of relevancy that I hadn't always believed prior.'

Pearler's founders are, in every sense, Australian founders. Australia is known for its 'tall poppy syndrome': an urge to cut down anyone seen to be growing too tall. It's a problem because it can hold back talent. But it's arguably also a boon because tall poppy syndrome prevents success from going to any talented person's head.

It's a natural bs barometer, built into Australian society. This is likely why so many major startups come from this region: from Airtasker to Canva, and of course, Atlassian. Buoyed by our proximity to Asia, a region also on the rise, the Australian and New Zealand startup scene is a quietly thriving hub. Not that anyone here would ever tell you. We're happiest as underdogs. So it's rather fitting that Hayden Smith would see success as incremental.

'Even right now, I know that the vast majority of Australians have never heard of Pearler,' said Smith. 'If I went down a random street in Wagga Wagga and I asked a local, 'Have you ever considered investing?', and they said, "Yeah, I'm thinking about investing in Pearler", it would feel like we'd reached the next stage of validation. So product–market fit for me is just an evolving story of milestones.'

Why is product–market fit so attractive?

When it comes down to it, there are only three ways to dominate a market:

- Be the first to market
- Be the best in market
- Own the market.

It's simple enough to state, but almost impossible to achieve.

Being first to market involves releasing an innovation so game changing that it effectively reorganises the entire market. It shifts how consumers purchase, and might even put long-established incumbents out of business.

Apple's iPhone is a good example. Not only did it obliterate the long-loved brick-like Nokias of the world, its swiftly evolving camera and video functionality rang the death knell for the entire photography industry. Gone were disposable cameras, and even the emerging digital camera market found itself unable to compete with the all-in-one, do-everything-you-can-imagine iPhone. Genuine innovations like the iPhone create entirely new product categories — in this case, the smartphone. Innovation meant Apple enjoyed first-to-market advantage.

Additionally, being the best in market is what every organisation aims for, but few can hold for long. This is the very nature of competition and the reason competition can be helpful. Few become the best and the few that do rarely stay the best for long. For example, while Apple enjoyed a first-to-market advantage, competitors like Samsung soon came along. Their competition created innovations and differences in price that provided a better choice for consumers.

Finally, you can own the market. This is literally the point of *Monopoly*. It's the goal of all capitalism. It's a goal so dangerous to consumer choice that most capitalist economies have a government-funded, independent body and extensive anti-competition laws to break up monopolies.

Nonetheless, it's what most organisations who manage to nail either being first to market or best in market ultimately aim to do. Grow swiftly, and buy competitors until there is no meaningful choice in the market.

Tesla has attempted to do this by owning an entire market vertical. Not only does Tesla make cars, but they also make batteries, chargers — the entire supply chain for their cars.

Australia's grocery market is dominated by four main retailers: Woolworths (37 per cent), Coles (28 per cent), Aldi (10 per cent) and Metcash, which owns IGA (8 per cent). That's 80 per cent of our grocery market. That doesn't amount to much meaningful choice, which is why the two biggest players, Woolworths and Coles, have been investigated for using inflation as a cover to increase prices and enjoy record profits. It's the kind of anti-competitive behaviour you can engage in when you own the market.

All three market states — being first to market, best in market or owning the market — are made possible by finding product–market fit. That's why it's such an attractive objective.

How do you find product–market fit?

So how do you find product–market fit?

We recommend the following four-stage process:

1. Run a low-cost experiment

2. Test and assess, maximising customer feedback

3. Pivot when needed

4. Don't go big or you'll go home.

It's always better to fail quietly. Steer clear of the desire to embrace empty, fanciful slogans like 'You have to spend money to make money'. This is the kind of catchy nonsense designed to part you from your money.

Great startups run experiments to find problems worth solving and ways to solve them. They run experiments to find how much people will pay for these solutions and who exactly will do the paying. They run experiments to identify users from customers. They are patient. They usually don't go all-in, quitting their day jobs gung-ho. They spend only what they need to garner market data. So when customers start to trickle in, they listen closely enough to determine which customers they want — and how to grow into untapped markets.

'It actually took us quite a long time to reach what I would call product–market fit,' explained LegalVision founder Lachlan McKnight.

McKnight, an ex-corporate lawyer, founded LegalVision in 2012 as an online legal documents business. Early adopters flocked to their user-friendly documents, which set LegalVision apart as a pioneer of the NewLaw movement — a push to make legal services accessible to a broader market, often through new business models and technological innovation.

As their users required more than just online legal documents, LegalVision expanded their service, offering to include an online marketplace for legal services. By 2014, LegalVision established an incorporated legal practice, allowing them to hire lawyers to provide legal services directly to an expanding client base of SMEs at scale.

In 2019, LegalVision again revolutionised the legal business model, introducing a membership model — an all-you-can-eat subscription product. Again a pioneer, LegalVision was the first law firm in the world to operate an unlimited legal services membership model. In other words, members can access LegalVision lawyers on an unlimited, on-demand basis.

Global growth followed. In 2021, LegalVision leapt across the pond to New Zealand, heading to the UK in 2022. This growth was fuelled by confidence in its all-you-can-eat subscription product: as the product grew, it was clear LegalVision had evolved to hit product–market fit.

'That's important when you're looking to expand: confidence in unit economics. Once you've nailed that, you can feel more confident launching in new markets', explained Lachlan.

Uh, so what is 'unit economics'?

The short version: what does each sale cost you? Once you know how much a sale costs, you can know how to grow.

To understand your unit economics, you need to clarify a few key considerations:

- *Customer lifetime value (CLV):* How much do you make, on average, from a customer? This goes beyond a single purchase. For example, SaaS companies calculate CLV as starting when a customer first signs on with a product, to when they cancel.

- *Customer acquisition cost (CAC):* How much do you spend in sales and marketing to attract a new customer? Spend too little, and you won't attract enough new customers to sustain your growth. Spend too much, and you're burning through cash. Figuring out how to spend exactly the right amount — the Goldilocks zone of CAC — is directly influenced by CLV.

- *Churn rate:* How many customers do you lose, on average, compared to how many you gain or retain? For example, how many customers cancel Netflix over the course of a year? The churn rate is expressed as a percentage.

- *Retention rate:* How many customers do you retain? For example, how many customers stay with Netflix over the course of a year?

- *Average customer lifetime:* Crucial to calculating CLV, this is how long, on average, a customer stays with you before they churn.

- *Total number of customers:* How many customers do you have during a given period?

- *Actual number of transactions:* How many transactions occur during a given period?

- *Total revenue:* How much do you make from your customers over a given period?

- *Gross profit:* What is your total revenue, less the cost of sales?

- *Average order value:* What is your total revenue divided by total number of sales?

- *Average gross margin:* What is your gross profit, divided by total revenue?

Taking the time to make these calculations can help you determine your unit economics.

While these metrics can apply to many forms of business, they are particularly suited to startups because the goal of startups is to grow exponentially — that is, to 'scale'.

Although professional services firms, hair salons and restaurants also aim to grow, startups bet big on innovative technology, exclusive IP or disruptive business models in the hopes of growing radically faster than a regular business.

Startups will 'burn runway' — that is, spend money without seeing profit — for far longer than a regular business to chase exponential growth. It's an approach that requires a constantly optimistic mindset, one grounded in pragmatism.

'On Airtasker, for every 100 tasks we see posted, between 40 and 60 become a completed task,' said Tim Fung. 'I see that as so amazing!

'We see things as glass half full rather than half empty. It must be so built into my brain to be so glass half full, because to me, those kinds of things are simply unit economics.'

How long will it take to find product–market fit?

Honestly? It depends.

Forage recently hit the Holy Grail of the startup journey: they exited through acquisition by US education firm EAB. Founded in 2017 and acquired in 2024, Forage found product–market fit through an openness to experimentation and relentless self-analysis. This helped them truly identify the problem they were trying to solve — and how best to solve it.

'We'd watched an online video from Y Combinator, and it included interviews with founders who talked about product–market fit,' said Pasha Rayan. Following the UNSW Founders' 10× Program, Forage enrolled in Y Combinator, widely considered the world's most successful startup accelerator. Its alumni include Dropbox, Airbnb, Stripe, Twitch and Reddit.

'In that Y Combinator video, they described product–market fit as nonstop demand from your customers for what you're trying to build. And honestly, when we [Rayan and co-founder Tom Brunskill] watched that video, we both felt sick because we knew we didn't have product–market fit.'

At this stage, Forage was a mentoring platform built in response to student surveys revealing that students wanted a mentor to help get a graduate job. Still, they didn't grow. They tried job boards. They tried job-matching through CVs.

'During those early days, we were known as a startup that changed our product every week. It almost would have been a badge of honour, if it didn't make us look so skittish. The good thing was, by experimenting so much, we really came to understand the problem,' said Rayan.

In an attempt to understand the problem, Forage spoke to over 600 students. They also had 3000 students on their platform. This led to their eventual pivot into virtual internships.

'We wanted to hold ourselves to the standard of some of the best companies in the world,' said Rayan. 'We knew we'd need a lot of work to get there. Part of our efforts included building out our team and bringing in amazing leaders from great companies. But the heart of it is making sure students around the world are getting value from what we offer them.'

Jenna Leo, co-founder of Like Family, found branding to be an unexpected impediment to product–market fit.

'When we first started, we'd named our company Home Care Heroes,' explained Jenna.

'Early on in that first year, we went to a disability expo. When we'd invite people to come and talk to us, they would say, 'Thanks, but I don't need home care'. We'd then tell them that what we actually did was help members and carers build relationships and get out into the community. When people started responding with, "Wow, that's exactly what I need!", we realised that we'd given ourselves the wrong name.'

Home Care Heroes originated as a service with carers who would come to a person's home and take them out into the community. However, within the disability space, 'home care' referred to in-home medical care or nursing.

'Back then, we didn't have the creative space to think of a new name, so we kept rolling as Home Care Heroes for a while,' said Jenna. 'Looking back, though, I see the confusion. It meant that effectively communicating what we did was a bit of a challenge at first. That's why we eventually changed our name to 'Like Family'.

How do you lose product–market fit?

Remember Kodak? Blockbuster, or Video Ezy? Any business can lose product–market fit if it fails to keep pace with new technology or business models — from the iPhone, to streaming services.

You don't need to be first to market to find product–market fit. Even first movers can lose their share of the market.

'Facebook wasn't the first social media company — MySpace and Friendster existed first. But the market was ready,' explained David Burt, Director of Entrepreneurship at UNSW Founders.

'Uber wasn't the first carshare company — there were other similar companies in the market. It is better to be a new company in a good market than a great company in a terrible market.'

Burt should know. He heads up entrepreneurship at UNSW, which has led to the *Australian Financial Review* naming it Australia's most entrepreneurial university. It is also one of the highest producers of unicorns of any university in Australia.

Indeed, both Pearler and Forage came through UNSW Founders' programs.

For co-founder Alexis Soulopoulos, maintaining Mad Paws' product–market fit hinges on consistently delivering high-quality service.

'Right now, we're the biggest in the market,' said Soulopoulos. 'A major reason for this is that we never forgot that the quality of our pet sitters is key. Our approval rate for pet sitters stands between one and two of the 10 who apply. This is because we maintain such high standards for our pet sitters.'

They know Mad Paws sells peace of mind to pet owners. After all, if you're looking for a professional to provide a service, you only want to consider the best.

'We applied that same mindset to choosing our pet service providers. I think that's also set us apart. As the business started growing, we raised more capital, which gave us more resources to spend on amplifying our reach,' explained Soulopoulos.

When you achieve product–market fit, everything changes: customer acquisition becomes easier, growth accelerates naturally and your startup gains the momentum it needs to thrive.

CHAPTER 10
GET PROFITABLE: RIDING THE MINI-UNICORN

In many ways, 2019 felt like the last good season of a long-running TV series. The calendar year ended with Black Summer, which marked some of the most catastrophic bushfires Australia had ever suffered. Before the SES had even cleared the ashen rubble in 2020, COVID-19 seized the planet in its sneezy grip. From there, our civilisation seemed to drunkenly career from one calamity to the next, until we arrived here.

Rewind to earlier in 2019, though, and Australia was a different place. Back then, most urban-dwelling Aussies complained about two things: real estate prices and the final season of *Game of Thrones*. It was against this sunny backdrop that Airtasker found itself with a champagne problem.

Still two years away from their IPO, Airtasker had started to scale in earnest. In fact, by that point, they'd earned around $100 million in annual turnover, a princely sum for an Australian startup. The only issue? They were still burning around $2 million a month in venture capital (VC) funds. They had cracked the

10-figure revenue range, but they still relied on investors to keep the lights on.

'The thing is, we were essentially an Australia-only business in 2019,' Airtasker founder and CEO Tim Fung told us.

'This was a problem, because Australia doesn't have the deep capital markets that you'd depend on to raise money when you hit that kind of scale. This meant we couldn't raise the money we needed to at that stage.'

'Oh, boo-hoo,' some early-stage founders may decry. 'You couldn't raise more funds for your 100 *million dollar* business. Cry me a river. Let me guess: you're also upset because your Ferrari doesn't have seat warmers, and your diamond boots are too tight.'

Well, while it may seem enviable, Airtasker's problem was actually anything but champagne. Per research by CB Insights, the number-1 reason startups fail is because they 'fail to raise new capital'. This ranked ahead of 'No market need' (number 2), 'Got outcompeted' (number 3) and 'Flawed business model' (number 4). In other words, a startup can find product–market fit, *and* beat its competitors and *still* fail to find funding.

So, what did Airtasker do? The only thing they could.

'We made the decision that we had to get profitable ASAP,' Fung said.

Now, there's a reason this chapter is called 'Get profitable: riding the mini-unicorn': for growing startups, profitability can be seen as elusive. Within some circles, it's even derided as counter-productive. Skip back to chapter 8 and you'll recall that, for young ventures, it's the domain of small business. Startups, by contrast, are built to scale. Surely, then, Airtasker's plan must have floundered.

'We thought [getting profitable] would take two-and-a-half years,' Fung recalled. 'It ended up taking eight months.'

Fung's tale doesn't only serve to silence the profitability naysayers — it also proves a vital point. When a startup starts to turn a profit while still scaling, it can wield a power over its problems. That's why, in this chapter, we'll explore:

- how to balance profitability with growth
- how to build the option of profitability into your business
- when to launch (or scale back) products to grow profit, rather than revenue.

Wait ... if I'm turning a profit, am I scaling enough?

As we mentioned above, we devoted an entire chapter to the myriad differences between small businesses and startups. A small business model, you may recall, works to turn a profit as soon as it can. In contrast, every dollar a startup saves is a dollar it *isn't* pouring into scalable growth. Sure, against a challenge like the one Airtasker faced in 2019, circumstances may demand a profit. But in fair weather, shouldn't a growing startup function like a government budget and spend its surplus on something worthwhile?

Hayden Smith, co-founder and CTO of Pearler, said it best: it's not always about doing it, but knowing you can. 'The best way I can explain it — and I'm speaking very generally from what I've seen — is that most growing ventures don't seek profitability,' Smith said to us.

'What they *do* seek is the option of profitability. And the option of profitability is really valuable because it's basically a downside protection.'

By 'option of profitability', Smith refers to a point at which a startup can stop spending, start saving and still function. For example, it could switch off a portion of its marketing budget and find itself in the black. Most of the time, such startups would choose to keep operating at a loss in the name of scalable growth. However, the option to do so can give a capacity to respond to recessions or murky economic climates.

Hard cash = soft power

This option of a profit doesn't only serve as an insurance policy — it can also give you leverage with investors.

'It's powerful, because profitability says you can't be held ransom by people,' Smith said.

'People who give out money in the startup space are ferociously smart and will, to some extent, take advantage of a poorly positioned startup. If they can sense that you're dead without them, you'll see that reflected in the terms of your capital raising. And that's not a negative value judgement — that's their job, and I'd probably do the same in their shoes.'

Perhaps the most famous Aussie case study of Smith's hypothesis is Atlassian. In 2010, after bootstrapping for eight years, they raised US$60 million in VC funding from North America–based Accel Partners. Given the nascent state of Australia's startup scene at the time, the size of the **cap raise** is notable enough. But it gets better: because they'd been profitable since 2005, and scaling since 2002, Atlassian's founders could negotiate favourable terms. As a result, Scott Farquhar and co-founder Mike Cannon-Brookes still owned the majority of the startup when it IPO'd in late 2015.

As far as cap raises go, it was a dream outcome for any founder. But how did the team behind Atlassian manage to turn a profit so early?

Within their first two years of operations, Atlassian had launched two products: Jira and Confluence. Historically, it was rare for early-stage startups to split their efforts across two products, instead of championing one. Anyone who's tried to cook dinner and bake dessert at the same time will understand why. In Atlassian's case, though, the decision proved shrewd.

Jira and Confluence integrated well with each other and — together — fulfilled the varying needs of the startup's target market: developers. In other words, they had spawned an almost textbook case study for 'product–market fit'. What's more, they removed the need for a sales team by using a freemium model. For other B2B tech startups, sales of an enterprise product depended on cold calls, long lunches and longer lead times. Atlassian, on the other hand, simply gave users a 30-day free trial — after which they would offer a paid plan. Their users loved the products, and were mostly paying out of their employers' pocket, so conversion rates were impressively high.

The result? After three years, Atlassian was earning enterprise prices for its products without the need for a bloated staff roster. Or, to frame it within the lens of this chapter, they were turning a profit.

When they *did* eventually seek VC funding, it wasn't to meet next quarter's payroll, but to bankroll product acquisitions. This gave the founders immense leverage because:

- as Smith observed about profitable startups, Atlassian had proven they didn't need the funds to survive

- it sold a more appealing vision to investors, who could be sure they were funding growth, rather than subsistence.

Sure enough, these funds empowered them to keep acquiring complementary products, which they continued to assimilate into their business. Their success became the stuff of biographies and *Australian Financial Review* articles … and the rest is history.

Atlassian's road to profitability won't offer sure footing for every founder. Even so, their principles can apply to virtually every founder. Find product–market fit, create a business that doesn't require an army and let your users be your marketers. Do this, and you may yet scale while staying in the black.

Key takeaways

- *'I can do that, but I don't want to.'* Not every startup needs to be in the black; sometimes, they may want to channel their resources into growth instead. Even so, your business should maintain the *option* of being profitable. Work towards ensuring you can funnel funds towards a net profit, should the need arise.

- *The more you can keep, the less you need to give away.* The option of profitability doesn't only protect you against a downturn. When you can show a profit to prospective investors, you'll be able to command more favourable terms.

- *Ask yourself: 'What can I scale without spending?'* Much like Atlassian scaled an enterprise-focused startup without a sales team, you find scalable solutions that cost you nothing. Before you spend on staff or expenses, question whether you could achieve the same result without the price tag. Whenever the answer is 'yes', you'll ferry yourself closer towards the Zen-like state of profitability.

The fastest route towards a profit? Sell more things to the same people

Honesty time: Atlassian's tale of low-cost user acquisition is as inspiring as it is rare. If it wasn't, Australia would have sprouted a forest of multibillion-dollar startups. In reality, there will be times when you need to spend money. Scaling without spending is the dream, but saving without scaling is the nightmare. Most startups don't eschew a profit because they hate money: they do it to feed the Growth Machine.

Not everyone can create a wholly word-of-mouth conversion **funnel**, or a B2B model that requires no budget. But if you *do* need to spend money earning users, there is a way you can make it count.

Put simply: once you've found people who use your product, find more products to sell them. After all, you've already acquired them, so earning more money from them will lower your total CAC. This will, in turn, edge you closer towards breaking even. We saw a pitch-perfect example of this with Atlassian: Jira users picked up Confluence, and Confluence lovers embraced Jira.

However, for their many zeros' worth of success, we recognise that the Atlassian case study might feel a bit niche. For a much more adorable example, let's look to Mad Paws.

During its early days of 2014, Mad Paws' business model could have fit on the back of a bar napkin. It ran a website. The website listed Sydney-based pet sitters. Local pet owners who needed a pet sitter would visit the website to find one. Mad Paws would take a small cut of the booking fee and provide insurance coverage during the booking. Depending on the napkin's size, there could be enough space left over to draw a little beach umbrella.

Skip forward a couple of years and you wouldn't need a much larger napkin. The process tightened, the number of sitters grew, the number of bookings surged, the area swelled from Sydney to Australia. Other than that, not much had changed — and why would it? At that time, the team at Mad Paws were solving bigger problems, like 'How do we ensure the quality of our pet sitters?' (Answer: vetting and training) and 'How do we stop people from meeting through Mad Paws, then taking the bookings offline?' (Answer: remove pet sitters who repeatedly do so. Advertise the benefits of pet sitting insurance coverage. Rinse and repeat).

What's more, with around 28.7 million pets in Australia, according to the RSPCA, pets officially outnumber humans. By the same figures, around 69 per cent of households own pets. In other words, to reach market saturation would be to reach two-thirds of our nation's homes. Mad Paws' growth team had a large enough target market to keep themselves busy for a decade. The target had grown big; the napkin was still small.

And now? You'd likely need to use one of those long cloths that bartenders always drape over their shoulders. At the time of publishing, Mad Paws offers five pet-focused categories: pet services; pet health; toys and treats; pet beds and accessories; and pet insurance. Within each category is a laundry list of offerings, from dog grooming, to chew toys, to pet medication. Yes, pet sitting is still their cornerstone, but it now stands as one of many in Mad Paws' mission.

From this vibrant cast of characters, there's a sweeping diversity in form and function. Pet sitting and dog walking reflect a classic double-sided marketplace model, while Sash dog beds and accessories are e-commerce 101. Pet insurance went to market on Mad Paws' watch, while Waggly's toys and treats were the result of an acquisition. But for all their differences, these mishmashed business sectors have one thing in common: they target the same user.

In what he refers to as 'ecosystems thinking', Mad Paws co-founder Alexis Soulopoulos spoke of the company's structure for cross-selling.

'The first few steps are the same language and consistent branding across all products: logical integration and the use of data to create a holistic loop,' he said to us. Or, to break it down into dog treat–sized chunks:

1. Attract a customer with one of Mad Paws' many pet products.

2. Based on their pet type, determine what else the pet owner might need. For instance, a dog owner who signed up for pet sitting may also be receptive to chew toys and treats. A cat owner who signed up for Mad Paws Pet Insurance will probably also need feline medication at some stage.

3. Ensure that every product under the Mad Paws umbrella reflects the same language and messaging. If a customer travels online from Pet Chemist to Sash dog beds and accessories, everything should feel consistent.

4. Through the power of data, email marketing and digital advertising, turn those insights from step 2 into customer segments. Someone pays for a pet product and they receive content showcasing other products their pet might need.

The more data you collect, the more specific your segments become. Before you know it, West Highland White Terrier owners are receiving emails about bacterial dermatitis cream after buying pet insurance. German Shepherd puppy owners are booking dog training sessions, then signing up to monthly chew toy subscriptions.

Holistic loop ahoy.

Like any thriving company, Mad Paws will always keep working to reach new customers. But by cross-selling to the ones they've already reached, they can earn more from the money they've already spent.

Key takeaways

- *Spend once, earn twice.* You've already spent time (and likely money) on acquiring your current customers. Sell them new things — things that complement your original product — and you'll earn more from your past efforts.

- *It doesn't matter where you're from, it only matters where you're going.* You may launch new products yourself, or you may claim them via an acquisition. Regardless of their source, make sure that the language you use to promote products remains consistent. Your customers have come to trust your brand, so they'll want to know you're behind any other products they're considering.

- *Keep your customers in the loop.* Use your knowledge of your customers to granularly tailor your cross-selling efforts. Beyond better serving your goals, you'll also be more likely to give your customers what they need.

How do I make sure I don't streamline my business *too* much?

Remember the COVID-19 lockdowns of 2020 and 2021? (We know that probably isn't a question you want to read, but bear with us.) When the lockdowns first began, state and federal governments rushed to define 'essential workers': those whose vocation required them to disregard the stay-at-home orders. Some people bristled at the notion, claiming that everyone's work was essential. However, at a glance, even the critics could understand (if not agree with) the government's rationale.

First responders?

'Makes sense.'

Healthcare workers?

'Um, how else are we going to beat this virus?'

Public transit drivers?

'Well, they can't exactly work from home, can they? Besides, someone needs to get those healthcare workers to the hospital.'

Supermarket employees?

'Well, we don't want to run out of toilet paper again, so fine.'

Bank employees?

'Yeah, I guess tha–... wait, what?'

No, we're not only talking about bank tellers. Yes, we're referring to those people who sit at their desks for most of the day looking at spreadsheets.

'But that's insane. They could do that from home! Well, if they're classed as essential workers, then why isn't everyone?'

These days, the lockdowns have joined sex, religion and politics as topics you should never discuss in polite company. Even so, they pose a poignant case study for any business aiming to cost-cut their way towards profitability. Had the governments slashed too many essential services, our society would have ceased to function. If they'd cut too few, they would have plunged into the red (or, in this case, watched COVID-19 sweep the nation).

And if they'd focused only on the 'essential' — healthcare, law enforcement, groceries — and less on the 'services'? If bank workers had stayed at home like most suits, and the systems that underpin our nation's commerce had crashed? Society may have survived, but it would have faced a mighty hurdle once the pandemic abated.

In a business, much like during the lockdowns, the criteria for what is and isn't essential isn't always clear. But listing the expenses you *could* switch off can act as profitability's last line of defence.

Is the juice worth the squeeze?

Hayden Smith and co-founder/CEO Nick Nicolaides of Pearler have a structured approach for creating such a list.

'Two or three times a year, Nick and I have a chat and ask each other: 'Okay, if, from tomorrow, no-one ever gave us a dollar again, what's our plan?' Smith told us. 'What services do we need to turn off? What features do we need to sunset? What headcount do we need to be reduced to?'

This process allows Nicolaides and Smith to prepare for the worst. But beyond that, it lets them identify which expenses are essential for *survival*, and which ones are essential for *growth*. After all, a startup that can't scale is simply a small business. For Pearler, certain products provide their startup with a growth engine, which makes them worth the expense during bleak eras.

'For example, tomorrow, we could wake up and say, 'Right now, Pearler has 15 staff. If we get rid of [Pearler products] US trading and micro-investing, and we cut the staff down to seven, then we're profitable,' Smith said.

'Sure...but what then? Now, as a founder, you're facing a mid-tier salary, in a high-risk business, with no prospect to alleviate stress. So yes, profitability is still important, but only if it leaves prospects to grow. Otherwise you just have indefinite survival mode, waiting for fatigue to find you.'

Unless you're launching an investing platform yourself, your growth engines will scarcely resemble Pearler's. However, Hayden's words ring true for any business. Identify what you could afford to cut—but recognise what you *need* to keep. Nobody wants to be stuck in lockdown forever.

Until Black Summer, 2019 might have been a quaint year for large-scale problems. However, it was a turning point for Airtasker. By turning profitable, they laid the foundations for their IPO in 2021. What's more, beyond solving their investor issue, they also kept growing.

Reflecting on that period, Tim Fung frames it as a high point in Airtasker's journey. 'My advice for founders: until you push yourself to do it, you probably won't do it,' Fung said to us.

'Getting profitable is a bit painful in the short term, but in the long term, it's the best thing you could ever do in the business.'

Now, if only HBO would rewrite that final season of *Game of Thrones*...

Key takeaways

- *Keep your wallet dry in stormy weather.* Turning a profit in a thriving market means little without a buffer in trying times. Create a list of your business' expenses, then deem which are essential and which aren't. This way, you'll be prepared to defend your profits if conditions turn against you.

- *... and plan for it when the weather is sunny.* Don't try to learn how to repair a ship while it's sinking. Build your Essential Expenses List from a place of stability, then revisit it every few months. The needs of your business might change, but the need for a list will not.

- *Don't slash yourself into purgatory.* At the risk of sounding like a fridge magnet: understand the difference between surviving and living. Before you add an item to the non-essential column, ask yourself, 'Could my business still grow without this expense?'

CHAPTER 11

BECOME A PROBLEM-SOLVER-IN-CHIEF

Have you watched the series *Succession*? Yes, yes — we finished the last chapter with an HBO reference too. It isn't our fault they've seized control of the Cultural Zeitgeist, you know. Anyway, if you haven't seen *Succession*, here's all you need to know: everyone has access to a helicopter, and no-one deserves your sympathy. (Well, maybe Roman, but that's a topic for a psychology textbook.)

In the series, there's a kind of masochism on display. At several points, the various heirs and magnates have the opportunity to sell their concerns. By doing so, they would become rich enough to buy and fund their own fleet of helicopters. They would also be able to bid a final farewell to all of their business headaches. Yet, time and again, they eschew their exit. They refuse to convert their holdings into a multibillion-dollar payout — all so they can keep facing complex problems *every day*.

Many viewers would have dismissed this central premise as a byproduct of fiction.

'Surely, no-one in *real life* would choose to embrace a life of sleepless nights and endless challenges,' they'd say, over their Pad Thai.

'Why would anyone want to keep facing strange new stresses, day after day, if there was another option available?'

Meanwhile, any business owner watching might have said, 'Hey, this episode feels a lot like last Wednesday!'

Back in chapter 3, we touched on the merit of 'just getting started'. That business is a parade of unknown unknowns, and the only way to solve new problems is to discover them. And, like the hydra of ancient legend, whenever you solve a problem, more emerge in its wake. Once you start a business, there is no stopping. No other side where your issues disappear. Your life becomes a gauntlet of solving problems you didn't even know existed yesterday. Facing challenges is now the status quo — and it always will be.

We don't tell you this to scare you, but to temper your expectations. You won't need to solve problems so you can get on with your job — solving problems will *become* your job. While this might sound daunting, it's actually a way of making peace with your future. A farm struck by a rogue snowstorm will face a meagre harvest; one beset by snowstorms every day will come to cultivate Arctic-friendly livestock. Accept your role as a perpetual problem solver and you'll feel more prepared for inclement skies.

In this chapter, we'll explore the typical life of a problem-solver-in-chief. This will include:

- dealing with imposter syndrome
- becoming an endless novice

- approaching challenges like a crime fiction writer (or a YouTube addict)

- prioritising the right problem at the right time (and not just the loudest one right now)

- knowing when you need to strive for perfection — and when near enough is good enough

- knowing when to delegate problems to your team

- accepting that your problems work like energy. They never cease to exist ... they only change shape.

Side note: not giving Arnold Schwarzenegger a cameo in *Succession* was a missed opportunity. He could have finished a business meeting with 'Now, if you'll excuse me, I need to get to the chopper.'

Fake it 'til you ... realise you don't need to fake it at all

Imposter syndrome can cast its shadow over any field, from business to bounty hunting (which, incidentally, is still a thriving profession in some countries). For many founders, its presence is particularly pronounced. Without a doubt, the weight of leadership is at least partially to blame. However, according to Lockpick Games founder Tash Jamieson, the demands of a young business are the chief culprits.

'There's always this low-key feeling that you never know what you're doing,' Jamieson told us.

'It's hard enough dealing with imposter syndrome in a normal career, but the real nature of startups is that you never, ever know what you're doing. And anyone who says that they know what they're doing is lying.'

To manage imposter syndrome, Jamieson suggests a mindset switch: become comfortable with uncertainty.

'It's counterintuitive for a lot of people — especially if they've been working a professional job,' Jamieson said.

'If you're an employee and your manager asks you to write a report, you're not going to write "I don't know what I'm doing". You're going to learn everything you can about the subject matter so that the report is perfect. In a startup, you need to be comfortable writing an incomplete report. It might say, "I need to do X. I've never done X. I don't even know if X is the right way forward".'

For most employees, being comfortable with the unknown is something they seldom need — and are rarely encouraged — to possess. It ranks alongside 'Not Hoarding Annual Leave' in the Column of Outlandish Employee Behaviours. By contrast, it's something that any founder will need to wear like a second skin.

'It can be scary,' Jamieson concedes, 'but you need to accept that not knowing is the nature of the job.'

Jamieson is far from the only founder to tout comfort with the unknown as a key trait. Mad Paws co-founder Alexis Soulopoulos similarly flagged it as one of his steepest learning curves in business. When asked how his perspective on business problems has changed, his answer was as direct as it was poignant: 'Before I ever started anything, I didn't know anything.'

'If you'd asked me before we launched, I would have told you that I knew there would be problems,' Soulopoulos told us.

'What I didn't understand back then was that I would be solving new problems on an almost daily basis.'

These problems were as diverse as they were frequent. One day, Soulopoulos would need to don his accountant's hat to balance Mad Paws' ever-evolving cashflow. The next, he would slip into his developer's apron and spend his life-force solving cruel and unusual website glitches. And the greatest challenge? Before Mad Paws, Soulopoulos had never worked as an accountant *or* a developer.

'It felt like each time we solved a problem, another problem would emerge,' Soulopoulos told us.

'Back then I kept thinking, "Once we've worked through these problems, everything should settle down". Eventually, I came to realise that working through problems isn't the exception — it's the rule!'

Become an endless novice

Across those first few months, Soulopoulos learned something that countless successful founders have come to accept. Wil Schroter, the US-raised founder and CEO of startups.com, describes it as starting as a freshman.

'We're creating a product that has never been built, in a market that doesn't yet exist, with a team that just came together five minutes ago,' Schroter said on his website. From the start, you're fundamentally unable to be certain, which restrains your confidence.

In his seminal book *The Medici Effect*, entrepreneur Frans Johansson goes a step further. He suggests that innovation often grows when people of differing expertise apply their minds to a new problem. By applying their fresh perspectives, the theory goes, the novice can find answers that the specialist would never even consider. As proof of his theory, Johansson cites that it was a geologist — Charles Darwin — who fathered the theory of evolution.

Any creative type who has wrestled with a spreadsheet for the first time may baulk at the Medici Effect theory. Likewise, the idea of being a startup freshman feels a bit … American. Instead, we'll offer a gentler suggestion: become an endless novice.

The idea behind being an endless novice is simple, if terrifying. Instead of striving to become an expert in one field, embrace the idea of being a beginner. Every time a strange challenge rears its head, acknowledge that it falls outside of your current expertise. Then, once you've composed yourself against the fear of the unknown, take three steps:

1. Assess everything you don't know about the problem.

2. Apply your existing skillset to solve what you can.

3. Fill the gaps in your knowledge to solve the rest.

Rinse and repeat this process every time a new problem confronts you and you'll be surprised by the results. With this approach, Souloupoulos turned cashflow management and technical glitch repair from 'daily headaches' into 'business as usual'. He's still not an accountant, or a developer, but put him in a room with either and he'll speak their language.

Not only will this mindset improve your problem-solving prowess — it will also create unique growth opportunities for your business. After all, Darwin didn't create his theory of evolution by looking at rocks all day. He did it by thinking like no geologist had thought before him.

Key takeaways

■ *Know nothing — and do it anyway.* The life of a founder is a constant exercise in humility. To quote Tash Jamieson: 'Not knowing is the nature of the job'.

■ *Your problems are your BAU.* You may have grandiose visions of how you're going to spend your day as a founder. In reality, you'll likely spend much of it extinguishing fires in areas that you didn't even know were flammable.

■ *Be an endless novice.* You'll encounter foreign problems that bear no relation to your existing skillset. All the time. And you know what? That's fine. Embrace your perpetual status as a beginner, and you'll foster two new skills: learning and problem solving.

Be a crime fiction writer: start from the end

When solving problems, you're not looking for mastery, you're looking for adequacy. Should a problem require more from you, your skills will sharpen in response to the need. And to achieve adequacy, you have every resource you need at your fingertips.

Nellie McQuinn of Moonbug Entertainment fame discovered this too. As we saw in chapter 9, Nellie came to pursue online children's content after a career in acting. At the time, it was a niche and burgeoning field, and her production company was at the forefront. While this granted them product–market fit, it also meant that:

● they had no existing templates to follow

● Nellie needed to solve problems in an industry she hadn't initially planned to enter.

In short, McQuinn faced a steep learning curve. However, she embraced the idea of the endless novice, and she put it into practice.

'I taught myself how to film, edit and do sound — whatever the project needed,' McQuinn told us.

'I loved the creative process, but I really did it out of necessity. I knew that if I was going to do something, it was because it needed to be done and no-one else would do it for me.'

Today, Nellie's skills as a content creator would meet most people's concept of mastery. Back then, though, she didn't worry about seeking the perfect avenue for learning.

Rather, she approached every unknown like a crime fiction writer: she started at the end and worked her way back.

'The way I work is that I look at the end goal and then map back the steps to determine what I need to do to get there.'

Once she'd crafted a plan to solve a problem, she would search online to fill any blanks in her knowledge.

'If I don't know how to do something, I'll just YouTube it, or read up on it,' McQuinn said. 'I hate not knowing how something works.'

Constant learning via YouTube or Reddit may not be one of the most touted aspects of leadership. However, to Nellie, it's a core aspect of any founder's identity.

'I think that's something I carry with me to this day: "Just work it out",' McQuinn said. 'If ever anyone says I have an entrepreneurial spirit, I think that's what they're referring to.'

Not all business problems have easily searchable solutions.

Even so, while the tools might change depending on the problem, the process remains the same. Lachlan McKnight,

CEO and co-founder of LegalVision, runs a business that shares little in common with children's online content (although if your toddlers love reviewing a legal contract, we won't judge!) Yet, despite his differences to this book's other Mc (that being Nellie McQuinn), McKnight describes a similarly direct approach to problem solving.

'When you're in that [post-launch period], you just *do* rather than think too much about what you're supposed to do,' McKnight told us. 'I think it's the same for a lot of first-time founders. Once you're in it, the needs of the business take over.'

Don't know where to start? Let your business be your guide

We get that 'just work it out' might not sound particularly useful. It can feel akin to telling a debut marathon runner to 'just run,' or George RR Martin to 'write faster'. The good news: your business will inform you of what you need to 'just work out', and what can wait.

'You've got marketing, you've got sales, you've got product... and they all demand attention at different times,' McKnight said.

'When you first start, you need to come up with an initial product, or the business isn't doing anything. Then, you might need to connect the product to customers, so you need to focus on marketing. Up next, you might find that you're bringing in lots of leads, but you're not converting them, so that becomes your priority.'

'You might then realise that you need to further improve your product to sell more, so you focus on product. Once your product improves, you turn your attention to marketing, and the cycle begins again.'

It's an approach much like crop rotation. Instead of trying — and failing — to focus on every issue at once, you rotate your attention between different areas. Much as the seasons dictate when to rotate crops, so will the seasons of your business steer your focus.

In LegalVision's case (as with most startups), the varying needs of the business don't go neglected between their cycles; there are product, marketing and sales teams addressing their respective areas year-round. However, as a co-founder and CEO, Lachlan's attention is determined by the cycles of the business.

After several such cycles, you'll also better come to understand the requirements for your different problems. Not all challenges are created equal, and some may demand a less complete solution than others. Knowing how much to give is a process we've named the Soulopoulos Score — for reasons you'll soon discover.

'When you're long enough in the business, you come to understand better what to prioritise', Mad Paws co-founder Alexis Soulopoulos told us.

'You know the answers to the questions, 'What do I need to get 100 per cent right? What am I happy to get 60 per cent right? And what am I willing to not get right?'

Concepts like business cycles and endless learning may *sound* profound, but they can feel hollow without a concrete example. That's why, to put these ideas into practice, we'd like to introduce you to Blue-ber.

Blue-ber: a kriller of a concept

The world's first whale-centric startup, Blue-ber connects blue whales with smaller sea creatures looking to migrate on their backs. (*Side note:* Blue-ber may or may not be a real startup. It definitely isn't, though — so Uber, please don't sue us.) As you'll see, Blue-ber provides a whalesong pitch-perfect example of problem cycles, endless novice skills, and the Soulopoulos Score.

Kim Seong Park is the founder and CEO of Blue-ber, a Brisbane-based startup with a humpback-sized mission. Thanks to rebounding blue whale numbers, and a demand for whale-centric migration from fish, there's supply on both sides of the marketplace. However, for all the startup's promise, Blue-ber is beset by a plankton school's worth of problems.

Seong Park's team is good at what they do, but there are some problems that only a CEO can solve. Luckily, Seong Park doesn't need to be everywhere at once. After a few months of steady growth and sleepless nights, he realises that not every problem is a CEO problem. In fact, Blue-ber's business needs dictate which problem Seong Park should prioritise — and how much bandwidth for error he's afforded.

In January, Blue-ber faces three key challenges: they need more whales, more users and a better platform. Seong Park has faith in his marketing team, and trusts that they'll address the first two problems. By contrast, the third problem poses a major obstacle; without a responsive platform, neither whale nor small sea creature will use Blue-ber. Kim is no coder — nor is he an HR professional — but the needs of Blue-ber care not for his limitations. Thus, he commits himself to both: coding to help his engineer improve the platform, and HR to find additional coders.

His aim is to hire a team of Steve Wozniaks and build the cruiseliner of apps. By the quarter's end, he's employed a team of grads, and cobbled together a rickety raft — not glamorous, but functional. His efforts fell short of his hopes, but whales and sea creatures alike are now able to use the app.

The Soulopoulos Score for Q1: 50 per cent

Endless novice skills: HR and engineering

Fast-forward to April, and Seong Park is helming an improved startup. Blue-ber is now meeting the UX standards of fish and whales, and his Q1 problems are sinking to the seafloor. However, in the depths of Q2 lurks a different issue: Blue-ber hasn't acquired enough new whales. The platform can now host increased traffic, but there are too few whales to meet demand. Some, doubtless, still haven't heard of Blue-ber; others were burned (or, rather, harpooned) by the platform's poor UX in Q1. In any event, the startup burned through a lot of runway when fixing its platform issues, and they need revenue. And without enough blue whales to meet sea creature demand, revenue will elude Blue-ber like plankton in a swift current.

So, what does Seong Park do? He dons his marketer's goggles and lives by a mantra for Q2: 'without our blue whales, our Blue-ber will fail'. Across three months, Kim works hand-in-fin with his marketing team, ensuring their projects align with the needs of the business. He also gives himself a crash course in whale psychology, to better grasp what motivates the giants of the sea.

By the end of June, Seong Park aims to have quadrupled the number of blue whale freelancers on their platform. By EOFY, they've only tripled. Any less, and they would have lacked the supply to meet the year's revenue targets. However, while he didn't reach his target, the result provided enough whales to meet the demand.

The Souloupolos Score for Q2: 75 per cent

Endless novice skills: Marketing and whale psychology

It's now a crisp July in the city of Brisbane. Blue-ber's engineers are solving tech glitches as they surface, and the marketing team are enticing a healthy balance of supply and demand. Of course, it wouldn't be Q3 without a fresh problem.

For every five sea creatures who have flocked to the platform, there have been three complaints. Users don't understand Blue-ber's features, from the 'Book-a-Whale' function to the 'pay in krill' currency. There have also been several disagreements between whales and sea creatures; some users expected a journey to Antarctica, and were irate when their rides dropped them off in Bass Strait.

Beyond some very public 1-star reviews — which damage the brand — these issues also raise insurance concerns. Should a poor journey lead to a sea creature injury, Blue-ber could be on the hook. In the face of such grim tidings, Seong Park decides to focus on two problems:

- *Improving the responses of Blue-ber's customer service*

- *Securing affordable but airtight insurance.*

Seong Park's next few months are a blur of customer phone calls, adaptable email templates and insurance meetings. Every time a user leaves a 1-star review, Seong Park and the customer service team workshop a response. Whenever an insurance provider declines Blue-ber, he learns why and refines his pitch for next time.

Winter wanes as he and the customer service team reflect on their efforts. Blue-ber's response time is now under 5 minutes, due to new comms templates for common queries and complaints. Better customer responsiveness has kept dissatisfied users from pouring their anger into Google reviews. Rates of new 1-star reviews have plunged by 90 per cent, while 5-star reviews have seen a 65 per cent increase. After months of shopping for insurance, Kim also strikes the right tone and finds a provider who will cover them.

There's still more to do, but Kim now feels content to hang up his customer service headset. His team can take it from here.

The Souloupoulos Score for Q3: 90 per cent

Endless novice skills: Customer service and insurance

Spring is here. The air is rich with pollen and promise. Blue-ber's supply and demand are in perfect balance, and the denizens of the sea are pleased with the platform. Yet, Seong Park knows the glowing reviews and growth charts don't address a looming problem: Blue-ber has almost expended its runway.

Like any young startup, Blue-ber has funnelled its earnings into new features and new users. They've become bigger, faster and better—but they can't do it forever. Not without more capital. After months of learning to solve different problems, Seong Park must once again convince investors to back Blue-ber.

For the year's final quarter, Seong Park returns to the pitching roots that earned Blue-ber its seed funding. But this time, the stakes are higher. Before he launched, the outcome for failed fundraising would be an unrealised dream. Now, it would mean a loss of employment for Blue-ber's staff—not to mention the whale freelancers. Fortunately, Seong Park can draw on nearly a year's worth of growth, improvements and learnings to attract funding. Much like the sea creatures that ride on the backs of Blue-ber's freelancers, his year's final efforts will ride the lessons of the past 12 months.

Seong Park delivers the best pitch in Blue-ber history. He knows the outcome is binary: either he raises his target amount, or Blue-ber beaches. A less prepared CEO may have floundered under the pressure—but not Seong Park. He has spent the quarter pre-empting every thorny question, justifying every flattering figure.

On New Year's Eve, Seong Park receives good news. He's raised their next series of funding. Blue-ber will swim proudly into the next calendar year. He truly is…a whale of a founder.

The Soulopoulos Score for Q4: 100 per cent

Endless novice skills: Capital raising

So, Seong Park's problems are over, right?... almost. That funding Seong Park accepted? It came attached with conditions. Those VCs want to see something concrete for their investment. By the end of the next calendar year, they expect Blue-ber's revenue to have skyrocketed. And to handle that kind of growth, Blue-ber will need an expanded engineering team—and some major platform updates.

As Q1 commences, Seong Park once again commits himself to HR and engineering, and prepares to don the true role of a founder: problem-solver-in-chief.

Key takeaways

- *YouTube is your friend.* A guide is good, and a business degree is always useful, but for quick upskilling, you can't go past AI, search engines and YouTube tutorials. Before you spend money, try to solve your problem with free tools.

- *Allow your business cycle to steer you.* You'll always have more problems than days in the week. Find which require your focus. When in doubt, ask yourself, 'Which challenge will lead to *more* challenges if I don't prioritise it?'

- *Know the Soulopoulos score for your problems.* Some problems are binary: you either find a solution, or you don't. Others offer a sliding scale of acceptable outcomes: 100 per cent would be ideal, but 60 per cent will still suffice. Knowing the threshold you need to meet for each problem—the Soulopoulos Score—will dictate how much effort you need to expend.

Solve it, then ship it: the art of knowing when to delegate

At this stage, you might find yourself wondering, 'What happens when a business faces more than one major problem at a time? Problems aren't always going to wait patiently for their turn in the business cycle, you know. I can't be everyone at once, so how do I know which ones I should tackle?'

It's a fair question — and a paradox. There are some problems only a business leader can solve, but unless your business involves advanced cloning, there's only so much you can achieve yourself. CEOs from Musk to Ma have found the fix to this, but we believe Tash Jamieson summarises it best.

'As a startup founder, the moment that you *do* know what you're doing, and it becomes a system, you should be passing that job onto someone else,' Jamieson told us.

'The second that something can be systemised, it *should* be systemised. It doesn't matter if your company has one employee, or 200 — the founder should always be taking on unfamiliar problems.'

In short: 'Solve it, then ship it'. And if you've followed the tenets of chapter 7, you'll have faith in those to whom you ship. From there, you can better systematise your problem solving and create more time for management.

'If you have good people around you, and you can empower them, then your job as a CEO becomes enabling them to do *their* jobs,' Soulopoulos added.

'When you do this, you can focus on managing your team, instead of worrying about every problem yourself.'

Like many of the notions we've explored in this chapter, 'solve it, then ship it' sounds both simple and obvious. After all, who wouldn't want to offload their stress? However, many leaders (especially new ones) bear an almost allergic aversion to delegation. Jesse Sostrin, PhD — Global Head of Leadership at Philips and author of *The Manager's Dilemma* — claims that many new leaders hoard work to feel practical. In doing so, though, they often sabotage their own goals.

'Too many of us are in a constant state of overextension, which fuels an instinctive reaction to 'protect' work,' Sostrin wrote. 'This survival instinct ultimately dilutes our impact through an ongoing, limited effect on others.'

Are you, too, guilty of holding on to too much? Ask yourself: If you had to take an unexpected week off work, would your initiatives advance in your absence? If your answer is 'no' or 'not sure', you're probably overinvolved. You want to extend presence through the actions of others.

Or, to frame it in unicorn terminology: solve it, then ship it.

But how? To paraphrase 1980s hip-hop icons Run-D.M.C: it progresses in a manner akin to that shown in figure 11.1 (overleaf).

As you can see, not *every* solution needs to be systematised. But if it solves a problem that's likely to recur, you should delegate the solution. Or if it addresses a unique, once-in-a-lifetime problem from which your team should learn, you should document it. By pruning stress from your mind, delegation will encourage your team members to become problem solvers. This way, you won't need to face tomorrow's uncertainties alone.

And that's the way it is.

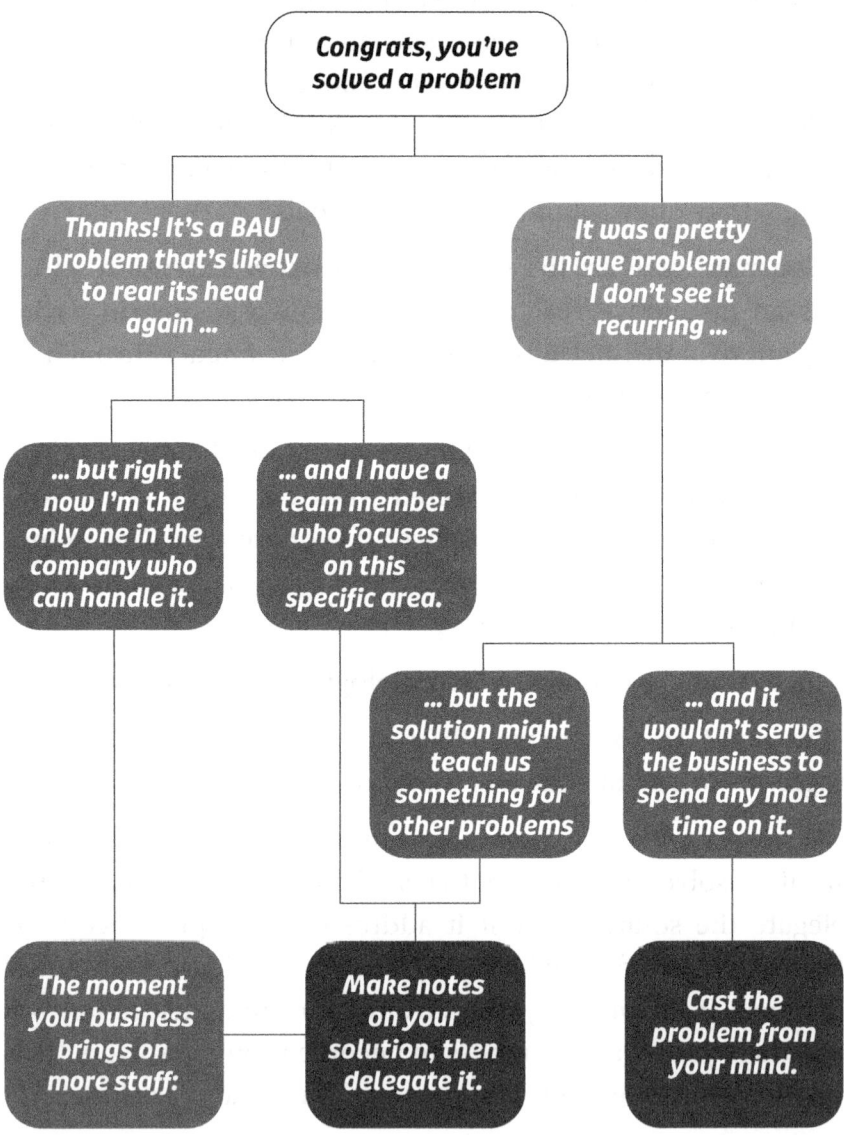

Figure 11.1: solve it, then ship it

Your problems work like energy (and that isn't a bad thing)

'I feel exhausted just reading this,' you groan, head in your hands. 'Can we skip to the part where I'm Scrooge McDuck, dive-bombing into a pile of money?'

Look, some founders *do* reach their Happily Ever After. Remember Tom from MySpace, the platform's co-founder and the first friend you'd receive when you created an account? (Zoomers and Boomers, you can refresh yourself on MySpace in chapter 1.) He sold Myspace for US$580 million in 2005, and retired around four years later. Since then, he's been golfing, hiking, scuba diving, flying drones and — in an ironic twist — posting travel photos on Instagram.

It's true. You *could* become the next Tom from Myspace. But becoming Tom from Myspace can't be your only ambition.

This is because the drive to scale a business doesn't work like a charging port; you can't simply switch it off once you reach an arbitrary threshold. It's like that guy who dreamed of being a rockstar 'so then I'll be famous'. He'll never grace the stage of Madison Square Garden because he doesn't love making music. But your other, quiet friend who plays piano four hours a day? You wouldn't be surprised to find them in the studio with Taylor Swift.

To be great at business, you've got to love the process of growing a business. This doesn't mean working until it kills you. Tim Fung swears by switching off by 7 pm every day. He turns up, solves problems, and goes home to his wife and family.

As your business grows, your problems will function like energy: they won't die, but they will change shape. Such was the case for Nellie McQuinn, after her acquisition.

In 2018, McQuinn had been problem solving for her production company, Grass Roots Media, for 12 years. She managed a team of six, so she lived a classic problem-solver-in-chief life: every problem from 'This project's scope is larger than we thought' to 'Our invoicing system is glitching' fell to her. Then, in September of the same year, Grass Roots Media was acquired by what would become Moonbug Entertainment. Following the acquisition, her role transformed from that of a founder into that of a corporate executive — pretty much overnight.

'My world was completely turned upside down in terms of the scale of the stuff I was working on,' McQuinn told us.

'Many of the crucial parts of people management — HR and team meetings and org structures — are never anything you do with five people.'

In short order, Nellie's role evolved from founder and doer-of-everything, to Vice President — Head of Production. Instead of leading five professionals, she managed 150. And rather than doing a bit of everything, she needed to do a *lot* of a few things.

'As you climb that corporate ladder and you manage more and more people, you do less of the hands-on stuff that you first fell in love with,' McQuinn said. 'My team grew, so I needed to pivot into a much more hands-off role, and focus on new skills.'

These skills included budgeting and cashflows; **mergers and acquisitions (M&As)**; due diligence; and liaising with clients like Netflix and Disney. A far cry from learning how to edit via YouTube, but no less challenging.

Nellie's fresh challenges after an acquisition differ from the pressures of an IPO or growing a company privately. However, they all have one thing in common: solutions are the journey, not the destination. Get comfortable with problems as a daily part of life and you'll be a step closer to your end game.

As life coach-y as it sounds, we believe that accepting your role as problem-solver-in-chief is one of the most powerful things a founder can do. Countless facets of commerce are beyond our control, but when we embrace this, we lift our outlook into a more proactive place. And that is something we *can* control.

Key takeaways

- *Solve it, then ship it.* Once you solve a problem, entrust the process to your team and let them own the solution.

- *Problems don't disappear — they just shift forms.* Your future self will fare better at problem solving than your present self. Much like willpower, problem solving is a muscle, and yours will grow along with your challenges.

CHAPTER 12
WHAT'S YOUR 'WHY'?

What is the craziest, hardest thing you've ever done? The one that hurt. That defied all reason? The one thing you did just to prove you could do it?

Maybe, like Nellie McQuinn, you moved from all that you knew on the promise of an opportunity. Like many of us at 17, university didn't feel like the right option — not quite yet, anyway. So she put it on hold for a year in the UK, hoping to hustle her way into a career in London's arts scene. There, she studied at the prestigious Royal Academy of Dramatic Art, co-founding Grass Roots Media at 19.

'Grass Roots Media fell into a niche,' said Nellie. 'We started by specialising in short-form content. Back then, it was a money decision: it was cheaper to make a three-minute episode than a 30-minute episode. We would create micro-series and publish them online before YouTube was a thing.'

The concept caught on, and their content has received over seven billion views. Along the way, Nellie happened to audition for a role as presenter.

'As part of the audition, I met with a guy from India who ran the operation. He told me he was looking for a production company that does short-form content,' said Nellie. 'He was looking for someone who could create content for children, so that's how we found our focus on short-form kids' content.

'The fates had aligned for me — this guy had been sent about 1000 sample tapes from production companies, and he'd only watched about 20, which he'd selected at random.

'While there's a lot to be said for the entrepreneurial spirit, there's also a lot to be said for being in the right place at the right time. If that guy hadn't opened my email, I don't know where my life would be.

'Because short-form online kids' content was such a niche back then, we became very specialised. We were the first ones building a name for ourselves in that space, so we grew very quickly.'

Grass Roots Media served clients like EOne, Peppa Pig and PJ Masks.

'A lot of much bigger players entered the space after us, and they took the concept into much bigger spaces. After that, we maintained an interesting niche by being at an accessible pricepoint. We had big companies coming to us because they couldn't afford to make content at the price that we could.'

The experience led to further opportunities, including joining Moonbug Entertainment as part of its founding team. Here she served as Vice President, Head of Production. Moonbug soon made a name for itself, enjoying a reported $3 billion acquisition by Candle Media. It was also recognised on FastCompany's 2023 World's Most Innovative Companies list. Ever the entrepreneur, she also founded Property 165, a specialist in residential flips, and went on to win New Property Investor of the Year. She's since founded AWAY Wills, bringing insights from other markets to the UK.

Quite a story. And it all started with what seemed a little crazy: leaving her home in Sydney to try her luck as an actor in London. Why did she do it? And what made her succeed?

Intelligence. Grit. Inventiveness. Plus a work ethic and stubbornness few others possess. And, as Nellie acknowledged, a little bit of luck.

There is no clever study or fancy formula for finding your 'why'. Believe us, we'd cite it if we could! Rather, as you explore your reasons for starting a business, let's discover what inspired others. We know you face huge odds. As *Harvard Business Review* won't hesitate to tell you, approximately 90 per cent of startups fail. But with the global startup economy valued at $3 trillion, it can seem like a gamble worth taking.

From banking to business: how the economic downturn freed Tim Fung to innovate

You don't need to drop out of university to succeed in startups. Sure, Bill Gates and Mark Zuckerberg succeeded without degrees, but Elizabeth Holmes, founder of the ill-fated blood-testing startup Theranos, is probably regretting it now she's serving an 11-year prison sentence for fraud.

According to data published in *Tech Crunch*, only 7.1 per cent of successful co-founders didn't go to university. Of these, only 3.9 per cent were university dropouts, and most of these dropouts came from well-established academic institutions like MIT, Harvard or Stanford.

What compels a clever, highly educated university graduate to pursue a high-risk career in startups?

In the case of Tim Fung, it was a recession.

'After university, I worked at Macquarie Bank, working in the property division,' said Fung. 'It was the GFC. Whole teams were laid off and consolidated. I was fortunately young and got a redundancy cheque from Macquarie.'

Inspired by hit TV show *Entourage*, Fung decided to take a hard left and work for a modelling agency, Chic Management.

'It was serendipitous,' said Fung. 'One of the directors of the agency worked with Optus, and invited me to work on a startup with him.'

Together, they set up Amaysim.

'It's important to surround yourself with smart, interesting people. I went on that startup journey with him,' said Fung. 'That's how I caught the startup bug. I didn't know you could just write a PowerPoint deck, raise money and do something.'

Amaysim was sold to Optus for $250 million in 2020. Fung has since founded Airtasker, which has gone public and expanded to the UK and the United States.

Without the GFC, Fung might have stayed in investment banking. Like many founders, economic turbulence spurred him to try new careers, creating companies that have grown globally and become household names.

Fung's startups join the ranks of many successful GFC ventures, including WhatsApp, Airbnb, Instagram and Uber. It is a testament to the unlikely value downturns can provide: as previous career paths close for talented, highly educated professionals, a new pool of founders finds themselves free to pursue high-risk, high-reward innovations.

From corporate law to LegalVision

Other founders, like Lachlan McKnight, might spend a few years working in a traditionally prestigious career path before deciding to start their own venture.

'I found being a corporate lawyer in a big firm wasn't for me. It's not a bad career at all, but after a few years in a role, you get to know what you're good at and what you're not so good at,' observed McKnight. 'You develop a real attention to detail by grinding out similar work every day, and that process taught me that I didn't want a conventional career in big law.'

McKnight opted to explore a broader range of career paths, completing an MBA at INSEAD as he figured out what he might do next. He's not alone in this. According to *Fortune* magazine, 54 per cent of *Fortune* 100 CEOs hold a graduate degree. Of these, 59 per cent pursue MBAs and 16 per cent undertake JDs in law, while the rest complete a PhD or other Masters degree.

It was while studying his MBA that McKnight decided he wanted to start his own business.

'When I was working as a lawyer at a big firm, I was just doing the work,' said McKnight. 'I was early in my career, and in my early to mid 20s, so I wasn't really thinking about how it all fit together. The drive to start my own business emerged after I saw other entrepreneurs talk about their ventures while completing an MBA. I then started exploring options for businesses that fit with my skillset and background. Because I was part of the legal milieu, and understood the space, I started to form the concept for LegalVision.'

LegalVision started life as an online documents business. It's since evolved to become a buffet of law, providing businesses with unlimited access to legal services at a fixed fee.

Make your mission clear — and make it matter to you

Jenna Leo and Mathieu Bertrand were deep in the grind of corporate life when they founded their first side hustle, a couples fitness business. Inspired by *The 4-Hour Workweek*, their first venture seemed like a no-brainer — Bertrand provided PT sessions after hours, and Leo taught yoga.

'When you ran the calculations against the business model, it wasn't scalable. And I didn't want to teach from 5 am to 9 am, in my lunch break and from 5 pm to 9 pm every day,' said Leo.

What they loved about fitness was the impact they could have.

During one of Leo's yoga classes, a woman burst into tears. Horrified, Leo rushed to her side.

'I put everyone else in child's pose and ran over to check if she was injured. I thought she'd torn a ligament! She looked up at me with this huge smile and she said, "I have anxiety and depression, and I've never taken a full breath for as long as I can remember. I just did for the first time because of your class, and I feel *so* good".

'It was a really scary and really rewarding moment. I felt good for making her feel good, and I realised that I wanted to do something that made me feel like this, rather than the daily grind of working for the sake of work.'

Until then, Leo had always imagined a future as a 'corporate big dog'. That's why she had studied business and law. But it was a moment she couldn't ignore.

'We came to see that the idea behind Like Family could make people feel *great*,' said Leo. 'So there was always an impact element that we wanted to provide.'

Democratising opportunity: how Pasha Rayan found his purpose

'I started Forage with Tom Brunskill in 2017,' said co-founder Pasha Rayan. 'After we graduated from university, Tom and I were helping students in our own ways. Tom, a corporate lawyer, did a lot of resume reviews and career coaching to help students enter the legal profession. Meanwhile, I'd been doing the same for business and consulting. Because of our backgrounds, we had a bit of a chip on our shoulders about wanting to help anyone get into "cool careers".

'Tom grew up in Wagga Wagga, and he didn't know much about corporate environments until he went to university. That's when he realised it could be a real process to get into law firms. I grew up about five minutes away from UNSW, which is the university where Tom and I met. I was from a single-parent family, and Mum had done a lot to raise us, so I lucked my way into a good career.

'I was able to join one of the UNSW business societies because I knew how to use Photoshop and InDesign,' explained Rayan. 'This is where I learned how to create a resume, how to apply for jobs and what internships were.

'I think both Tom and I had this chip on our shoulders that the opportunities we'd found felt like luck. Many of our childhood friends hadn't been as lucky at landing cool jobs after high school or university. We wanted to help people reach that next level.'

Now, don't get us wrong. There are plenty of talented nepo-hires in the world. If Francis Ford Coppola hadn't bankrolled his daughter's first film, we wouldn't have *The Virgin Suicides*, *Lost in Translation* or Bill Murray back in our lives.

But for every Sofia Coppola the writer/director, there is a Sofia Coppola the actor. (Seriously, watch *The Godfather III* if you don't believe us.)

Forage was founded to provide a platform for people with more talent and fewer opportunities.

'It's really cool to hear stories from people who have landed their dream jobs through Forage. We hear them every day,' said Rayan. 'The stories come from people of different backgrounds, from different places with different starting points in life.

'We've had single mothers who have landed jobs in major law firms while raising their kids. We've had students from underrepresented backgrounds in America who have been the first in their families to land a job at a big corporation. Because of their effort and their work, they were able to get the attention they deserved through Forage. The fact that I got to wake up every morning and hear these great stories is a real honour.'

A home for the get-rich-slow crowd

Did you love *The Wolf of Wall Street*? Then Pearler is probably not for you.

'Nearly all of the mature platforms people use for long-term investing were built for the use of short-term traders,' said Pearler co-founder Hayden Smith.

Smith and co-founder Nick Nicolaides had a hunch that most people didn't want to spend their lives architecturally at one with their trading apps. They just wanted to work, tuck away some savings and live their lives.

'We decided to build a fit-for-purpose tool to do what we believed everyday Australians were trying to do with their money,' said Smith.

'Until Pearler, long-term investors were using platforms built for short-term traders. It was like using a book as a monitor stand. It might work, but there was still the opportunity for someone to build a monitor stand and improve the solution.'

Pearler embraced an ethos of 'get rich slow'—which is about as far removed from Lambos and Quaaludes as you can get. While Jordan Belfort was busy crashing yachts and marrying super-models, Pearler's helming a movement where the only thing getting high is their customers' compound interest—a movement so popular, they've surpassed $2 billion in funds under management.

High kicks and quick wits: how Dua Shkara found her 'why'

How do you know you're an entrepreneur? You're the kind of person who would work 80 hours a week just to avoid working 40 hours for someone else.

With 485k followers on Instagram, 6.9 million likes and 330 000 followers on Tik Tok, you might be surprised to find that Dua Shkara 'kinda fell into content creation.'

In her life before content, Shkara was a study in contradictions. Her taekwondo talents earned her a place representing Team GB internationally, but she sensibly started her career as an accountant in London.

'Working in finance allowed me to understand different kinds of businesses from a financial standpoint, whether it was salons or restaurants,' she says. 'I also paid close attention to how they marketed themselves.'

An e-commerce stint with The Athlete's Foot exposed her to content creators. Now she's the face of Reebok, emblazoned on billboards — you might have seen her on your drive home.

'It's fascinating how much we've changed as a society in terms of advertising,' Shkara explains. 'Consumers are savvier than ever and can easily spot inauthenticity. That's why businesses are increasingly turning to micro-influencers who have built a trusted and engaged community. It's not just about follower count. Engagement and authenticity are what matter most. Micro-influencers have a curated environment and brand culture that resonates with their audience. Because they don't have a massive following, consumers perceive them as more trustworthy. They see someone with 10 000 followers genuinely talking about a product, unaware that a brand might be behind it. Imagine Kylie Jenner promoting a product versus someone with a highly engaged, niche following. As consumers and marketers, we've learned to "spot the fake" when it comes to product endorsements.'

Like a true-born entrepreneur, Shkara has mined every job she's worked for insights to inform her business. Accounting grounded her in the fundamentals of business finance, while e-commerce introduced her to the potential of building your own brand as a business.

'Up until 100 000 followers, I didn't make a dime,' said Shkara. 'I think in the foetal stages of your Instagram account, you should not focus on monetisation at all. You shouldn't sell anything or talk about money. It should just be who you are, and what you have to offer.'

Shkara first went viral for a truly impressive kick landed in one of her first Sydney fights. From there, she focused on figuring out what made her unique — and taking her followers on her journey.

'I found a niche I was passionate about. It kept growing, so I was able to create this beautiful audience. Even in the comments they'd reference things about my life, inside jokes, and brands would pick up on that. That's a green flag for a brand nowadays. I've created a narrative.'

She's since been picked up by an LA-based agency and gone on to create promotional content for One Championship.

'Polished ads with expensive cameras just don't resonate as much anymore,' said Shkara. 'People trust someone in their pyjamas raving about a product more than a staged commercial. There's a huge shift towards more genuine content, perpetuated by Tik Tok. The psychology of today's marketing world is being able to relate to a content creator. If they're in their PJs in a darkly lit bedroom talking about a hair product they just found, you might watch and say, "Hey, I have that same duvet cover!" That bedroom looks like mine.'

For Shkara, her drive — her 'why' — is intrinsically intertwined with her own identity. Her content is a reflection of who she is, so she's selective with the brand partnerships she accepts. Her businesses also align with her experiences as an athlete, and she developed a knee mobility program alongside her own knee surgery and recovery.

In a world where 90 per cent of startups fail, your 'why' isn't just a nice-to-have: it's your light in the dark of sleepless nights and uncertain futures, a purpose as unique to you as your fingerprint. Your 'why' can emerge from unexpected places: a redundancy payout, a moment with a yoga student, a kick of such parabolic elegance it captivates the world just for a minute. Find yours, and you'll find the fuel you need to forge forward — and perhaps, someday, ride your unicorn dreams.

CHAPTER 13
HOW TO AVOID THE GROWTH CEILING

A growth ceiling is a classic good problem to have. It's when you've hit max reps at the gym, devoured an entire KFC Family Feast, or binged every episode of *Bake Off*.

You'll know you've hit a growth ceiling because you'll feel your revenue even out to a soothing plateau. As with any plateau, it's a sign you've scaled great heights. Congratulations!

Look, we promise we're not searching for problems to throw your way. We just want to ensure you don't go to bed with dreams of launching the next Atlassian, only to wake up with a mid-level consultancy in the 'burbs.

And that's not meant to throw shade at consultants — we've seen their expertise save startups more times than we can count. Even so, a consultancy requires a different track from a startup. You may remember that we delved into these differences in chapter 8. For now, we'll say this: if you want a startup life, you need startup growth. And nothing stymies startup growth like the growth ceiling.

Have you hit your growth ceiling?

Do you feel like you're working harder than ever — but accomplishing less? When innovation means a new colour for an old feature, or a new cast for the same old story (*Star Wars* prequels, we're looking at you).

Hitting your growth ceiling is like rearranging furniture when you need a bigger place: a temporary manoeuvre to delay an inevitable investment.

Here are a few signs you've hit your growth ceiling:

- You've hit 85–90 per cent utilisation of your key resources (time, money, people, technology).

- You've served 70–80 per cent of your total addressable market. This means you're close to market saturation.

- Your productivity-to-effort ratio is flattening. In other words, your efforts are yielding minimal additional results.

- Your innovation velocity is slowing.

- Your competitors are growing significantly faster than you are.

You might even catch yourself using bland corporate-talk — after all, 'We're in a strategic plateau phase' sounds so much better than 'We're stuck'. Much like saying 'I'm on a nutritional sabbatical' sounds better than 'I binged a KFC Family Feast solo'.

No matter how you sell it, you're starting to see diminishing returns on your efforts. At this point, you can either choose to optimise your operations, deprioritise growth — and the significant expenses investing in growth will incur — and take the off-ramp to create a long-term, sustainable business. This is an excellent result. Your business is thriving enough so you don't need to work for someone else. You might have more freedom, even a few employees and a stable customer base.

However, if you are looking to grow, you'll need to push past this 'strategic plateau'. Let's explore how a few startups did so and how they transitioned into scale-ups.

Wait ... what's a scale-up?

So, what is a scale-up? As the name suggests, it's when you grow, and change in scale. This is when you have:

- *stabilised your business model* to provide a reliable source of recurring revenue
- *industrialised your core product* so it can be produced and sold to a broad market
- *proven your commercial viability* through a loyal customer base.

The OECD and Scale-Up Vaud provide several helpful calculations to reflect scale-up status:

- Your turnover is $1–$3 million.
- Your team is growing by over 10 per cent per annum, with at least 10 employees on permanent contracts.

Once your business has reached these milestones, it no longer exists in a state of extreme uncertainty. It has braved storm-lashed seas and sailed into the clear skies of scale-up life.

In short, a scale-up is a startup that's *made it big*.

Startups, unlike businesses, must break through the growth ceiling. Investors expect exponential returns, and startups have often burned significant capital ('runway') on the promise of capturing a major share of the market.

This means the next stage of a startup is to:

- *grow* ... into a scale-up. Examples of this include Airtasker, LegalVision, Canva and Atlassian
- *exit* ... by going public through an IPO, or acquisition. Forage, for example, exited by acquisition to EAB, a US education firm
- *sad exit* ... oh no! You've run out of runway. It happens to everyone who takes a big swing. It's happened to most founders. Chin up. You'll live to dream another day.

We should know. We've seen all three.

Scale-up by solving the right problem: Mad Paws

Mad Paws set itself apart from other pet sitting operations early on.

'We focused early on the demand and supply issue,' explained Mad Paws co-founder Alexis Soulopoulos. 'This was the difference between us and our 30 or so competitors.'

This meant ensuring Mad Paws had enough qualified pet sitters to meet demand.

'Sometimes this meant spending hours on the phone connecting pet sitters with pet owners,' said Soulopoulos. 'It was really hard work. There were some days when I would make over 100 phone calls, but I needed to bring energy to each one as if it were the first.'

'At the time, it didn't occur to me how far those phone calls would take us. I didn't realise that this effort would be the key ingredient to our early success.'

By spending hours each day on the phone, Soulopoulos laid the foundations for Mad Paws to eventually scale-up: he created a sustainable, double-sided marketplace. With reliable pet sitters available to care for your furry friends, Mad Paws swiftly distinguished itself from its 30 or so competitors.

'Once our website was ready, we had sticky customers and highly engaged pet sitters ready to take bookings,' explained Souloupoulos. 'From there, we were able to scale in a way that we wouldn't have if people hadn't stuck around.'

From here, they could focus their investment on helping Mad Paws scale, implementing automated text messages and notifications, calendars of pet sitter availability and pet insurance to reassure pet owners in case of adverse events.

'As some of our competitors didn't seem to focus on solving demand and supply, it was much harder for them to scale. Because we addressed this marketplace issue at the outset, it was easier for us to go from zero to one.'

Going 'from zero to one' is a reference to Peter Thiel's iconic startup manifesto of the same name. It refers to creating something from nothing, the act of creation that underscores true innovation.

For Mad Paws, their innovation wasn't the *idea of a pet sitting platform*. This idea was already being played out in many ways, both online and informally. How Mad Paws differed was *how they operated their pet sitting platform*. No other platform provided pet insurance, or such diligently qualified pet sitters. No other founder was hitting the phones up to 100 times a day. You see, no business will ever have enough money. It's what you do with the money you have that makes all the difference.

When COVID-19 banished the world indoors, pet ownership exploded. However, with pet owners banned from non-essential travel, the demand for pet sitting imploded.

'When COVID hit, our revenue dropped from good levels to, in the worst weeks of lockdown, literally $0,' said Souloupoulos. 'It was a similar revenue drop to what many airlines would have experienced, and it was extremely scary.'

In an emergency meeting, the company didn't mince words: runway was running out, and with the entire fate of Mad Paws at stake they needed a big pivot, fast.

'Dominating the pet care industry was always part of our vision from day one,' said Alexis. 'Initially, with a small team and limited resources, we didn't want to lose focus on our core offering: pet sitting. COVID prompted us to expand.'

Seizing the chance to serve the pet-owning households of Australia — which rose sharply to 70 per cent through COVID-19 — Mad Paws launched a pet food line. This sustained the startup long enough to grow into other verticals, including Pet Chemist.

Mad Paws listed on the Australian Stock Exchange in 2021. Our own furry friend, a feisty West Highland Terrier with no shortage of self-esteem, helped mark the milestone by ringing the opening bell. According to Professor Schnoozy MacDuff, it couldn't have happened without her.

Scale-up by listening to the right feedback: Pearler

'I think user feedback is everything,' said Pearler co-founder Hayden Smith.

'When you first build a platform, you're building it for 10 people,' said Smith. 'Then you're building it for 50, then 100, then 500, then 1000, and it echoes on beyond that. The first time you get some usable feedback, you don't spend a lot of time thinking about what it looks like to someone in Perth or Adelaide. You're just thinking about those 10 people you have in Sydney, and you're trying to make them happy.

'When you start looking at more people, you widen your scope. A natural part of growth is that, as you build your product for more people, there can be a trade-off,' said Smith. 'Sometimes, to do something that's going to satisfy 40 people, you might need to do something that will upset the first 10. And that's just the natural product growth story.'

Learning to listen to the right feedback is crucial to figuring out how to grow and scale. It's better to have 1000 customers eager to invest every month than 100000 vaguely interested in investing someday. Building your product to meet the needs of the right group is crucial to scaling up successfully.

But how do you choose who to listen to?

'You have to consider a few things,' said Smith. 'If a small minority of your earliest customers want something, and your newer customers want something else, you have to balance the sheer scale of it. You need to look at which group has more customers, but you also need to ask yourself, *Which group has the more engaged customers?* If those first 10 customers are powerhouses that bring lots of new referrals, then it's not possible to weigh 30 customers against 10 in a three-to-one ratio.'

This is particularly important for Smith, who heads up development for Pearler. Every day, Smith's team decides what to build and what to shelve. It's a difficult process. You have to resist the urge to build everything for everyone.

'There are also two other things to weigh up,' said Smith. 'The first is *what's true to the brand.* In this case, sometimes a smaller group's desires might become more important because of how much more clearly their desires align with our brand. The second is *how future customers might respond.* Sure, the first 10 and the next 40 customers might disagree, but what do the next 1000 look like?'

'Sometimes you can feel like you're dealing with something that's inherently controversial. A good example is our "goals" feature, which is much more opinionated than a more generic goal-setting tool,' said Smith. 'We know we're going to annoy some new and some old customers with its rollout, but others are going to respond really well to it.

'We're also thinking about those future customers who are going to benefit from it. Because we're going to annoy some people regardless, we can afford to take a bet on the longer term since we have high conviction of where this will evolve in the next two years.'

Highly engaged, incredibly loyal customers have proven to be the engine powering Pearler's growth. Pearler is putting itself in pole position to scale-up by making hard choices about where to innovate, what products to provide and how to serve its customer base.

'None of these things become easy decisions, and involve quite a lot of discussion,' said Smith. 'We talk with our customers, talk with our employees and spend a lot of time thinking it through.'

Scale-up once you've proven a concept: Forage

Forage provides a classic example of how to grow from startup to scale-up. They started with mentoring, which they pivoted through customer research to virtual internships. Once they built their virtual internship platform, they set their minds to growth.

'Now that we were proving the concept, we knew we needed to expand,' said Forage co-founder Pasha Rayan. 'Tom [Brunskill] did a great job of approaching the law firms we already knew and saying: "Hey, we've got this product. Students are pretty interested in finding out what it's like to work as a lawyer". We were able to get [law firm] King & Wood Mallesons on board, which took a lot of security and compliance work. Luckily, because of our backgrounds, we knew what it meant to be secure from day one.'

'Once we brought King & Wood Mallesons on board, we were able to run our first job simulation. We'd proven the concept with the H2 program, and then we built the official version with King & Wood Mallesons. Next we got KPMG on board, then followed with other employers. That's how we got to our core product, which was the virtual job simulation.'

The rest, as they say, is history. By refining their virtual internships, Forage proved popular with university students, and cost-effectively delivered graduate recruits to their sponsors, graduate employers. To grow, however, Forage knew they needed to leave home turf.

'Tom Brunskill, our CEO, moved to the US so we could land one US corporate partner while still growing in Australia,' said Rayan. 'From there, we could start building a network of employers and students in the United States, as well as Australia.

'Our big break for global expansion was getting our first US partner, the law firm White & Case,' said Rayan. 'That partnership helped us prove that we could operate a global model with global partners. Eventually, this helped us get into Y Combinator, which also helped to accelerate our discussions with companies like JP Morgan.'

While Brunskill brokered deals in North America, Rayan continued improving the platform. 'Every week, we were applying feedback and pushing through new code,' said Rayan. 'It wasn't only a few big steps — it was also lots of little steps.'

'One of the appeals of Australia comes from the size of the market,' said Rayan. 'In a small market like Australia, there are lots of traps around building too many product lines. You can also suffer from over-optimising for a few big clients. If you're in North America, the market is so big that you can create a unicorn from one world-class product. Then, when you move to Australia, your product has already benefitted from another five or six years of R&D investment. All this extra refinement usually puts the product ahead of whatever the local solution is. Your American competitor can then clean out the local market because of the intense focus their bigger market allowed them to have.'

By expanding to North America, Forage was able to overcome the growth hurdles of staying in the smaller Australian market. Their client list includes the likes of Red Bull, JP Morgan, Lululemon, Bank of America, KPMG, Goldman Sachs, Citibank, PepsiCo and ... well, you get the idea.

'Today, we have major banks based in the United States who see around 40 per cent of their internship cohorts come from Forage,' said Rayan. 'In the UK, we have top-tier law firms who report 60 per cent of their interns having completed a Forage program. We've also been told that students who come through Forage are more diverse — because Forage interns come from everywhere.'

It's a triumph for a platform that's always been about breaking the grip of nepotism and 'insider knowledge' in graduate recruitment. In 2024, Forage was acquired by EAB, an American education firm — a mere seven years after the company was founded.

Scale-up to new international markets: LegalVision

Understanding market size is crucial for identifying growth ceilings. LegalVision's founder, Lachlan McKnight, recognised this early on.

'You've got to think about the size of the market,' he explained. 'If you think about the dollars, the big money will always be at the big end of town. We're talking about big corporates paying tens of millions of dollars to big law firms on an annual basis to handle big deals. If you look at a top-tier firm like Allens, they might bring in around three quarters of a billion in turnover annually. Do I think LegalVision, or any other NewLaw firm, is going to generate that sort of revenue in Australia alone? No, because we target a different customer base and type of work.'

This insight was critical to Lachlan's growth strategy for LegalVision. By serving a different customer base to a top tier firm, LegalVision was free to explore an alternative business model: an all-you-can-eat buffet of legal services available year-round. This move away from billable hours is what's allowed it to achieve scalable legal services.

'If we tried to be Allens, could we generate a couple of hundred million in revenue? Yes, the size of the Australian market means it's possible. It would be a great result, but we'd not really be doing anything innovative, new or interesting,' he stated.

LegalVision's success lay in understanding its market and innovating a different business model.

'For us, this is why we've expanded to New Zealand and the UK — if we want to truly scale, we need to be global,' McKnight emphasised. 'Because the Australian and NZ timezones are so similar, we could run a number of teams out of Australia. By launching in New Zealand as our first international market we were able to give ourselves a test case for international expansion. We worked out how to operate in another jurisdiction, and ironed out some things. This gave us the confidence to launch in the UK.'

'For us, the UK is a really big market,' said McKnight. 'Its legal services market is over four times larger than Australia's. The digital side of things is also about four times bigger, so we had a huge opportunity to grow rapidly over there.'

LegalVision launched in the UK as the first provider of a membership-based model of legal services. By 2024, LegalVision saw top line revenue of $50 million for its Australian and New Zealand businesses, and $13 million from the UK. Lachlan has his sights set on reaching $100 million revenue by 2027. With ambition like that, LegalVision's all-you-can-eat business model is scaling faster than a lawyer can bill by the hour.

Scale-up through acquisitions — aka 'How to buy other people's growth'

If you've reached this stage in your journey, you've done something right. Brilliant work. You're now in a position to buy other people's growth. So how do you do this?

Nellie McQuinn is no stranger to buying growth. Her entertainment company, Moonbug, acquired CoComelon, a YouTube children's channel that became one of Netflix's most-watched children's shows, viewed over 200 million times in the second half of 2023 alone.

'Moonbug works by looking for smaller companies that are doing well in one specific area — normally YouTube,' explained McQuinn. 'They would then acquire the company, and wrap this industry around it.'

'For instance, we'd give it a proper licensing and merchandising team to sell toys, a proper production and creative team, things like that. Before the acquisition, it would usually be a small Mum-and-Pop operation pumping out YouTube videos in a garage. They would have tapped into something that made their content a huge success online, but they wouldn't have that industry infrastructure. There'd be no feature film, or their branded bed linen wouldn't be for sale in Kmart. After the acquisition, we would wrap the business around the creative.

CoComelon was already a huge success on YouTube when Moonbug purchased it. Then, after the purchase, we did our wraparound.'

Merchandise revenues continue to rise, and Nellie led as executive producer of CoComelon's three-season, three-special Netflix deal.

CoComelon's acquisition reflects the best-case scenario when it comes to buying growth because both sides benefitted from the acquisition. Moonbug brought the expertise and capacity to commercialise CoComelon, scaling it to a global audience and tying in merchandising opportunities. CoComelon proved, as any good startup would, to be a disruptive force in children's entertainment — and what could be more startup than running a production out of a garage?

Hayder Shkara is a disrupter in a field far more traditional than online entertainment: he buys law firms.

'There's a very strong reason why I started acquiring law firms, and it was quite a conscious decision,' said Shkara.

Shkara founded his family law firm in his mid 20s with $20 000. But it wasn't his first foray into business. Ever the hustler, this Australian Taekwondo Olympian started a martial arts club at 18. Operating from a community hall, it was the first time he encountered the concept of a 'growth ceiling'.

'I realised that the size of clubs didn't change much,' said Shkara. 'Clubs and coaches might grow from 50 to 60 members over a decade. What I also discovered is that big clubs managed to stay big. A club with 300 members would tend to stay at 300 members.'

Why was this happening?

'With every business, you're limited to your market size, demographics and offering,' said Shkara. This is true for both martial arts clubs and law firms. Breaking through the growth ceiling is expensive, and it might simply be easier — and more profitable — to just open in a new location.

'As I grew my law firm, I knew I offered a niche service with a somewhat limited market. You're confined to the people in the area, and especially in the legal industry, [in terms of] whether they can afford your services.'

Shkara has grown by buying firms in new locations. Starting in Sydney, he's since bought firms in Victoria and Queensland, allowing him to establish a dominant foothold across Australia's eastern states.

'The main thing I look for is how reliant the firm is on the vendor outgoing principal,' said Shkara. In law, that is usually the outgoing partner.

'You've got to be careful that your acquisition isn't just based on that person's goodwill with the community,' said Shkara. 'The value of the business can't be largely dependent on one person.

'Financially, it needs to make sense,' said Shkara. 'You want to make sure that the business that you're operating is fairly specialised. It just helps with how things are set up, how to market it and how it's viewed in the market as well. A law firm doesn't normally make financial sense unless it's somewhat niche.'

Shkara then sets about making changes as early as possible.

'I'm a big believer that when you first take over a business, you've got a golden window of opportunity,' said Shkara. 'You come in with a fresh perspective, and for those first two-to-three months, you can look at what the business is doing and start changing things appropriately.

'The most valuable resource you have is every single team member, particularly those working in the firm's admin. They tend to know more about processes, and what's inefficient in the business. So if you ask them, 'What do you think could be improved?' they often have answers, but they've never been asked before. For me, it's important to build trust with team members so you can figure out what needs to be done and implemented.'

Once he's committed to making a series of changes — often to operational processes, technology or marketing — he won't hesitate. 'You've got to capitalise on change before people get accustomed to the way they do things,' he explained.

Scale-up by pivoting to new content

YouTuber Wengie (13.3 million subscribers) attracted her first million subscribers through makeup and lifestyle videos.

'These tags and trends in the beauty community were really popular at the time,' explained Wengie. 'But it wasn't until I pivoted to life hacks that my channel took off.'

She also improved her production quality, persuading her then partner to help with her shoots.

'Prior to this, it was just me, my tripod and a slider, and creative editing!' said Wengie.

'Life hacks were a trending category, but no other creators applied a "brand" to it,' explained Wengie. 'Once I injected my aesthetic and curated life hacks that seemed useful and made sense to me, my channel took off.

'To avoid hitting a growth ceiling, I always tried to beat my previous performance. I kept a keen eye on analytics, and obsessed over using every single second of my video. I'd comb through edits and cut out anything — to the second — that felt slow or didn't add value. I'd do this multiple times. I think this is why my videos performed so well. I valued my audience's time and subconsciously understood that attention spans are a key factor to creating a good video. I'd follow what topics were trending, and try to insert our content into popular keywords or trends. Consistency-wise, I rarely skipped a week in eight years.

'I saw my thumbnail aesthetics as a way to "brand" myself,' said Wengie. 'All my thumbnails look consistent, so you can tell it's my channel even if you can't see my face.'

Wengie's commitment saw her become one of Australia's biggest YouTubers, landing her an LA agent and brand partnerships targeting the far larger North American market. She's since pivoted from YouTube into crypto gaming, raising $13 million for NYAN Heroes at a $200 million valuation. Not bad for an accountant who told her Asian parents that YouTubing was 'just a hobby'.

Wengie's YouTube success shows how the right mix of commitment, applied to the right channel, at the right time, coupled with a willingness to experiment and learn your way to a solution can make for more than a great YouTuber. It's the stuff of great founders.

Should I stay or should I grow?

Only you know the answer. Ultimately, it comes down to how much risk you can afford to take, and what you hope to achieve.

As Tim Fung told us, 'It's just as hard to run a startup as it is to run a small business. That's why I chose to run startups.'

CHAPTER 14
GROW WITH YOUR BUSINESS

For a few years there, Chloe Zhao was a darling of the independent film scene. After earning festival acclaim with her debut film, Zhao became the talk of Sundance with her 2017 sophomore, *The Rider*. However, it was her 2020 film *Nomadland* that catapulted her into the global spotlight. Produced on a budget of US$5 million, *Nomadland* won Best Actress, Best Director and Best Picture at the Oscars. It was resplendent in its sparseness: the type of movie that film studies students would cite as an influence.

Of course, films are labours of commerce as much as works of art. In this, *Nomadland* excelled as well. By the end of its cinematic run, it had earned US$39.5 million—nearly eight times its production budget. This figure is doubly impressive given the release coincided with the aftermath of COVID-19, when theatres were still recovering. Before *Nomadland*, Zhao had proven herself to be a skilled artisan behind the camera. All of a sudden, she was a master of the balance sheet as well, someone who could turn a shoestring budget into golden lace.

It's fair to say, then, that Zhao had proven herself as an indie filmmaker. How, then, would she handle a blockbuster?

Cue *The Eternals*. Riding the coattails of the Marvel Cinematic Universe's golden age, *The Eternals* was forecast to be a major earner. Disney also saw it as an opportunity to create a higher tier of film. With such a lofty goal in mind, Zhao seemed like a natural choice to helm the project. Between her track record and the franchise's goodwill, a budget of US$236.2 million probably seemed like too much money (!).

However, the market — much like reviews — can be brutal. Shortly after its release, *The Eternals* became the lowest-rated MCU film on review aggregators Rotten Tomatoes and Metacritic. Indeed, it holds the dubious honour of being the first MCU film to score a 'rotten' classification on Rotten Tomatoes. Critics and viewers alike raised a slew of issues, from a stilted screenplay to an unfamiliar cast of characters. Yet there was one target that fell into the crosshairs of most naysayers: Zhao's directorial efforts.

Few doubted her intentions, or her commitment to the project. Still, many felt that the quiet splendour of her earlier works was lost in the blustering noise of a blockbuster. The sentiments of most critics were perhaps best distilled by Peter Rainer in, of all places, *The Christian Science Monitor*:

> *I don't think Zhao should be chided for attempting a film so seemingly outside her comfort zone. No director should have to commit to a career of specialization [sic]. The only qualm I have about Eternals is that it's not better.*

Financially, the film was a disaster. Officially, *The Eternals* earned over US$400 million — a fortune for most films, and nearly double its budget. However, after deducting distribution costs and cinema takings, Disney was left $35.1 million out of pocket. The next month, *Spiderman: No Way Home* grossed $1.9 billion — so

MCU fatigue wasn't the culprit. By Disney's standards, and by those of the fandom, the film had failed.

This entire anecdote must suggest that we harbour some blood feud against Chloe Zhao. Chloe, if you're reading this: we're sincerely sorry for the drivebys, and we know how talented you are. The reason we raise Zhao's story is because it mirrors that of many startup founders. Zhao excelled at bootstrapped creative pursuits, and her success propelled her to a higher level. However, the traits that allowed her to thrive at a small scale hampered her performance on a larger stage. A threadbare budget requires a different strategy from a nine-figure one. An indie studio will harbour different demands from one of the largest media companies in the world. A work of art with two cameras differs from a spectacle with 20. And film festival aficionados show up for different reasons to a box office crowd.

As Chloe Zhao knows all too well, the skills that help us to reach the top aren't always the skills that will help us stay there. In chapter 11, we explored how your problems will change shape as your business grows. Now, we'll detail how you can evolve to be the leader your latter-stage business needs you to be.

We'll do this by highlighting:

- the differences in traits between promising early-stage business founders and **Fortune 500** CEOs
- the changes in your day-to-day life when your business finds success — and how you can prepare for it
- the LEGO-isation of your decisions: they'll transfer from many choices to a few major choices
- the steps you can take today to prepare both yourself and your business for growth.

Now, let's get to ensuring you're less *Eternals* and more *End Game.*

From chief doer to executive

At a glance, the chasm between leading a young business and a large company may seem obvious. An early-stage founder can spend 12 hours a day with all five of their employees; a Fortune 500 CEO can work 12 years without meeting 5 per cent of their staff. A founder can lose sleep over making monthly payroll; a CEO can stay awake fretting about the impact of tariffs on next FY's forecasts. One deals with the problems of a household, while the other grapples with GDPs.

Nellie McQuinn said as much to us after steering businesses through not one, but two acquisitions. First, her shoestring production company was acquired as part of Moonbug Entertainment's launch, which she joined as a founding member. Suddenly, the number of employees in her company 10×'d, and the business morphed into a different beast. A few years later, Moonbug was acquired by Candle Media for US$3 billion — and the business changed again.

'In some ways, it's easier as a smaller company because you know what everyone's doing,' McQuinn told us.

'When you work in a senior role in a huge company [after an acquisition], you might find there are entire departments whose specific workload eludes you.'

McQuinn noticed that, after each acquisition, the differences stretched beyond extra zeros on the balance sheet. Indeed, the very nature of her job evolved from 'chief doer' to 'executive'. And while the stakes may not feel so high in such a role, you also don't enjoy the same degree of involvement.

'When you're in a team of five, you know *everything*, because you're all sitting within five square metres of everyone,' McQuinn said.

'You can't get away with underperforming because there's no fat in the team to protect you; you're fully exposed.'

Granted, McQuinn's experience is informed by her acquisitions. After exiting, she joined her creation in its new home and saw how it grew under someone else's hand. Not every founder will set the same target for themselves, so some will live a different experience of growth (see chapter 15). Even so, McQuinn's post-acquisition days convey an insight for any founder: For your business to evolve, you'll need to trust others to do the work you used to do.

From a master of one to a jack-of-all-trades

When you launch a business, you're likely to spend most of your time plying a specific skillset. Perhaps this relates to your pre-business vocation, or maybe it involves your venture's core offering — like cooking in a food truck. Either way, once your baby grows, you'll spend more time on the business of Business.

When investing platform Pearler first launched, co-founder and CTO Hayden Smith chiefly spent his days doing CTO things. This made sense for many reasons, such as:

- There were only three co-founders, Smith was the CTO, and someone needed to build the platform.

- He had interned at Microsoft, worked for years as a web developer and lectured on computer science. His skillset matched what the business needed.

- He spent his spare time coding; building and racing solar cars; and otherwise giving every indication that he loved solving technical problems.

That was 2018. Now, Smith contends with a starkly different daily reality.

'From my specific experience as a CTO, I've found that I'm much more of a business person — as a proportion of what I do every day — than I was five years ago,' Smith told us.

'In terms of day-to-day changes, I've gone from dealing with a large volume of minor issues to a small volume of critical issues.'

Business growth or not, the 'T' in 'CTO' doesn't simply disappear because the workday has other plans. Any technical issues still fall under the purview of the CTO, which means the buck stops with Smith. This is where he sees a marriage between the business and the technical: people management.

'I think that tango between 'founder' and 'CTO' is always an interesting one,' he said.

'For me, at least, the 'founder' element has started to become more relevant as we've brought on people who can do the technical work.'

In a sense, Hayden's role requires him to imbue his staff with the skills that made him an effective CTO. He'll never be able to build every platform feature and fix every glitch — but he *can* ensure his team does. By doing so, he scales Pearler's technical output while still retaining that which made him shine in Pearler's early days. Or, in the parlance of our Chloe Zhao rant: he's making a successful *Nomadland* for the MCU.

Key takeaways

- *You can't grow your business without trusting others.* There will come a point where you can't manage and 'do' at the same time. At this stage of your business cycle, you'll need to find your comfort with delegation (revisit 'Solve it, then ship it' in chapter 11). Trust your team to do the work you used to do, monitor their output and magic will happen.

- *Nurture a team of mini-yous.* On one hand, a larger business requires you to be a leader, not a doer. On the other, your business will only have grown if you excelled at your early efforts, and you don't want to deprive your company of quality labour. The solution? Hire team members who possess the same technical skills as you. Set clear goals for their output, and they'll be well placed to replicate your success.

- *Embrace the business of business.* Maybe you spend your days in a kitchen. Perhaps you labour in different coding platforms. Maybe you're at your best with a tool in your hands. Whatever your skillset, it will play a much smaller role in your future. Any skilled professional can replace your labour, but there can be only one CEO (or two, at most). Beyond people management, your days will belong to the business of Business — the decisions you *can't* delegate.

Mark the Founder and Zuck the CEO: a tale of two leaders

The differences between an early-stage founder and the CEO don't begin and end with day-to-day stresses. Indeed, the most crucial distinction may be a strategic one: how each leader thinks they can best achieve their goals. This detail might seem trivial next to operational issues, like the gap between a six-person payroll and a multinational budget. But as we saw in chapter 11, a good leader can learn to conquer new daily challenges as they emerge. By contrast, a dated strategic outlook can hamper a mature business from growing as it did during its youth.

Perhaps no-one embodies this truth better than Mark Zuckerberg, the founder who inspired a biopic before Steve Jobs. There's nothing we can say about Zuckerberg that hasn't been said by more authoritative sources. The man doesn't need an introduction, and we won't bore you with another origin story. Rather, we'd like to visit him at two different years of his life: 2006, when he was still a founder; and 2022, when he was very much a CEO. This way, you can see how the traits that spawned his success stalled his company's growth.

For ease of reference, we'll call the 2006 version 'Mark', and the 2022 version 'Zuck'.

2006: MySpace, mould-breaking and Mark's mission to move fast

Back in August 2006, the World Wide Web was nearly unrecognisable from its many-tendrilled form today. MySpace was the world's largest social media platform, with around 100 million users. The iPhone had yet to see its release, and smartphones in general were a fringe item. As a result, nearly everyone with a social media account logged in via their desktop or notebook. And Facebook — barely more than two years into its lifespan — was suffering from growing pains.

Sure, its meteoric rise would have been the envy of any mid-noughties startups. What had begun as a Harvard-only social networking platform in 2004 had spread to campuses across the United States. By the time Justin Timberlake's *SexyBack* hit the charts in mid 2006, it had wooed around 7 million users. In barely more than 24 months, Facebook had become a byword for the American college experience. Perhaps it hadn't reached MySpace's 100 million, but it was showing promise. See figure 14.1 for a timeline of Facebook's 14-month rollercoaster.

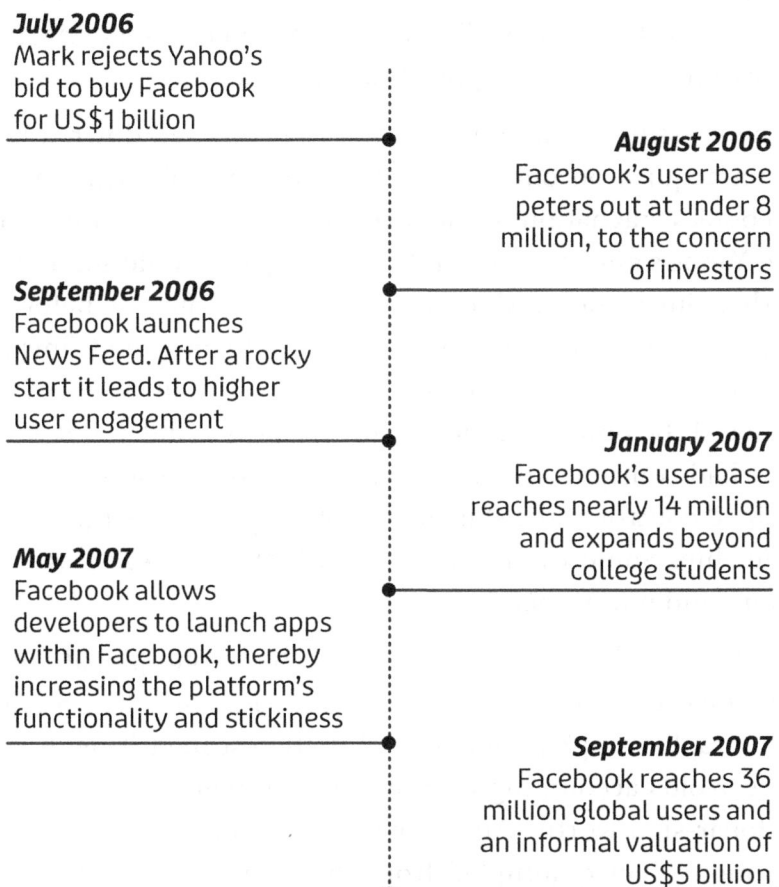

2006-07:
Mark Moves Fast

July 2006
Mark rejects Yahoo's
bid to buy Facebook
for US$1 billion

August 2006
Facebook's user base
peters out at under 8
million, to the concern
of investors

September 2006
Facebook launches
News Feed. After a rocky
start it leads to higher
user engagement

January 2007
Facebook's user base
reaches nearly 14 million
and expands beyond
college students

May 2007
Facebook allows
developers to launch apps
within Facebook, thereby
increasing the platform's
functionality and stickiness

September 2007
Facebook reaches 36
million global users and
an informal valuation of
US$5 billion

Figure 14.1: A brief timeline of Facebook's 14-month rollercoaster

Even so, the secret to Facebook's early success had become a barrier to its growth. Namely, the platform was struggling to find usage with anyone who wasn't a university student. It had gained acclaim as a college networking tool — so a college networking tool was all anyone saw. Mark's goal was to steer Facebook beyond beer pong and frat houses, and into the mainstream. He'd said as much to Facebook's investors; they had given Mark nearly US$38 million to realise the dream, and they wanted results. Instead, after 11 months of failing to crack the high school–aged market, Facebook had stalled south of 8 million users. MySpace, meanwhile, showed no signs of slowing.

The pressure compounded when Mark turned down a US$1 billion acquisition offer from Yahoo in July. Following fears of Facebook's stagnation, some investors and board members had seen Yahoo's offer as a graceful exit. Everyone would see a return on their investment. Mark would pocket 10 figures before his 23rd birthday. And Facebook's founding team would finish on a high before the startup could decline on their watch. When he closed the book on Yahoo, many insiders wondered if Mark's pride had consigned them all to a sinking ship. And while Mark retained control of the startup, doubts began to emerge over his leadership. Some even questioned whether he was less a boy genius, and more a petulant brat.

Fast-forward a year, and Facebook had gone global. Forget 7 million users — Facebook had 5×'d to 36 million. The US college demographic trap? Facebook had deftly escaped it, with over-35-year-olds accounting for the fastest growing user base. And its dollar-sign worth? According to industry VCs, its valuation had more than quintupled from the prior year's US$1 billion Yahoo offer.

So, what changed to allow Facebook to reverse its fortunes? In a word: nothing. In a sentence: Mark stayed true to the vision that had first incited him to launch Facebook. For all its customisable backgrounds and tailored profile soundtracks, MySpace didn't differ all that much from the era's online forums. Profiles didn't require real names or photos, and any users could connect with strangers as easily as friends. If you wanted to create an alter ego online, MySpace could help you make it happen. Observers saw Facebook as a would-be rival to Myspace, but Mark didn't *want* to create a MySpace clone. Rather, he sought to hold an online mirror to users' existing, real-life connections — what he dubbed the 'social graph'. In doing so, he hoped to digitise the grapevine, office water cooler, family email chain and morning newspaper. Facebook would be to social media what Google was to search engines.

In September, Mark and his team launched News Feed — the bedrock for our current relationship with Facebook. After some teething issues around user responses, News Feed became a mainstay of the platform. When Mark then opened Facebook to the wider world, signups soared, and the user base nearly doubled by January 2007. But as the user base grew, Mark wanted to ensure they never had a reason to log out. Remember, Mark didn't dream of a new MySpace — he dreamed of a new Google. He wanted a platform that engrained itself in its users' daily routines. To keep users engaged, Facebook would need to incorporate a near-limitless number of apps. That way, users could remain logged in for their daily online habits, from browsing Marketplace to sharing life status updates. However, Facebook's plucky team of devs couldn't predict every app use case, and even if they could, there weren't enough hours in the day. But, once again, Mark's vision yielded an uncharted solution.

Facebook: saying 'there's an app for that' before it was cool

In May of 2007, Mark invited external developers to build, launch and monetise independent apps in Facebook. For non-technical readers (these authors included), such a jargon-y sentence may have summoned a forecast of brain fog. However, at the time, the app integration was akin to pairing wheels with an engine. Yes, the tech existed — but nobody had combined it like *this* before.

And in doing so, Facebook spawned the most successful multi-level marketing campaign since Avon.

Thanks to News Feed, a user's Facebook friends would learn whenever they downloaded a new app. These friends may then download the app in question, which would further promote it to an even wider network. The approach worked like a digital chain letter, and app developers flocked to Facebook. Previously, developers had needed to list their apps on Google and hope that their target market found them. It was the equivalent of self-publishing a book, cramming it onto a store shelf and hoping for the best. With Facebook, these devs could depend on their users to refer their products simply by using them.

Suddenly, cash-strapped devs who had never left their postcode could connect their apps with users in different time zones. They could then profit by either charging users or advertisers. Users and usage surged, as Facebook's app-friendly interface ensured they never needed to log out.

Facebook had created a self-sustaining growth machine for both ends of the marketplace. For apps both great and small, it had ushered in a new age of meritocracy. For anyone with an internet connection, it had drawn a new roadmap for how people would interact online. And for Mark, it was a vision fulfilled.

Why Mark the Founder thrived

Over these two years, Mark doubtless needed to hone new skills, like people management and **board whispering**. In the end, though, he solved the challenges of 2006 with the traits he leveraged to launch Facebook:

- *A deep understanding of the digital landscape*, and a vision for how Facebook would reshape it

- *A tech-led strategy* for how Facebook would find an ever-growing product–market fit
- *An iron nerve to back his vision,* regardless of mounting pressures.

His now-famous motto, which has inspired books, articles and T-shirt prints: 'Move fast and break things'.

All in all, a bona fide success story, no? Now, let's see how these same virtues serve Zuck the CEO in the not-too-distant future.

2022: Zuck and the Metaverse of Madness

Facebook the startup was now Meta the conglomerate. It owned Instagram, WhatsApp and the attention spans of people across the planet. Its army of techs had pioneered smartphone access for social media; and in doing so, had irreversibly changed our collective rapport with our phones, friends, dopamine receptors and bathrooms. Around 10 years prior, its IPO had raised US$16 billion — the third largest in US history at the time. Since then, the tech giant had been a planning ground for uprisings, a vessel for election interference and a literal mine for personal data.

While younger users flocked to Tik Tok and Instagram, Facebook's brand recognition was on par with Coca-Cola or McDonald's. In short, Facebook had become less a company, and more of a new world order.

And Zuck was still in charge.

A founder retaining leadership after an IPO is incredibly rare. What's more, Zuck controlled 61 per cent of Meta's voting shares, essentially granting him the power of a corporate monarch. But while the company's challenges had evolved since 2006, Zuck was still using Mark's toolkit to fix them.

To fully grasp how Zuck dug his own hole, we need to rewind to a year earlier. Back in 2021, Zuck had announced that the company behind Facebook would change its name to Meta. The title change was more than a brand refresh: it was a declaration of intent. Its aim was to align with Zuck's vision of a 'metaverse company', replete with the latest virtual reality tech.

Given Zuck's feted record for daring revamps, many investors welcomed the move. After all, Facebook had plateaued at around 3.5 billion cumulative monthly users in 2021. At the same time, social media rival Tik Tok was luring younger users from Facebook and Instagram. On the upside, the Cambridge Analytica scandal was starting to slowly recede from the public's recall. Facebook and Instagram had also seen a spike in e-commerce advertisers, as COVID-19 lockdowns required record numbers to shop online. True to their playbook, they channelled their winnings into human resources, with staff numbers nearly doubling between 2019 and 2022. Zuck then paired his Meta rebrand with his next thrilling frontier: virtual and augmented reality.

Based on the traits that made him a darling of innovation in 2007, this move made sense. It involved a big swing that would challenge the way people digitally engaged with each other. It bet on a vision that largely stemmed from Zuck's mind. And, if it paid off, it would once again cement Meta as market-leading innovators. Much as Facebook had reframed the role of social media, Meta aimed to reinvent the way we socialise. Imagine *The Matrix*, but more benevolent. Trip to Venice? Head to the Metaverse! Game night with neighbours? Play with anyone in the world...through the Metaverse!

The only problem: Meta was now too unwieldy to solve its issues with One Big Idea. See figure 14.2 for a timeline of Meta's two years in the metaverse.

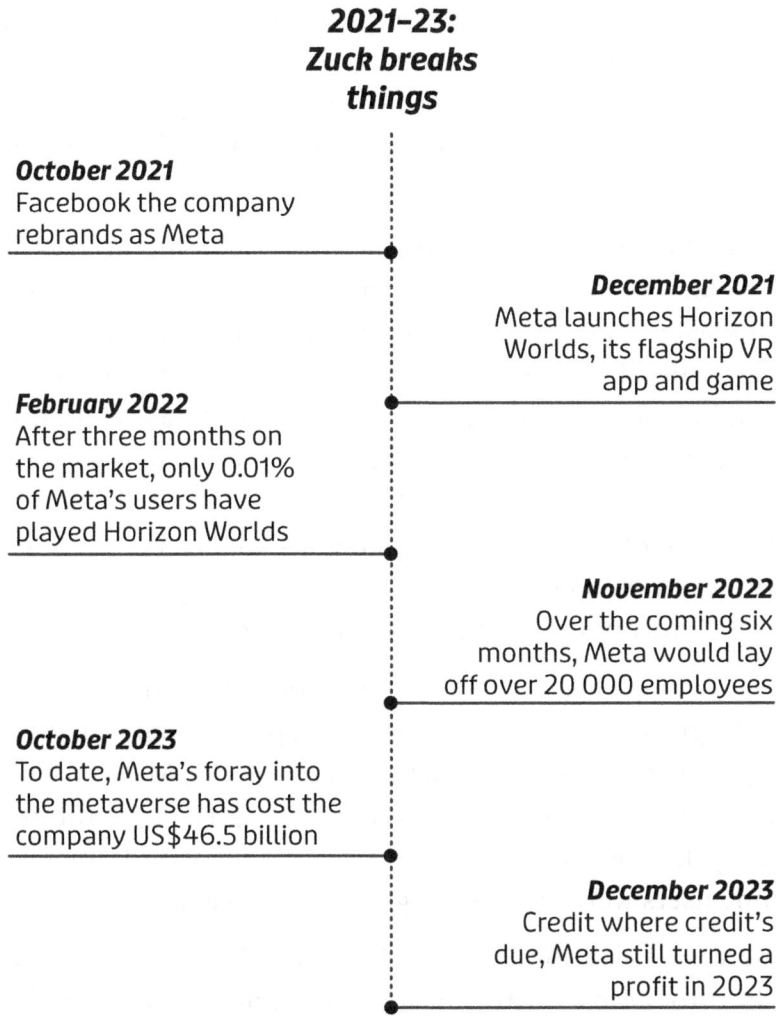

2021–23:
Zuck breaks
things

October 2021
Facebook the company
rebrands as Meta

December 2021
Meta launches Horizon
Worlds, its flagship VR
app and game

February 2022
After three months on
the market, only 0.01%
of Meta's users have
played Horizon Worlds

November 2022
Over the coming six
months, Meta would lay
off over 20 000 employees

October 2023
To date, Meta's foray into
the metaverse has cost the
company US$46.5 billion

December 2023
Credit where credit's
due, Meta still turned a
profit in 2023

Figure 14.2: A glimpse into Meta's calamitous two years in
the metaverse

Move slow and debate things

The stagnant growth of new users was the least of Meta's worries. Despite the surge in e-commerce revenue, 2022 served Meta the types of problems that only a multinational corporation can attract. For starters, privacy changes to Apple's mobile operating system crippled Meta's advertising model to the scale of billions of dollars. Within the same period, Meta's share price plummeted by more than 60 per cent — despite Zuck's bold claims about the metaverse's promise.

Meta's financial state cast a pall over Zuck's metaverse plans. In the face of bitter market sentiment, investors feared that the metaverse would earn too little to reverse Meta's fortunes. Sluggish initial uptake of Horizon Worlds — Meta's VR flagship app and game — also didn't help. Based on Meta's own publicly released numbers in February 2022, only around 0.01 per cent of Meta's user base actively played the game. Meanwhile, hundreds of millions of users were flocking to metaverse games like Fortnite and Minecraft. There was clearly a hunger for metaverse content — just not the content Meta offered.

A generous critic may argue that other factors shaped Horizon World's glacial rate of adoption. Perhaps the metaverse was a young person's game, and in a post–Tik Tok era, Meta's user base was too old. After all, Facebook's demographic skewed towards the grey. By contrast, over 80 per cent of the world's metaverse gaming users weren't old enough to drink in a bar.

There was also the fact that Horizon Worlds required a VR headset to access. This meant that, unlike 2007 Facebook, Horizon Worlds came with a price tag. While Meta's Quest 2 headset outsold the competition in 2022, its cost was always going to deter most Meta users.

What's clear is this: the metaverse rollout was a victim of Meta's success. It's easier to pivot a small thing than a big thing, and we don't need a Meta insider to tell us this. But a Meta insider we have — in the guise of gaming great John Carmack. Geeks of a certain age may have enjoyed his earlier works like

Commander Keen, Doom and *Wolfenstein 3D*. Twenty tens VR lovers will recognise him as the CTO of Oculus, a VR business that Facebook acquired in 2014. And those startup scenesters who live for drama will know him for the searing memo he circulated when he left Meta in 2022.

In his now-infamous parting shot, he blamed company bloat for many of their metaverse struggles: 'We have a ridiculous amount of people and resources, but we constantly self-sabotage and squander effort'. In subsequent podcast appearances, he further cited that corporate bureaucracy had taken the 'Meta' out of 'metaverse'. Zuck, it seemed, was trying to run startup software on Big Corporate hardware.

None of these stumbles would have mattered if Meta's VR foray had paid off. Alas, the balance sheets echo John Carmack. Reality Labs — the erstwhile Oculus VR and Meta's VR and AR subsidiary — cost Meta US$6.6 billion in 2020, US$10.2 billion in 2021 and over US$13.7 billion in 2022. By the end of 2023, Meta's VR efforts had lost the company over US$46.5 billion. For context, and as *Fortune* journalist Paolo Confino noted, the figure outstrips the revenue of some Fortune 100 companies. That's a lot of rejected 2006 Yahoo bids.

'It's not about the money — it's about the people'

Now, at this point, it must be said: Reality Labs' losses didn't scuttle its parent company. In fact, thanks to its trio of Facebook, WhatsApp and Instagram, Meta still reaped a profit in 2023. It also isn't fair to compare Reality Labs' overheads to, for example, those of Facebook. After all, Facebook exists in the online ether, whereas Reality Labs builds hardware — a markedly more costly product to build.

Even so, a US$46.5 billion loss is a bad day in the office for any leader. Between November 2022 and the following May, Meta laid off over 20000 employees. Remember that 2021 COVID-19–fuelled hiring wave? Within six months, these layoffs undid those HR gains. A 2023 in the black would have been a relief to Meta's shareholders, but it was cold comfort to those who lost their jobs.

On a more philosophical level, the very concept of One Big Idea belonged to a different era in Meta's lifespan. In 2007, Facebook was only three years old and had yet to settle on an ironclad business model. By 2022, Meta's market cap was larger than the GDP of Luxembourg. One was a high school wonderkid who everyone assumed would go far; all they needed was to choose a direction. The other was a wealthy, middle-aged banker with several properties, several mortgages and a strained marriage. For the former, One Big Idea — pursued with effort and care — is all they needed to succeed. For the latter, it feels like a midlife crisis.

During his early years at Facebook, Zuck led by the tenets of his motto, 'Move fast and break things'. And in 2007, it served Facebook well. Fifteen years later, Meta had become too large and unwieldy to move fast into the metaverse. And the only thing they'd broken…

…

…

… was the budget.

Why Zuck the CEO dived

Okay, 'dived' is far too strong a word for a Fortune 500 CEO who turned a profit for his company. Even so, we have a rhyming theme to maintain.

Zuck's startup outlook failed to monetise the metaverse because he didn't foresee the new realities of Meta:

- The *sprawling bureaucracy* that sustains a major corporation, but hampers any fast movement or glass-breaking

- A global, 10-figure user base, which requires a *much bigger price tag* to enact One Big Idea

- A *publicly-listed status and tens of thousands of employees*, which creates higher stakes for failure than an early-stage concept.

Despite all appearances, the aim of this case study isn't to suggest that Zuckerberg is a bad leader. Meta is one of the largest tech companies in the world, and Zuckerberg's stewardship helped to make that happen. Since his foray into the metaverse, Zuckerberg has also presided over some ringing monetary triumphs, such as the incorporation of AI into Meta's suite of products. In fact, in 2025, off the back of its AI revamp, Meta saw its most profitable first quarter *ever*. That's a far cry from the metaverse alarm bells of 2022.

All we mean to highlight is that Zuckerberg's problems changed. Had he evolved his approach by 2022, Meta may have avoided some of its pitfalls and become even more successful.

And like the tech that underpins it, Zuckerberg's leadership style is still evolving. Years from now, sources like this one may reflect on a future Zuckerberg as the very model of a modern major CEO.

Can I avoid these problems by 'pre-growing'?

Growing with your business is a lot like advancing through grades in school. Try and skip grades too quickly, and you'll be failing calculus when you should be learning your times tables. Move too slowly, and you'll wake up one day to find yourself repeating kindergarten for the third time. Lay your learning foundations in your early years, though, and you'll be well placed to become the school dux.

Growing with your business is much the same. You can't 'pre-grow' to meet tomorrow's needs, much as you can't pre-solve the unknown unknowns we covered in chapter 12. However, you can create an early framework that will allow you — and your business — to grow productively.

Rem Oculee is the founder and CEO of Confidence Wealth Management, a California-based financial firm that specialises in preparing business owners for exits. He is also the author of *The Exit Mindset*, which seeks to lay out a roadmap for exit strategies. We haven't met Rem Oculee, and can't attest to his current state of mind. However, based on his business-leading vocabulary and Wall Street Chic headshot, we're confident he wouldn't use a phrase like 'pre-growing'. Even so, much of his body of knowledge applies to anyone looking to pre-grow for their business.

In his hypothesis, Oculee refers to (among others) four steps a founder can take to prepare for future growth:

1. Assemble a seamless infrastructure

2. Build in scalability

3. Identify bottlenecks

4. Get buy-in.

In the vacuum of a list, these tips feel devoid of meaning, so we'll expand on them here.

1. Assemble a seamless infrastructure

The goal here, as Oculee describes it, is to structure your business like a car. Much as a car's parts work cohesively, and survive the malfunction of one specific component, so, too, should your business. This might seem obvious at first read, but many owner-doers overlook the basics here. They (quite understandably) become so engrossed in solving daily problems that they fail to structure their systems. As a result, when the business begins to grow, its ad-hoc processes often buckle under its own weight.

To ensure you don't fall into the Owner-Doer Pit, ask yourself the following questions:

- *'Do the systems we've created across the business integrate, or did they just spring up in response to a need?'*

- *'Are our processes as efficient as they could be? Have we phased out any superfluous steps?'*

- *'When a change occurs, do my team members await further instructions, or do they proactively adapt? And as their leader, have I empowered them to?'*

- *'Am I assessing our systems objectively, or am I looking at them through rose-tinted lenses?'*

2. Build in scalability

'Scalability' is a word you'll encounter a lot in books like this. And by now, you likely have a handle on its meaning. For the purposes of this list, 'scalability' simply refers to the automated, self-operating systems in our business. By building scalable processes, your output should grow with your consumer demand — without you needing to clone yourself.

Have you built in scalability? Try asking yourself these questions:

- *'Which parts of my business work exactly the way they should? What can I learn from those processes, and how can I apply them to other corners of my business?'*

- *'Do my systems reliably deliver the same result every time? If not, what can I change to ensure they do?'*

- *'What are the most common recurring issues that slow or derail the processes in my business? Why are they occurring, and what can I learn from them?'*

3. Identify bottlenecks

In Oculee's words: 'A system can only run as fast as its slowest component, and that's what bottlenecks are'. Most often, bottlenecks manifest as makeshift solutions to high-volume, low-priority problems.

During the early days — and years — of your business, you might be able to survive bottlenecks. Your invoicing system doesn't work correctly, so you manually override it. You don't have a designated HR manager in your team, so you handle any workplace issues directly. The A/C doesn't work on hot days, so you hang a wet cloth over a fan.

But what passes for a hack in a young business can, with time and success, fester into a crisis. When you have six employees, you might think your workaround has offered a jar in which you can encase your issue. When you have 60, that jar will sprout a neck, and in doing so, will morph into a bottle. And then? It's going to do what bottlenecks do.

That manual override for your invoicing system? It isn't enough to meet the influx of payments that define a large company. Your homespun HR approach? It's failed to quell a few workplace scandals — for which you have unwittingly become liable. And that wet cloth/floor fan combo has triggered a wave of resignations.

Never fear! We're here to help you break the bottle…before it becomes a bottleneck. When assessing your solutions, ask yourself:

- *'Has this solution caused delays in other areas of the business?'*

- *'Is this solution easily reproducible by others? In other words, am I the only one who can handle it? Or could I confidently ask a team member to take responsibility for it?'*

- *'Would this solution work just as well if my business employed 10 times as many staff?'*

4. Get buy-in

Some CEOs like to claim their job is to 'inspire'. Many middle managers might claim their role is to 'manage expectations'. As is so often the case, there's a shred of truth to both — and a missed opportunity.

Just as managers can feel their CEOs demand unrealistic results, business leaders can sometimes conclude that staff are 'making excuses'. When you set a deadline or launch a project, you might hear 'That isn't possible' or 'We don't have the resources to do that'. If you do, you might feel as if your team aren't fully committing themselves to the problem. However, this line of thinking will disempower your team and fail to decentralise responsibility — which will stunt your business' growth.

Instead of losing either your drive or your patience, involve your team in the conversation. Ask *them* a series of questions, such as:

- *'Well, knowing what we're trying to achieve, what would you suggest we do?'*
- *'What resources would you need to reach this target?'*
- *'How have you solved problems like this in the past?'*

What Chloe Zhao and Zuck have in common

Chloe Zhao still attracts courtship to write and direct major motion pictures. Mark Zuckerberg is still Mark Zuckerberg. If they constitute failure, we couldn't begin to imagine success. Even so, you can learn from their public stumbles — and ensure you minimise the chances of making your own. Lay the right foundations today, then be prepared to evolve with the demands of tomorrow.

Do so, and your legacy may truly be...

...

...

... eternal.

CHAPTER 15

HOW TO EXIT YOUR BUSINESS (OR STAY WITH IT FOREVER)

You have to be a little bit crazy to go into business. It's so much more *uncomfortable* than working for someone else. Its highs are Everest, but its lows can bankrupt you. You could deliver a smartphone into the hands of every urbanised person in the world. Or you could ride your food delivery app into a startup graveyard.

But hey, all of life is a gamble. Even being alive is a little bit unlikely. At any other point in human history, it's unlikely that you would have lived in an era stable and affluent enough for you to read this book... or consider a wild startup adventure.

So, congratulations! You've believed in yourself and made it this far. You're officially through your harrowing early days and people are buying what you're selling. The only question that remains: where should you go next?

This is the million-dollar question. Or perhaps the billion-dollar one.

Tim Fung knows a thing or two about exits. He's experienced every angle of a business: worker bee, founder, investor. On Tuesday, 21 March 2021, he added a new angle: CEO of a listed company. Airtasker (ASX:ART) closed its first day of trade at $1.05, climbing 60 per cent above the $0.65c IPO price at which the company raised capital. For Tim, however, it was just the start of the next stage.

'From my perspective, I saw it had a good start, which is fantastic, but we're really here for a 5–10 year journey, and we're focused on that long-term perspective,' Fung said. Having expanded to Ireland, New Zealand, Singapore, the UK and the United States, the listing could help Airtasker consolidate its foothold in new markets and launch new products and services.

'Airtasker started as an app for cleaning and gardening, but people can now buy experiences and lessons,' said Fung. 'If you want a drag queen to come over to your party and entertain your guests, you can buy that on Airtasker now.'

So if an IPO is not an exit, what is? Well, it's really up to you.

Startups are full of false starts. First, you have a big idea that *could change everything!* So, you create an MVP and test it with early users. You revise, and you launch. You pivot, and you grow. Along the way, you find co-founders, team members, C-suite leaders, customers, partners.

How you progress can't be captured by a neat little roadmap. Life is too untidy. Luck plays too big a part to ignore. Perhaps — like Canva co-founder Melanie Perkins — you could kickstart your business by taking up kitesurfing to meet VCs.

You see, finish lines are much the same as starts: they're individual to everybody.

When Cathy Freeman crossed the finish line to win Olympic Gold — a sporting moment voted as Australia's most iconic — it changed how this part of the world viewed itself. No longer were we merely 'Oceania', the opposite of historically thriving hubs like London, New York or Paris. Instead, we were winners. It built on the clout earned by Antipodean pioneers like Kiwi Sir Edmund Hillary, one of the first two people to definitively reach Mount Everest's peak; or Aussie Lionel Rose, the first Indigenous Australian to win a world boxing title. When *Australia II* won the 1983 America's Cup, ending America's 132-year winning streak, we saw much the same effect. New Zealand then went on to distil this magic by claiming the Cup a further *four times*.

What these victories showed us is that we could be winners. Our part of the world is rich with resources, highly educated and relatively affluent. It's also characterised by a *willingness to try*, a certain appetite for risk. Successive waves of hopeful immigrants refresh our ranks with vigour, skills we need and work ethic. These are all the ingredients you need for a thriving entrepreneurial scene.

It's no surprise then, that the likes of Airtasker, Atlassian, Canva, McCarthyFinch and Like Family would come from this part of the world. So let's indulge a little daydream. Imagine you've built a business from the ground up. It's profitable. You're comfortable. And you're wondering what you should do next.

What are your options?

For most businesses, there are three ways you can exit:

- Initial public offering (IPO)
- Mergers and acquisitions (M&A)
- Exit? What Exit?

Exit stage left: IPO

Going public via an Initial Public Offering (IPO) is the gold standard of success for many founders. When it comes to 'What's your exit strategy?', IPO usually tops most lists. Between media roadshows and a glossy prospectus, it's a statement that you've made it.

For investors, it can be an opportunity to exit. For startups like Airtasker, Mad Paws and Meta, it can be a chance to raise funds for fresh ideas or expansion.

Matthew Hodgkinson, founder of Papillon Lawyers, has steered both listed companies and M&A deals in his years as a general counsel involved in high-stakes corporate transactions. He's well aware of the promise and pitfalls of an IPO.

'Being pessimistic here, the administrative burden of being publicly listed is massive,' warned Hodgkinson.

'I think a lot of companies don't understand exactly what that entails when they move to an IPO. If you've got a founder who likes to be in control and likes to be agile, a lot of the administrative things that come with being in a listed business can slow you down. You've got company secretarial requirements, issues around boards and establishing committees. You've got an entire layer of bureaucracy that doesn't exist in a private business, or certainly not to the same extent.'

While this might sound like a champagne problem, Hodgkinson is quick to assert that it can cause an administrative hangover.

'This is a layer of bureaucracy that you're putting on top of the leadership in a listed business. And it does slow you down. And if you don't like lawyers, then you can have a lot of problems.'

DOES A PUBLIC LISTING SUIT YOUR BUSINESS?

'Shareholders have a completely different time frame for results,' explained Hodgkinson. 'They have a different understanding of the impact and speed in which results can occur.'

Given these pressures, you must ask yourself: do you even want to be listed?

'It's important to look at the type of business that you have,' said Hodgkinson. 'For example, I think that professional services businesses are just not a good fit for being listed. They don't have a good alignment with shareholders wanting a continuous return. There are success stories, like Accenture, but when you see the broader market, the most successful professional services businesses rarely get listed. They've either avoided a listing or they've gone through a listing and had terrible issues. Look at Slater & Gordon. When you're considering an IPO, it's really important to look at your own business and understand what the drivers are and how shareholders would react to the sort of long-term thinking that you potentially need to have for a successful business in certain industries.'

However, for some startups, an IPO is ideal. For Mad Paws, it meant they could raise the kind of funds necessary to drive grand ambitions — like dominating the pet care landscape.

'It was already our vision from day one to build a pet-care ecosystem,' explained co-founder Alexis Soulopoulos.

'Ignoring COVID-19, the idea of expanding had always raised a resource question. COVID-19 helped with the resource question because our staff couldn't focus on the core business of pet sitting. The good news was, our business was already reaching a pretty interesting stage in which we could raise larger amounts of capital. If COVID-19 hadn't occurred, we likely would have looked to scale into other pet-care industries anyway. COVID-19 definitely accelerated our scaling plans; it created a need for other revenue streams and gave us the resources to focus on scaling.'

Listing has also suited Airtasker, fuelling its acquisition of Zaarly to accelerate its US expansion. Going public reportedly made Tim Fung $20 million richer, and he is now based out of Los Angeles to lead the company's American expansion.

However, as an Australian-born-and-bred company, it was important to Fung that Airtasker list in Australia, as a signal to encourage our next generation of entrepreneurs to thrive globally.

Get help from your friends: M&A

Acquisition can also be an appealing exit strategy. Unlike an IPO, it doesn't come with the administrative burden of going public. As many startups disrupt an existing market, acquisition by a larger rival can make sense.

For Nick Whitehouse, exit by acquisition meant his startup, McCarthyFinch, could achieve more in the vast North American market.

'The McCarthyFinch journey was crazy. We took three and half years from founding to exit — it was lightning fast,' Whitehouse told us. 'We were the first New Zealand legal AI company to exit, and I think we were one of the first legal AI businesses in Australasia to exit.'

COVID-19 threw a shutdown-sized spanner into the works. McCarthyFinch went from demo-ing to 50 US clients a week, and closing 25 per cent, but the pandemic shutdowns stretched their usual one-month sales cycle to three, four, and eventually, five months.

'This put significant pressure on our burn rate,' said Whitehouse. 'Did we have enough cash to keep the lights on? It was a juggle. We had to consider next steps. Most companies in our position were likely going to be consolidated through or post COVID-19.'

Brokering an acquisition by American legaltech Onit through COVID-19 was 'probably the busiest and craziest point' in his life.

'We were trying to do an international M&A transaction while in complete lockdown, trying to persuade the board on an acquisition instead of raising more cash. All of this alongside the public health crisis: would key team members even stay alive? We all forget that at this point, the COVID-19 mortality rate was relatively high,' said Whitehouse. 'Oh, and I was moving house!'

The Twilight Zone life of COVID-19 meant that the first time Whitehouse met Onit's CEO and key staff was right before fronting up to the media nearly two years after acquisition. It was the corporate equivalent of meeting your bandmates for the first time moments before playing at Bluesfest.

'We were heading into a full media interview with journalists at Legal Week in New York,' he said. 'I was like, "Hi, how's it going? Let's do media!" That was a lot of fun.'

So, what's Nick's life like post-acquisition?

'We've tripled our team size,' he said. 'We grew 900 per cent in our first year. Our average deal size was $3500 prior to acquisition — the first deal we did post-acquisition was about $400000. It was like being pulled up into the stratosphere.'

Suffice to say, the numbers looked good for McCarthyFinch. However, after the acquisition, they had a Big Brother who was watching. And that Big Brother had specific criteria in mind.

'We were the fastest line item growth for Onit for three years,' said Whitehouse. But with this comes the "private equity" thesis.

For a five-year investment, they want a 5× return on their cash. So if they put in $200 million, they want a billion-dollar exit.'

The product changed too.

'We had really good AI, but the friction isn't the AI,' said Whitehouse. 'The friction was how people learned to use and work with the AI. We focused a huge amount on user experience. This wasn't necessarily about making something pretty, but making something *frictionless*. That's how we could grow 900 per cent a year at Onit. We thought about our users a lot, and we removed that friction.'

Few founders stay on with a business post-acquisition. Whitehouse is very much the exception, and he puts this down to the fact that, prior to starting McCarthyFinch, he worked within large organisations. This allowed him to switch between a founder's mindset and being part of a leadership team. Philosophically, he also entered his post-acquisition era like a Buddhist monk with a tech agenda.

'Your business is your baby,' said Whitehouse. 'When you sell that business, it's still your baby. You want to see it do well. What a lot of founders struggle with is that it's rare that somebody's acquiring your baby for your baby to remain a baby. When you're selling your "business baby", it's more like you're selling the organs. You're selling an organ transplant. You're selling spare parts for the acquisition business. If you don't understand this, it's pretty horrifying when you see them get out the scalpel and start cutting and stitching it to other parts of their organisation.'

This didn't trouble Whitehouse too much.

'I was building intelligence. I don't care what it looks like. I just want to get it into people's hands. Onit was a great company to acquire us: there was a huge amount of synergy between our thinking. The product changed, but that didn't matter because our mission stayed the same. Now our goal was all about scaling, integrating and transforming.'

What really changed was what Whitehouse did day to day.

'I no longer worried about how much money I had in the bank,' he said. 'Or how I was going to pay my staff. Post-exit, I hired 40 people and helped acquire companies. That's my day job now — less about the day-to-day of Onit and more about strategy, go to market and acquisitions for the company in general. As Chief AI Officer, I travel to America once or twice a month. As a founder, I've been able to successfully exit, work internationally across time zones and keep my marriage going. I think I've been successful in that respect.'

It's also about a perspective shift. Many founders, quite understandably, focus on how their product or service will change the world. As a byproduct, this outlook can create a sense of Main Character Syndrome. Staying on after an acquisition can transform a founder into a supporting character for someone else's story. But from Whitehouse's point of view, that isn't a bad thing.

'In a startup, you have this crazy, naive dream that you're going to *change everything*,' said Whitehouse. 'Whereas at Onit, we're part of a story — part of a shift that's going to be 15 to 20 years in the making. That shift probably isn't going to happen in my working lifetime. But what part do I want in that story? I've got enough cash in my back pocket now that I don't need to keep doing this, but for some reason, I am. I'm still excited by it.'

Nellie McQuinn had a similar experience when she joined Moonbug Entertainment as part of its founding management team. Moonbug, the commercialising force behind CoComelon and Blippi, was acquired by ex-Disney heavyweights Candle Media for

$3 billion in 2021. The acquisition proved fruitful: Moonbug made FastCompany's World's Most Innovative Companies for 2023.

'When we were acquired, we weren't finding our feet as a team. We'd already grown as a team, and we knew what we needed to do,' explained McQuinn.

'In terms of getting prepared for an acquisition like that, I think you've got to be prepared to fake it 'til you make it. You think that these big, multibillion-dollar companies are completely slick and have everything sorted. They have all the wheels greased, and they're a well-oiled machine. Now that I've worked with many partner and contractor companies, [I] realise that everyone's finding their feet. It surprised me to realise that a small, five-person company can have many of the same foundational issues as a bigger company.'

Matthew Hodgkinson brings a non-founder's perspective to the table. He was general counsel for Arq Group when it was acquired by Singtel.

'Through an acquisition, you have to be aware there may be a massive cultural change,' said Hodgkinson.

'Your business can move from a fast-moving startup to one that's run in a much more bureaucratic and big organisation style. Our experience was an initial acquisition followed by a long period of integration. That really changed how the business approached clients and even its staff, which impacted every facet of the business. As a founder, you need to think about this.'

Hodgkinson realises that many founders only see the dollar signs when they think of an acquisition. However, acquisition means another company taking control of your business — and steering it any way they choose. Hodgkinson advises founders to do their research on a company proposing to acquire them.

'This decision will shape the future of your business, so it's very important as you consider acquisition as a potential exit,' he said.

'But sometimes, you just won't have a choice. If you've given away equity early on, or needed private equity to expand, other stakeholders may pressure you towards acquisition, especially if a large chunk of your business is no longer owned by you. This is why it's advisable to bootstrap your growth for as long as possible.'

In Hodgkinson's experience, private equity can transform an acquisition from 'bold new chapter' to 'gun pressed against your head.'

'Private equity investors are going to be more financially driven than most founders,' he said. 'This can mean private equity funding can lock you into a process over which you may lose control.'

Founders are best placed to assess the competing needs of investors, customers and team members. Acquisition can bring an influx of resourcing, infrastructure and connections, as well as access to a far larger client base, allowing a business to scale heights it might never otherwise achieve.

Even so, the very nature of an acquisition means surrendering your vision to a larger mission. For an example of how badly this can go, look no further than Disney's acquisition of *Star Wars*. Its latest trilogy triggered a slew of 'somehow, Palpatine returned' memes. In the eyes of long-term fans, it was a disagreement on par with whether 'Han shot first.' (He did, by the way. We all know he did.)

Keep growth private

Few founders bootstrap forever, and even fewer do it solo. However, if you're inclined to rickroll your way through your startup experience, you'll enjoy more control and profits.

Private growth was how Wenee, one half of our authorial team, chose to grow her first startup, Survive Law. As a young founder (she was 21, and still studying law), private growth provided plenty of room to fail fast, fail quietly and find what worked to grow. Six years later, when Survive Law was acquired by one of its largest advertisers, it meant the leadership team of three was streamlined enough to make the decision quickly.

Private growth reflected Wenee's circumstances. Graduating into the GFC, funding from friends or family wasn't an option. Survive Law had to grow on its own.

'It's important to consider your personal situation,' said Hodgkinson. 'The problem with startups is that there's often an obsession with "How much capital can I get from private equity?" or "How much capital can I get from an IPO?"

'The money can blind everybody to the fact that you are giving up control of your business. You're giving up the agility that you initially had when you put your business together, not to mention any of the financial benefits of running something yourself and bootstrapping it to a certain size.'

This loss of control doesn't only affect day-to-day operations, or an eventual payday. In some cases, it can also hinder your long-term plans for the business.

'That loss of control can be significant when it comes to potential conflicts between a founder who wants to build a long-term successful business and the demands of private equity, or shareholders in the market,' said Hodgkinson.

'You may be dealing with individual investors who may have a horizon for their investment. If so, there's going to be a conflict. That's why you need to understand exactly what you're getting into, and if there is a way you can do things without jeopardising your level of control. Bottom line, there will be a way that you, the successful founder, want to do things — and you want to hold onto that.'

Pearler co-founder Hayden Smith believes focusing on outcomes, rather than specific exit strategies, is a better way forward.

'I have a fairly simple aim, which is to earn some kind of financial security,' Smith said.

'My goal is for Pearler to become a company that provides me with the ability to take undue financial stress off my family and those I care about. It doesn't specifically need to be an IPO, or an acquisition; it could be a high salary, for example.'

Smith recognises that, to many people, launching a startup wouldn't seem like the simplest path to 'financial security'. However, he believes the opportunities it offers outweigh the headaches and late nights.

'Starting a business hopefully gives you the chance to impact the world positively while doing so in a way that can transform your life,' he said.

'I'm privileged enough to be able to start something from an idea and then benefit from it. I meet people who say things like, "I would never sell my startup", or "I would never IPO it". To me, even the idea of coming to the end of this with a modestly healthy outcome already feels like a blessing. That's why I don't get too caught up in the details.'

Tim Fung's experience is a testament to not getting too caught up in the details of an exit. In 2022, Airtasker turned 10. Reflecting on the experience from a WeWork in San Francisco, Tim Fung insisted it wasn't an overnight success.

'If I'd sat down at the beginning and planned the next 10 years, I probably wouldn't have started in the first place,' Fung told *Startup Daily.*

We can relate. In July 2025, Catmosphere celebrated its 10th birthday. It's no Airtasker, but it has provided refuge for rescue cats and cat lovers alike. Launching it in five months with no bricks 'n' mortar business experience taught us a lot about business. We've been learning ever since — and if we're lucky enough, we'll never stop. Like Tim Fung, we probably wouldn't have started any of this if we'd consigned it to some sensible 10-year plan.

We can't tell you what to do, but we hope a 10-year plan won't derail you from *your* dreams.

CONCLUSION

If you've read this far, you might feel daunted. You've seen a series of success stories, and in each, every founder admits how hard it felt along the way. But you don't run a marathon by thinking about every kilometre in the marathon (it's 42.195 kilometres, by the way). You take one step, followed by another, and you get a little further every day. Eventually, you might find yourself at any number of exits: an IPO, an acquisition, private growth or a sad exit, because this time, on this try, things didn't work out.

That's okay too. You learned a lot along the way. After all, in his quest for growth, the Very Hungry Caterpillar didn't always make the right choices. Yes, his initially healthy diet allowed him to scale, but his foray into junk food almost cost him his gains.

However, much like many of the case studies within this book, the caterpillar extracted crucial learnings from his mistakes. It was this hard-won data that steered him back on course towards his exit. And an exit from a chrysalis is a laudable exit by any caterpillar's standard.

Well, what are you waiting for? Go on. The world will be richer for whatever you do next. And while you may not find a butterfly on the other side, like our many-legged muse, you may just find …

…

…

…

… a unicorn.

GLOSSARY OF TERMS YOU'RE TOO EMBARRASSED TO ASK ABOUT

accelerator   You know those fitness boot camps that promise to get your body beach-ready before the summer? Accelerators are pretty much the startup version of those. Instead of personal trainers, you're paired with business mentors, and instead of repping out burpees, you hammer out business models. By the accelerator's end, you'll feel the burn… of industry expectations.

angel investor   Angel investors are a lot like a fitting birthday gift for your dad: you know they exist, but you have no idea where to find them. The myth goes that angel investors appear during the early stages of a business's lifespan. They provide much-needed funding and guidance, although their spiritual role is more limited than their name implies. Unlike venture capitalists (see below), angel investors are chiefly private citizens rather than investment funds. As a result, no-one can seem to agree on the best way to source them. To date, the most widely accepted answer is 'graduate from a private school'.

business as usual (BAU)   Like 'Old mate' or 'Chur', it's a flexible term that can mould itself to an array of meanings. One day, it might refer to a workplace's typical, ongoing workload; the next, it might refer to the status quo. To avoid any confusion with steamed buns, we suggest you say each letter ('B-A-U') rather than pronouncing it as a word ('Bao').

board whispering   Harbouring an innate talent for swaying boards of directors. If you've never handled a board before, trust us when we say that it's a skill both rare and crucial.

bootstrap/bootstrapped/bootstrapping   It's November. You want to avoid the looming family drama and flee to Bali for the summer holidays. Problem: December flights are pricey, and you only have a few thousand dollars in your bank account. You think about putting the trip on your credit card and staying in a White Lotus–style hotel. Instead, you decide to couch surf and hostel crawl on your meagre savings. No-one will mistake you for Jennifer Coolidge, but you'll retain full control of your holiday without owing money to anyone. When you're launching a business, bootstrapping would be your version of Bali couch surfing.

burn rate   It sounds like the title of an 1980s action film. It's not. Really, 'burn rate' is just a dramatic way of referring to how quickly a young business spends its money. The faster your burn rate, the sooner you'll need more.

customer acquisition cost (CAC)   CAC reflects the average amount of money you'll pay for each new customer. For instance, if you spend $10000 on advertising and sales, and you earn 100 new customers, your CAC will be $100. Like so many aspects of sales, it isn't always an exact science. And if you feel like a heartless corporate robot for putting a dollar value on people, welcome to marketing.

cap raise   In some distant moment, for reasons lost to the sands of time, founders took a stand against the phrase 'fundraise'. Perhaps they thought it sounded too charitable. Maybe they didn't want to be mistaken for a school cake stall. Whatever the reason, they seemingly swore an oath to refer to fundraising efforts as 'cap raises' (short for 'capital raises'). Not wanting to incense the Ghosts of Founders Past, all business leaders since have followed their example.

customer lifetime value (CLV)   Aka lifetime value (LTV), this figure approximates the net profit you'll make from a customer during their relationship with you. Depending on your product or service, this amount can vary wildly. For example, the CLV of someone buying a car might begin and end with their car purchase. By contrast, for a drug maker, a person with a chronic illness might offer a CLV that spans decades. If that last sentence filled you with ick, welcome to marketing.

double-sided marketplace   The startup version of that acquaintance who describes themselves as a 'connector' or 'nexus of people'. Think Airbnb (homeowners, meet holiday-goers), Mad Paws (pet sitters, meet pet owners), and Uber Eats (diners, meet restaurants/ghost kitchens). When you run a double-sided marketplace, the challenge of supply and demand kicks into overdrive. Too much of one, and your customers' needs go unmet. Too much of the other, and you have a horde of unhappy suppliers. Find the right balance, and everyone wins — namely, the marketplace, which usually earns points on each transaction.

elevator pitch   Whoever named this approach clearly did so before the advent of smartphones, because everyone now spends their lift rides doomscrolling. In its original form, an elevator pitch referred to a short presentation, typically delivered to someone whose support you seek. As the name implies, you should be able to deliver yours during an average lift ride. Best-case scenario: they agree to a meeting where you can provide a more detailed pitch. Worst-case scenario: you've ruined the flow of someone's morning doomscroll.

exit (*verb*)   Captain Ahab has his White Whale. Leprechauns have their pot of gold at the end of a rainbow. And business founders have their exits. In business parlance, to exit is to cash out. Sometimes an exit takes the form of an IPO (see below), while in other cases, it involves an acquisition (like when Meta bought WhatsApp for US$19 billion). An exit is what stands between a founder and their dreams of sipping Mai Tais on their own private island. That's probably why so many founders talk about it more than their own loved ones.

family office   It sounds like the title of a 1990s legal dramedy series. It's not. When a family holds more wealth than it could feasibly manage, a family office is born. Equal parts fund manager, financial advisory and life admin service, family offices seek to future-proof the fortunes of their charges. For founders, a family office can sometimes provide a conduit to private funding. Just don't align yourself with any one particular sibling, in case their rival inherits control of the finances.

Fortune 500   An annual list of the 500 largest US companies based on total revenue. When someone says they hold a C-Suite role in a Fortune 500 company, they're generally expecting you to be impressed. It's the corporate equivalent of claiming you only serve Parma prosciutto, or only drink sparkling white from the Champagne region.

funnel   In marketing terms, a funnel embodies the stages of a consumer's connection with a brand. At the top of the funnel, you'll usually have something like 'awareness' or 'attention'. This is the 'Huh?' stage of the process, during which consumers hear about you for the first time. The final stage — usually some spin on 'loyalty' or 'retention' — is what keeps them coming back for more. The stages in between mark the slow descent from 'What's the deal with this product/service?' to 'Okay, I'll bite'. As a business owner, it's your (or your marketer's) challenge to present the right message at the right stage of the funnel. The term still faces some pushback in Australia … probably because the word triggers fears of funnel-web spiders.

gross merchandise value (GMV)   We're sorry to break this to you, but we've only scratched the surface of startup initialisms. This one relates to e-commerce, and equates to the total amount a platform earns from sales within a certain time frame (such as a quarter). Every time you make a late night, wine-fuelled purchase online, Temu's GMV increases.

incubator   At first, accelerators and incubators might seem like Coke and Pepsi: they claim to be different, but they're not *really*. A more apt comparison, however, might be Coke and *Cuba Libres* (rum, Coke and lime juice, in case you're looking for an easy highball). Incubators host would-be startup founders at a much earlier phase, and often help them to refine their ideas. When they're ready for their *Cuba Libre* phase, the founders may throw some rum into the mix and join an accelerator. Half of this book's writing team is allergic to liquor, so only one author is to blame for this ham-fisted analogy.

initial public offering (IPO)   IPOs herald the moment when a private company becomes public. At this point, everyday investors can buy shares in the business via the stock market. For financially robust companies, this can allow founders to exit by selling some (or all) of their stake. They even get to ring a bell on the stock-market floor.

mergers and acquisitions (M&As) The two words arc often heaped together, but they actually mean different things. A merger involves a union between two organisations, whereas an acquisition occurs when one company buys another. To the business newcomer, the former might sound more empowering than the latter. After all, mergers conjure images of marriages and superhero team-ups, whereas acquisitions sound like invasions by hostile forces. In response, we invite you to look up how much money the WhatsApp founders made when they were acquired. We'll wait.

moat We're so sorry to disappoint you, but 'moat' (in this context) has nothing to do with castle defence. Rather, it refers to the unique or rare advantage that protects a company's status in the market. A moat doesn't need to be one specific feature; for example, McDonald's' moat depends on brand recognition, ubiquitous global presence and a scalable franchise model. Less of a moat factor was that creepy clown, which could be why Mickey D's have given Ronald some distance.

minimum viable product (MVP) Since we've devoted an entire chapter to MVPs, we won't explore them in too much depth here. But, in case you want a sentence-long definition: it's the cheapest, simplest thing you can get to your consumers that still does what it needs to do. Team sports fans will also have a *really* hard time not thinking 'most valuable player' whenever they read it.

pitch deck Remember the elevator pitch? Well, the pitch deck is what you get to deliver if your elevator pitch lands. A pitch deck is like an alibi: too vague and you won't convince, too long and you'll lose your audience. At a minimum, your pitch deck should detail what your business is, why people need it and how it will make money. Just as crucially, it must detail why you're the ideal person to bring it to life. By the end of your pitch, your audience needs to believe that you're the Chosen One. (They should also want to give you money, but that doesn't sound quite as epic.)

proof point Yet another marketing term, a proof point is an item of evidence that stresses a product's quality beyond reasonable doubt. For example: 'Pedro Pascal is the sexiest man alive. Proof points: his face and personality'.

prospectus As part of an IPO, a prospectus serves as a guide for potential investors. It provides an overview of how the business runs, whether it makes money yet and how it intends to grow. Depending on how business leaders craft their prospectus, it can either lead to a payday or a poisoned chalice. Do it well, and you may set the market ablaze with fervour (and a desire to buy your founding shares). Treat it like a night-before high-school essay, and you could go the way of WeWork's 2019 IPO attempt.

runway In aviation, it's practical. In fashion, it's chic. In Startup Land, it's a frequent source of panic. The yin to a burn rate's yang, a runway represents the time left until you run out of funds. The faster the burn rate, the shorter the runway.

SaaS SaaS stands for 'software as a service', and it describes products like Zoom, Slack and Salesforce. Whenever we hear it, though, we immediately think of a stern parent, rolling pin in hand, shouting, 'I'll have no sass under this roof, d'you hear?!'

scale/scalable/scalability A scalable business can grow in output without a commensurate increase in operating costs. This is huge because it hints at the prospect of limitless profits. For a deeper insight into how this works, see chapter 13.

seed (and pre-seed) funding Seed funding marks the point at which an early-stage startup says, 'All right, we haven't really done much yet. And we're a long way from making a profit. And, sure, you could invest your money in a low-cost index fund that tracks the US's largest companies. But if you invest in us, we might just become the next unicorn.' Basically, it's the good-looking but underemployed love interest in every romcom, asking the starlet to choose him over James Marsden.

Series (A/B/C) funding   Once the seed funding is done, you'll start working towards Series A, B, C, and sometimes beyond. Each round of funding will usually offer a different class of shares. In a perfect world, the startup valuation would increase with each round, meaning earlier rounds of shares carry more value. Think of it like band merchandise: back in 2009, few Australian and New Zealander fans would have committed to buying Taylor Swift T-shirts. In 2024, when Tay-Tay travelled to the Antipodes, those who had would have worn their shirts like they were tiaras.

small-to-medium enterprise (SME)   Are you a company with fewer than 200 staff? Congratulations! You're an SME.

unique selling proposition/unique value proposition (USP/ UVP)   What makes your product or service stand out from its rivals? What can it provide that the alternatives don't? And why will your consumers never go back once they've tried it? Once you can answer these questions, you'll have your USP/UVP.

UX   You may have heard insiders describe all things tech as 'engineering'. That would make UX — or 'User Experience' — the architecture. UX or product professionals also often act as intermediaries between tech and marketing. This is important because otherwise the two factions would likely kill each other.

valuation   The perceived worth of a startup or business in the eyes of the market. Sometimes, it can be based on tangible factors such as revenue, infrastructure and money in the bank. In other cases, it can be based on a hope and a whisper — or, as famed Australian lawyer Dennis Denuto would say — *the vibe.*

vanity metrics   Have you ever known someone who has said something like, 'Why can't I find a girlfriend? My freestyle rapping skills are off the charts!' They're measuring their virtue as a partner by vanity metrics. In businesses, vanity metrics rarely (if ever) relate to freestyle rapping, but instead focus on wins that don't generate revenue. Social media engagement or press mentions can fall into this category if they don't serve you new consumers. Try to be better … keep your eyes on the cheddar.

venture capitalist (VC)   They see your potential. They entwine their future with yours. And for all they invest in you, their criticisms keep you up at night. And no, we're not talking about your high-school sports coach. Unlike retail investors, who buy shares in public companies, venture capitalists don't always expect to see their money back. In fact, their business model assumes that the majority of their investments will *fail*. So, why do they do it? To oversimplify: because they're searching for unicorns. If they invest in 25 startups and one exits for billions, it doesn't matter if the other 24 go bust. It's little wonder, then, that every fundraising meeting with them can feel like an interview with the Gestapo. However, *unlike* the Gestapo, they want you to succeed. Just ensure that you enter every sit-down with your data loaded.

ACKNOWLEDGEMENTS

Like any great startup, it takes a village to ride a unicorn.

'Well, that's a stupid metaphor,' you might say. 'What kind of a village keeps unicorns? And what kind of a unicorn can fit an entire village on its back?'

Look, cut us some slack, okay? These are the acknowledgements, so we no longer need to maintain a veneer of sanity.

We're certain that, as soon as we submit this to our editors, Jordon and Chris, one of us will shriek, '*gurgling shrieky sound*, we forgot to thank [INSERT NAME]!' If this happens to you, please know: we are *so sorry*, and it's no reflection of your importance to us. Our brains are simply scrambled from writing a book, and we promise we'll make it up to you.

With that said, here are just a few of the people we'd like to thank.

First, thank you to our editor, Jordon Lott, for taking a chance on this book. In our current climate, most publishers will judge a manuscript on the number of Tik Tok followers its author/s boast. Jordon, however, read our draft, looked at our meagre socials presence and said, 'Let's give these two lovebirds a shot'.

Since then, she has played the juggling roles of strategist, cheerleader and mentor to us. Publishing has become a ruthless jungle with razor-thin margins, and Jordon really rolled the dice when she backed us. *Grazie mille, Padrina.*

We'd also like to give thanks to all our interviewees for taking time out of your busy lives to discuss *that crazy unicorn book*: Tim Fung, Nellie McQuinn, David Burt, Alexis Soulopoulos, Jenna Leo, Lachlan McKnight, Wengie, Hayden Smith, Nick Whitehouse, Alinta Furnell and Ismat Kabbara, Pasha Rayan, Dua and Hayder Shkara, Beste Onay, Matthew Hodgkinson, Lorenz Braysh, Beena Ahmed, and Kristen Phillips.

Startups are unlikely gambles, and you're the humans who make them happen. Without you and people like you, our world would be absent of the innovation that transforms how we live, and how well we live.

At UNSW Founders — the OG inspiration for *Riding the Unicorn* — they say they *make change happen.* But change doesn't happen without people like you making it a reality. Hopefully, this little entry into the startup/business pantheon of knowledge helps more people make change happen in their world, however they need it. You'll find some of the smartest, most committed people you'll ever meet working in startup hubs. Many might earn far more elsewhere, but they stay for the impact they might have.

In startup land, we mostly celebrate the lone billionaires who make it big. But it's people like those you'll meet at UNSW Founders — David Burt, Dina Titkova, Nina Juhl, Kristen Phillips, Rita Wu, Joseph Po, Julie Pham, Zac Rafidi, Tori Tucker and Sasha Whittle, and staff alumni like Jason Whitfield and Lucas Hakewill — who help founders scale great heights. Teams make dreams, and all that. But they really do.

Friends

Thanks to our friends who faithfully checked in over the two-and-a-half years it took to write this book.

Thomas: I'd like to thank Ai Ikeda, who has supported me through a medley of wacky shenanigans since we were 13. Akeysey, I always feel so proud whenever I get to refer to you as my best friend. Thanks to the Brotherhood of Monthly Banter (although it's more quarterly these days): Chetch, Crab Claw, Dougie, Felipe, Jimmy and Oleg. You've stood by me through fun times and failures, and you're never afraid to call me on my BS.

Jono, your laundry list of loathsome qualities is a ceaseless burden to me, and to everyone you know. If there is one silver lining to your life, it's the existential relief that your vomit-inducing face instils me. Someday, I'll leave the mortal bonds of this world, and I'll never again need to look upon your anaphrodisiac of a visage.

(Also, sorry I haven't visited for a while. Let's lock in an overdue weekend soon.)

Wenee: I'd like to thank Chantal McNaught (who cheered me on during my 5 am pre-work and Saturday morning writing sessions, then preordered five copies); and Angelique Lu, whose Tik-Tok and social-media strategy meant we felt a lot more Gen Z ready than older millennials have any right to be. Thanks to Emily Cordes, Sarah McNeill, Lauren Nissen, Maria Chan, Karen Tong and all our friends who are always up for encouraging our side quests, whether it's a book, cat café, rap battle, sailing or sumo.

Family

Thomas: I'd like to thank my mum, Gwogue, for planting the idea of ever being a writer. When I was too young to talk, she didn't just read me bedtime stories — she did the voices and everything! As I grew, she would listen to me waffle on and on (and on) about different book ideas. Even though she was a single mother with bills and rent to pay, she always found some wellspring of patience. Some people achieve their goals *despite* their upbringing, but I've only been able to co-write this book *because* of mine. Gwogue, I won't ever be able to thank you enough.

Daddy-o, it's fair to say that you and I breathe new life into the adage 'chip off the old block'. I didn't spend my teen years under your roof, but I'm so grateful that we've made up for lost time. You're a guiding light in my life, and I feel lucky to have absorbed so many of your traits. This book — and my outlook on life in general — wouldn't have been possible without your wisdom, encouragement and support. And Jane, thank you for always supporting me and Wenee, and giving us such a warm and welcoming haven!

To my brothers, Liam and Jack, and my brother-in-law Juwin: you guys give me hope for the future! It's my good fortune to watch you evolve into amazing humans. Whether it's by blood or law, I'll always thank my lucky stars that we're a family.

Wenee: I would like to thank my mum for raising me on *Back to the Future* optimism. My mum was a computer scientist before it was cool. She was the first woman in our family to study abroad. Her Honours research at Brighton Polytechnic, in handwriting recognition technology, undertaken in the 1970s/1980s, was pioneering. She raised me on sci-fi, and whenever I felt discouraged or overwhelmed, she'd remind me of what they say in *Back to the Future:* 'If you put your mind to it, you can accomplish anything'. That's as true for business as it is for any other field of endeavour, and it's the reason my CV looks like it does. Because if you put your mind to it, you might not always win. Sometimes, you'll lose. But you'll always learn. And you can accomplish more by trying than prevaricating on the sidelines.

I'd also like to thank my dad, who started a furnace and fire-testing business, an experience that caused him to advise me never to go into business because it's such a hard life. He's not wrong. When I ignored this very sensible advice, he quietly kicked emergency funds into Catmosphere to deal with an unexpected fire safety compliance requirement, allowing us to open within our ridiculously ambitious five-month time frame.

I have the kind of parents who encourage you to dream big, but dream pragmatically. Thank you.

• • •

Finally, a huge thanks to friends, family and total strangers who preordered months in advance! We can only capture everyone who got their order in at the time this was written, but we are honestly so appreciative to all of you. Thanks to Nina Juhl, Chantal McNaught, Minh Hua, Rose Raffaele, Lauren Nissen, Anita Uppal, Felipe Jara (who snapped our author photos), Lorenz Braysh, Lucas Hakewill, Saliha Rehanaz, Kathleen Notohamiprodjo, Jack Singleton, Liam Singleton, Jane Sherlock and Kim Singleton, Jose Opazo, Hayder Shkara, Nick Whitehouse, Melissa Lee, Emily Cordes, Tom O'Neill, Peter Mullen, Rita Wu, Maria Chan, Eric Wan, Shaon Diwaker and Yanko Leskovar.

As this book goes to great lengths to detail, a unicorn is a startup valued at over $1 billion. To us, though, it's a proxy for any dream that warrants your time. You know the ones we're talking about: the naysayers said you shouldn't try them and your loved ones said you must. Go find your unicorns, beautiful people, and ride them to the end of the rainbow!

BIBLIOGRAPHY

AAP (20 October 2010). How Australian techies created Google Maps. *The Sydney Morning Herald.*

AG Staff (18 June 2010). 20 Australian inventions that changed the world. *Australian Geographic.*

Allen, D. (2015). Getting things done: The art of stress-free productivity. Penguin Australia.

Animal Medicines Australia (2022). Pets in Australia: A national survey of pets and people AMAU008-Pet-Ownership22-Report_v1.6_WEB.pdf.

Artificial Lawyer (28 November 2022). Josef bags $3.48m in tough market as no-code fight grows. Artificial Lawyer.

ASIC Newsroom (14 January 2020). ASIC bans former Guvera director. Australian Securities & Investments Commission.

Australian Bureau of Statistics (26 April 2022). Australia's population by country of birth. Australian Bureau of Statistics.

Australian Bureau of Statistics (9 July 2024). Job mobility. Australian Bureau of Statistics.

Australian Investment Council (n.d.). Investment: How does venture capital work? Australian Investment Council.

Babych, M. (8 December 2021). A review of the minimum viable product approach. *Forbes.*

Baldassarre, G. (24 January 2017). Customer intelligence startup Local Measure raises $4.5 million to expand across the US and Middle East. StartupDaily.

Beaton, J. (25 February 2022). The idea that university degrees don't matter is a Silicon Valley fantasy. TechCrunch.

Bell, K. (25 May 2023). Meta is laying off employees for the third time in less than three months. Engadget.

Bertrand, M. LinkedIn profile, viewed 4 February 2025.

Blake, D. (30 November 2022). Delivering disaster: Why Send, Voly and Deliveroo collapsed in Australia. Inside FMCG.

Bonyhady, N. (19 February 2023). Every new customer cost Milkrun $57, then they bled cash on orders. *Sydney Morning Herald.*

Buelva, A. (27 December 2022). National survey reveals Australians spending on pets. Pet Food Industry News.

Casciaro, T., Gino, F. & Kouchaki, M. (6 October 2014). The contaminating effect of building instrumental ties: How networking can make us feel dirty. *Administrative Science Quarterly*, 59(4), 705–735.

CB Insights (3 August 2021). The top 12 reasons startups fail.

Chang, C. (2 February 2023). 'End of an era': What the 'tech wreck' means for Australian workers. SBS News.

Chapman, T. (31 October 2020). Tutoring in Australia is a billion-dollar industry. *Australian Financial Review.*

Chierotti, L. (26 March 2018). Harvard professor says 95% of purchasing decisions are subconscious. Inc.

Confino, P. (28 October 2023). Mark Zuckerberg's $46.5 billion loss on the metaverse is so huge it would be a Fortune 100 company—but his net worth is up even more than that. *Yahoo! Finance.*

Confino, P. (4 February 2024). Could AI create a one-person unicorn? Sam Altman thinks so—and Silicon Valley sees the technology 'waiting for us'. *Yahoo! Finance.*

Constantino, A.C. (29 September, 2022). 7 steps introverts can take to become 'master networkers'. CNNB Make It.

Cremades, A. (13 January 2019). The pros and cons of bootstrapping startups. *Forbes.*

CrunchBase (2023). Company Financials—Atlassian. CrunchBase.

CrunchBase (2024). Company Financials—VantagePoint Capital Partners. CrunchBase.

Davies, H., Goodley, S., Lawrence, F., Lewis, P. & O'Carol, L. (12 July 2022). Uber broke laws, duped police and secretly lobbied governments, leak reveals. *The Guardian.*

Dedovic, A. (31 May 2023). Operator behind Sydney vegan food chain Soul Burger aims to raise $1.6m. Business News Australia.

Demopoulos, A. (12 January, 2024). Stanley cups took the world by storm. Then the backlash began. *The Guardian.*

Di Stefano, M. & Sier, J. (11 April 2023). Milkrun to close doors, all staff made redundant. *Australian Financial Review.*

Dixon, S. J. (29 August 2023). Leading countries based on Facebook audience size as of 2023. Statista.

Ergas, C. (18 November 2021). An environmental sociologist explains how permaculture offers a path to climate justice. *The Conversation.*

Feigen, M., Jenkins, M. & Warendh, A. (July–August 2022). Is it time to consider co-CEOs? *Harvard Business Review.*

Fox News. (26 June 2014). Catching up with 'Mambo No. 5' singer Lou Bega. Fox News.

Fundable Staff. Types of investors. Fundable.

Fung, T. (8 April 2022). Tim Fung on 10 things he's learned in 10 years of building Airtasker. startupdaily.

Giradin, M. (26 May 2023). Venture capitalist vs angel investor. Forage.

Guillebeau, C. (2017). Side-hustle: From idea to income in 27 days. Crown Currency.

Hammond, M. (1 June 2011). Half of SMEs fail after insurable loss. Smart Company.

Hare, J. (2 February 2024). UNSW claims title of Australia's most entrepreneurial uni, again. *Australian Financial Review.*

Harroch, R. H. (13 April 2019). 15 key questions venture capitalists will ask before investing in your startup. *Forbes.*

Hearst Autos Research Editorial Staff. (14 May 2021). Everything you need to know about DoorDash insurance. Car and Driver.

Hecht, J. (8 December 2017). Are you running a startup or small business? What's the difference? *Forbes.*

Hopewell, L. (4 July 2013). Roamz is dead. Gizmodo AU.

Huddleston Jr, T. (20 January 2023). The 3 biggest reasons startups failed in 2022, according to a poll of almost 500 founders. CNBC.

Hunt Export Advice. (n.d.). Australian market overview 2024.

IBISWorld. (22 August 2023). Professional services in Australia: Market size (2008–2029).

IBISWorld. (August 2023). Professional services in Australia: Market size, industry analysis, trends and forecasts (2024–2029).

Jan Kamps, H. (23 September 2022). Looking at 320 pitch decks, here's what science tells us works best. TechCrunch.

Jansen, C. (14 November 2023). The rise of the Stanley tumbler: How a 110-year-old brand achieved viral success. Retail Dive.

Johansson, F. (7 April 2017). The Medici effect, with a new preface and discussion guide: What elephants and epidemics can teach us about innovation. Harvard Business Review Press.

Kelly, G., Zucker, J. & Doherty, R. (6 July 2022). Here's how the best leaders can drive 'outsized growth' in times of crisis, according to McKinsey's research. Fortune.

Knight, B. (28 September 2023). Will tighter regulations on short-term letting work? UNSW News.

Koehn, E. (15 May 2017). What happened to Guvera? A timeline of the troubled music streaming startup. SmartCompany.

Kushner, D. (2003). *Masters of doom: How two guys created an empire and transformed pop culture.* Random House, pp. 63–74, 142.

Lee, L. (2 November 2013). Welcome to the unicorn club: Learning From billion-dollar startups. TechCrunch.

Like Family's Instagram. (22 September 2023). Like Family has ranked 5th at the Top Startup Employers Awards. Instagram.

Mac, R., Frenkel, S. & Roose, K. (9 October 2022). Skepticism, confusion, frustration: Inside Mark Zuckerberg's metaverse struggles. *The New York Times.*

Mallaby, S. (15 February 2022). The power law: Venture capital and the art of disruption. Allen Lane.

Marks, G. (31 January 2021). Entrepreneurs are great, but it's mom and dad who gave them their start. *The Guardian.*

McDuling, J. (15 May 2017). Guvera debacle is a wake-up call for Australian start-ups. *Australian Financial Review.*

Melbourne Institute. (1 October 2020). Study shows Australians happy working from home, men and women are looking to upskill, but young people feeling the pinch. Melbourne Institute of Applied Economic and Social Research.

Mier, J. (7 August 2023). What's the difference between a startup and any other business? *The Conversation.*

Mitham, N. (8 October 2023). The Metaverse reaches 600m active users. KZeroWorldswide, LinkedIn.

Moon, M. (16 December 2022). John Carmack leaves Meta with a memo criticizing the company's efficiency. Engadget.

Motley Fool staff. (2 August 2023). Uber is profitable. For real this time. The Motley Fool.

Mumbrella staff. (4 April 2022). 88% of Aussie customers to maintain or increase their spend on Amazon post-lockdown. Mumbrella.

Napier-Fitzpatrick, P. (2017). The Art of remembering names: An all-important soft skill. The Etiquette School of New York.

Nikolovska, H. (17 February 2023). Metaverse statistics to prepare you for the future. Bankless Times.

Nix, N. (30 April 2023). How Mark Zuckerberg broke Meta's workforce. *The Washington Post.*

Oculee, R. (26 January 2023). How leaders can build scalability in their businesses. *Forbes.*

OECD. (n.d.). Helping SMEs scale-up. OECD Programme.

Oxford English Dictionary, s.v. (February 2024). 'side hustle (n.)', https://doi.org/10.1093/OED/8939913486.

Patrick, A & McDuling, J. (29 May 2017). The great Guvera mystery: where did $180 million of investors' money go? *Australian Financial Review.*

Perdew, K. (28 September 2023). Understanding the VC power law: Why fund size matters in venture capital returns. Leadership Prevails on Medium.

Pigeon Loans. Loan or borrow money with friends & family.

Pincock, C. (14 June 2008). Colin Murdoch. *The Lancet*, p. 1994, volume 371, issue 9629.

Plunkett, L. (25 March 2014). Facebook buys Oculus Rift for $2 billion. Kotaku.

Pm archive. (25 June 2007). The Pmarca guide to startups: The only thing that matters. Pmarchive.

Polaris Market Research Staff. (April 2022). Private tutoring market share, size, trends, industry analysis report. Polaris Market Research.

Powell, R. (12 October 2015). Why Jonathan Barouch killed his big idea at Roamz so Local Measure could live. *Australian Financial Review.*

Price, R. (4 January 2016). How a giant inflatable ball took the world by zorb. *The Sydney Morning Herald.*

Prikhodko, A. (6 July 2023). With STEM you can: Unlocking the code to tech entrepreneurship. CSIRO News.

Rainer, P. (3 November 2021). 'Nomadland' director brings her vision to Marvel's 'Eternals'. The Christian Science Monitor.

Redrup, Y. (6 May 2021). Atlassian's Scott Farquhar tells founders not to bootstrap. *Australian Financial Review.*

Reid, C. (13 February 2023). Eternals was over budget says Marvel. *Forbes.*

Reily, S. (3 October 2024). Census results reflect Aotearoa New Zealand's diversity. Stats NZ.

Ries, E. (3 August, 2009). Minimum Viable Product: A guide. Startup Lessons Learned.

Ries, E. (15 October 2011). The lean startup: How today's entrepreneurs use continuous innovation to create radically successful businesses. Random House USA Inc.

Ritter, T. & Pedersen, C. (13 April 2022). An entrepreneur's guide to surviving the 'death valley curve'. *Harvard Business Review.*

Rogers-Anderson, S. (24 December 2022). Why a recession offers opportunities for agile startup success. *The CEO.*

Rolfe, B. (6 March 2023). Grocery delivery app Milkrun criticised amid inability to meet early promises. news.com.au.

Santoreneos, A. (25 May 2023). 'Good to be back': Failed grocery delivery startup Milkrun bought by Woolies. *Forbes Australia*.

SBS (20 June 2016). Guvera to discuss blocked IPO with ASX. *SBS News*.

Scale-Up Vaud. (n.d.). OECD definition of scale-up. Scale-up Vaud—Apply.

Schroter, W. (19 April 2023). Founder imposter syndrome never goes away. Startups.

Scorer, O. (16 January 2023). Woolworths launches new one-hour delivery service. *New Idea*.

Sequoia staff. (14 December 2018). Two-sided marketplaces and engagement. Sequoia Capital Publication.

Shah, H. (2024). How Atlassian built a $10 billion growth empire. Nira.

Shontell, A. (5 September 2014). How 3 startup CEOs gave up fortunes to turn half their employees into millionaires. *Business Insider*.

Silicon Valley Bank staff. Raising startup funds from friends and family the right way. Silicon Valley Bank.

Smith, P. (2 November 2020). Optus buys Amaysim for $250m. *Australian Financial Review*.

Sostrin, J. (10 October 2017). To be a great leader, you have to learn how to delegate well. *Harvard Business Review*.

Sundich, N. (24 March 2021). 'We're here for a 5 year journey': Here's Airtasker CEO Tim Fung on life after listing. Stockhead.

Taneja, H. (22 January 2019). The era of 'move fast and break things' is over. *Harvard Business Review*.

Thiel, P. & Masters, B. (16 September 2014). Zero to one: Notes on startups, or how to build the future. Currency.

Thomsen, S. (27 January 2023). Milkrun, the last local grocery delivery standing, is still trying to find fresh capital after raising $75 million. StartupDaily.

Thomsen, S. (9 April 2024). Blackbird-backed job simulations edtech Forage exits to US merger. StartupDaily.

Turner-Cohen, A. (16 February 2023). Milkrun lays off 20 per cent of staff as tough market conditions bite. news.com.au.

UNSW staff. (n.d.). UNSW Founders 10× Accelerator.

UQ Communications staff. (11 November 2022). UQ's 'Frazer Institute' honours retiring vaccine co-inventor. UQ News, University of Queensland.

Vogelstein, F. (6 September 2007). How Mark Zuckerberg turned Facebook into the web's hottest platform. Wired.

Vogue Advisory Group staff. (2022). Guvera collapse. Vogue Advisory Group.

Walsh, L. (21 January 2022). Years after Guvera collapsed, investors are still fuming. *Australian Financial Review.*

WeFunder. Invest in founders building the future.

Whistler, K. (28 September 2019). New Fortune 100 CEO study: The top graduate schools attended by Fortune 100 CEOs. *Forbes.*

Wilson, B. (15 January 2024). How smart marketing, scarce supply and unique colours made the Stanley cup a must-have item. CBC, Chapter 9.

Wilson, F. (16 March 2011). Airbnb. AVC.

Wollaston, S. (23 March 2023). 'We don't do deep emotional discussions': Why men lose their friends—and how they can make more. *The Guardian*, Chapter 2.

World Population Review. (2024). Immigration by Country 2024. World Population Review.

YEC. (5 August 2021). Startup employee equity: What every founder should know. *Forbes*.

Zane, L. (6 September 2018). How and why does consumer behaviour change? *Forbes*.

Zider, B. (1998). How venture capital works. *Harvard Business Review*.

Printed and bound by CPI Group (UK) Ltd, Croydon, CR0 4YY

09/10/2025

14749193-0001